Hitler's Loss

Hitler's Loss

What Britain and America Gained
from Europe's Cultural Exiles

PETER OWEN PUBLISHERS

LONDON & CHESTER SPRINGS

in association with

THE EUROPEAN JEWISH PUBLICATION SOCIETY

PETER OWEN PUBLISHERS
73 Kenway Road, London SW5 0RE

Peter Owen books are distributed in the USA by
Dufour Editions Inc., Chester Springs, PA 19425-0007

First published in Great Britain 2001
by Peter Owen Publishers
in association with the European Jewish Publication Society,
PO Box 19948, London N3 3ZJ. Website: www.ejps.org.uk

ISBN 0 7206 1107 5

A catalogue record for this book is available from the British Library
Printed and bound in Great Britain by MPG Books Ltd, Bodmin, Cornwall

The quotation from Sir Winston Churchill's letters is reproduced with
permission of Curtis Brown Ltd, London, on behalf of the Estate of
Sir Winston S. Churchill.

The European Jewish Publication Society is a registered charity which
gives grants to assist in the publication and distribution of books relevant to
Jewish literature, history, religion, philosophy, politics and culture.

For Meeda and Raymond

Contents

Introduction

Perhaps the only virtue that the Nazis possessed was their bizarre consistency. Seldom did an official of the Third Reich deviate from party policy on any matter whatsoever. Nowhere was this more apparent than in the implementation of racial policy. That it led to Germany being denuded of much of its intellectual and artistic life seemed of no consequence to either Hitler or his cohorts. Even the military consequences of losing so many important scientists, particularly the nuclear physicists, counted for nothing when compared to the one essential of state policy – the eradication of any taint of Jewishness from German society. Wealth or past services to the state saved no one, as Germany's most famous chemist, Fritz Haber, was to discover. Nor did world opinion count for anything with Germany's new rulers as they pursued a ruthless purging of Jews and modernists from German culture. International condemnation of this policy led by Britain and the USA served only to provoke Nazi wrath.

The Nazi onslaught on the Jews and on 'alien' culture was pursued without ambiguity, whether by the toe of a storm trooper's boot or by the most sophisticated legislation. Its comprehensiveness was breathtaking, its spiteful detail shocking. It left the German nation not only without independent artistic talent but, more importantly, without a conscience, as integrity went into exile with Thomas Mann, Arnold Schoenberg, Bertolt Brecht and Stefan Zweig. In the broader context, hundreds of thousands of highly educated individuals were driven into exile by Nazi policies not only from Germany but later also from Austria, Hungary, Czechoslovakia, Italy and France. Hungary, in particular, was to provide not only a numerically large contingent of refugees to Britain and the USA but also some of the most talented. The world had seen nothing in modern times like this exodus of intellectuals as Nobel Prize winners were reduced to writing job applications to the USA and eminent artists took posts as domestic servants in London. But these, after all, were the lucky ones; they had the intellectual, artistic and scientific talent that was to prove an international currency in the free world unlike their less gifted fellow Jews who found it far more difficult to start a new career in exile.

Those who left, driven out by diktat or mob hate, suffered enormously, but so did their Aryan colleagues who remained silent in Germany. These 'lucky ones' were so compromised by the need to sublimate their consciences and integrity to the orders of the Third Reich that they became almost ghost-like figures. Even the German film industry, which remained as prolific as ever under the Nazis, produced only strange, escapist productions totally divorced from contemporary reality. Where Soviet Russia under Stalin had its Shostakovich, prepared to play a dangerous game between artistic freedom and totalitarian control, Nazi Germany had no one. No wonder so few of the exiles bothered to return to their homeland after the war; the cultural landscape had been denuded by the Nazis as surely as Germany's cities had been levelled by Allied bombers.

However, this book is concerned with those who left rather than those who stayed, and with the profound influence they had on the culture of their adopted countries. Although the most comprehensive work on their achievements, the 1,000-page *Weimar en Exile* by the French scholar Jean-Michel Palmier, still remains untranslated, the American experience has been widely documented in such books as Anthony Heilbut's *Exiled in Paradise* and Laura Fermi's *Illustrious Immigrants*. Surprisingly, the important contribution that the exiles made to British culture has been largely neglected in recent years, although this deficiency has been countered to some extent by perceptive newspaper and magazine articles by Paul Johnson and Daniel Johnson among others. *Hitler's Loss* attempts to redress the balance in the form of a personal selection of the exiles who influenced both

British and American culture. It also draws attention to the work of Varian Fry, the courageous American who saved so many of Europe's endangered artists and creative intellectuals from Vichy France in 1940. Fry's declared reasons for attempting his dangerous mission is a noble statement of gratitude to the artistic genius of Europe that the Nazis sought to destroy. His achievement in rescuing so much creative genius deserves the recognition that has only recently been given him in the USA and that he will now, it is to be hoped, receive in Britain.

The effect of these refugees on the British people was profound. Few in 1933 had met or even seen that strange beast, a European intellectual. As George Orwell observed, the British had an innate horror of abstract thought and felt themselves without a need for abstract philosophy or a systematic world overview. Britain was an insular country with bad memories of Germany in the First World War and with a consummate belief in her own natural superiority over other nations. The great majority of British citizens in the first half of the twentieth century had never travelled to Europe other than with a rifle in hand. When the émigrés arrived in London they were amazed to find that the British had little interest in them and that they were not required to assimilate into society as they had been in Germany. Rather, they were accepted for what they were, harmless but tiresome refugees from the Continent. To anyone educated in Europe these British were strange beings. Arthur Koestler, who progressed from penniless refugee to become a fine and influential writer in English, was intrigued by a society where the social norms were the very opposite of his own. He found that these strange people admired character rather than brains, prized stoicism rather than temperament and displayed nonchalance rather than diligence in most things. Where but in Britain, he wondered, 'would the tongue-tied stammer be thought more sincere than displays of unbridled eloquence'?

While Britain provided a more immediate refuge for the exiles, the USA was to offer them a far more prosperous future, but first they had to cross the Atlantic at a time when a long and expensive sea voyage was the only means of travel from Europe. Those who settled in Britain were aware that they took a risk. Until 1941 it was still possible that the Germans would invade the island, and it was not until the great reversal at Stalingrad in 1942 that it became apparent that Germany would lose the war. For this reason Britain appeared to many as merely a temporary refuge from danger in which to draw breath before moving on to full sanctuary in the USA. To the pessimists, the annexation of Austria in 1938 and the later fall of both Czechoslovakia and France must have made their choice of refuge in Britain seem merely a postponement of the inevitable disaster.

But the great majority of the émigrés, whether in Britain or the USA, flourished in exile. To many it was to be an illuminating experience and to some a personal artistic and intellectual fulfilment that might not have been possible in their homelands. What this immigration from Nazi Europe proved beyond all doubt was that the émigré brings far more to the adopted country than he or she will ever take from it. The USA is a country born out of this principle and Britain a nation that would do well to remember the constant waves of immigration even in the past three hundred years or so that brought the Huguenot weavers of the sixteenth century and the Kenyan Asians of the 1970s. The lessons of immigration are as relevant today as they were in 1933. What makes the events of the 1930s almost unique in history is the intellectual talent of the refugees. That so many of them immediately identified with their adopted lands was not surprising. The same principles that motivated the British determination to fight on alone against Hitler and that were behind Franklin Delano Roosevelt's patient and consistent drive to bring the USA into the war were those of the émigrés themselves – the preservation of moral integrity and intellectual freedom of the individual. One brief snapshot of the period sums up for me this union. It is of the writer Arthur Koestler – the European intellectual *par excellence* – on weekend leave in London, standing glass in hand at a literary soirée. He is the only man in the room in uniform, giving dignity and status to the rough khaki uniform of a private soldier of the lowly Pioneer Corps. The noble words of August von Platen, often quoted by Thomas Mann in exile, come to mind:

> But he whose soul despises evil
> Must one day face an exile from his native land
> When evil's worshipped there by fawning slaves
> Far better then to quit that land for ever
> Than live in tyranny under blind mob hate.

Prelude

On a spring day in 1933 Fritz Lang, Germany's most famous film director, put on his best suit and took a taxi to the Ministry of Propaganda in Berlin. He had been summoned by Joseph Goebbels, Hitler's second-in-command and Reichsminister for Enlightenment and Propaganda. At the door he was met by two jackbooted SS guards, men in black uniforms who marched him briskly to a bare waiting-room and left him there alone. Lang must have considered his film career, if not his life, would soon be over, for he had been told that that his last two films, *The Testament of Doctor Mabuse* and *M*, the story of a child murderer played by Peter Lorre, had infuriated the Nazis. After an hour's wait, the guards returned and led him down more echoing corridors to a vast office where the Reichsminister awaited him. As Lang entered, Goebbels did not get up from his desk but indicated that he should sit down. Then, looking up from the papers, Goebbels demanded to know what exactly Lang thought he was doing in attacking the people who had always been his friends. To put matters right with the new regime Lang was immediately to revise the ending of *The Testament of Doctor Mabuse* in line with the Nazi policy.

At this point Goebbels smiled. Did Lang realize, he asked, that the Führer was, in fact, one of his keenest admirers and had been delighted with Lang's earlier film *Der Nibelungen*, but most of all with *Metropolis*, even owning a copy himself. Goebbels paused, then, to

Lang's amazement, told him that the Nazi leadership would like him to become director of the new state film industry – he would be the most powerful man in German films. Goebbels then explained his proposition in detail. 'Now go home,' said Goebbels, 'and think about this great opportunity.' Lang stood up, shook hands and left the office, retracing his steps down the long corridors with an SS man on either side. However, instead of going on to his editing session at the Universum Film Arbeitsgruppe (UFA) studio, Lang took a taxi home, went up to his bedroom and carefully packed a single suitcase. That evening he caught the night sleeper to Paris. He never returned to Germany.

1

All That There Is Is Lost

When Fritz Lang got on that train to Paris he was just one of many to leave Germany in those first months of Nazi rule. Some of Germany's most eminent artists, writers, musicians and academics had already gone in what has been described as the greatest cultural migration in Western history since the fall of Constantinople to the Turks in 1453. Of those who left, the great majority were Jews, but with them went many Christians, communists and socialists who had opposed Hitler's rise to power. Most honourable of all were the small number of Germans, such as the conductor Fritz Busch, neither Jews nor political activists, who left on principle, outraged by the cruel and unjust treatment of their Jewish colleagues. The most famous exile of all was Albert Einstein, the world's best-known scientist. He had reached Ostend on his way home from a lecture tour of the USA when he was told that Hitler had been elected Chancellor. Loathed by the Nazis for both his race and his theories, Einstein turned away from his homeland and took the next ship back to New York. He never set foot in Germany again. Seizing the opportunity to please their new masters, both the Kaiser Wilhelm Institute of Physics and the Prussian Academy of Sciences voted to eject him, and the government revoked his German citizenship.

Einstein had been one of over half a million Jews living in Germany in 1933, a group that, in spite of Nazi propaganda, had never comprised more than 1 per cent of the entire population. Although small in number, Jews had, since the turn of the twentieth century, become ever more visible in German society. They were now prominent not only in business and finance but also in such high-profile professions as journalism, medicine and law. Their importance in German education was apparent to anyone who attended a university or college, as one in eight of all university professors and a quarter of all Germany's Nobel Prize winners were Jewish-born. Once the nation's underdogs, German Jews had by the 1920s become confident enough to involve themselves openly in politics, generally joining liberal or left-wing groups. They asked nothing more than to be fully integrated into German society like other citizens, and to many Jews this longed-for assimilation did, indeed, seem to have at last begun. Nor had they shirked their patriotic responsibilities in the First World War, when as many Jews (in proportion to their numbers) as Christians had volunteered for the army and 12,000 had been killed. Jews and Christians in Germany seemed also, to the Jews at least, to share the same ethical beliefs that included a respect for learning and culture and a capacity for hard work.

There were other reasons for Jewish optimism. Since the late nineteenth century the unified German nation had increasingly aspired to world cultural leadership. Nor did this appear to be over-optimistic, as Germany had become the first nation to achieve universal adult literacy and German universities were internationally regarded as the best in the world in most academic disciplines. In the arts, too, Germany under the post-war Weimar Republic was the crucible of the new and dynamic modernism that was influencing every branch of creative activity in Europe. The Jews of Germany, unlike those of Poland and other Eastern European countries, had by the 1920s rejected the cultural protection of the ghetto and had moved out into the mainstream of German life. They saw their new role as being net contributors to both German and international culture. If other European Jews, such as Mahler and Freud, could become world figures, why not those of Germany? Surely even the Nazis could not reject such a talented, valuable and sympathetic group within their own country who asked only to be integrated into the German whole?

But events were to show that Jewish confidence was misplaced. In reality, anti-Semites throughout the country saw these aspirations as a threat to the German nation and the Jews themselves as a hostile and alien minority acting collectively to exploit and dominate the majority. This historic fear and resentment had been exacerbated by the defeat of Germany in the First World War. In the search for scapegoats, latent anti-Semitism exploded into outright persecution led by right-wing groups. Shackled with enormous financial reparation payments by the victorious Allies (incredibly, they were scheduled to continue until 1989), many of the German people turned on the Jews. To the average German nationalist the Weimar Republic, the parliamentary democracy forced upon Germany by the victorious allies along with the abdication of Kaiser Wilhelm II, was a disgrace born out of defeat, characterized by easy-going liberalism and dominated by the Jews and their international allies.

The despair that gripped Germany changed it in a few years from being the most law-abiding society in Europe to one of the most violent and chaotic. Prominent in this disorder were Jewish politicians and intellectuals such as Kurt Eisner and Ernst Toller, who helped to establish a short-lived and violent communist regime in Bavaria in 1919. Support for the revolutionaries came from left-wing magazines, often edited and produced by Jews, who were equally prominent in the emergent pacifist and feminist movements and who also championed a more liberal approach to sexual matters. In the German public's perception it was the Jews who were behind this left-wing conspiracy to undermine and eventually to control German society. The right-wing response was immediate and brutal. In the four years between 1919 and 1922 almost four hundred communists and left-wing sympathizers, all but a handful of them Jews, were murdered on the streets of Germany by right-wing groups. As a result, Jews became more wary of political involvement and began to stand back as politics in the last years of the Weimar Republic became ever more violent. A decade later, in the 1932 elections, not one of the five hundred communist candidates was a Jew.

To German nationalists this threat was perceived as not only political but also cultural. They were associated in the public mind with everything that was modern, outrageous or international in the arts. Jews were particularly prominent in publishing, the press, film and theatre. For example, it has been estimated that Jewish-born artists made up half of all Germany's leading Expressionist groups. Expressionist artists believed that inspiration came from the artist's inner feeling rather than from a classical or theoretical view of the world – a concept that was anathema to the Nazi theorists. Any work of art that was thought to be daring or ultra-modern could, to the average German, confidently be attributed to a Jew. Often they were mistaken, as when a sexually explicit play, *Spring Awakening*, by the non-Jewish dramatist Frank Wedekind, provoked riots because of the erroneous belief that it was the work of a Jew. Many thought this modernism a deliberate attempt to undermine traditional German culture and values. Nor was it the right-wing alone that suspected a conspiracy. Conservative opinion in both town and country, encouraged by the academic defenders of traditional German culture, was convinced that such a Machiavellian plot did, indeed, exist. Their fears were shared by the right-wing critic Paul Fechter who, when invited to address the Association of National German Jews in 1930, warned that their own 'anti-Germanism' was inflaming the nation and was the cause of the mounting anti-Semitism. They were, Fechter told them, far too prominent in the arts for their own good. To traditional German anti-Semitism had been added a new fear and resentment of Jews born out of military defeat and a widespread loathing of the internationally imposed and 'un-German' Weimar Republic. It took a decade of this festering resentment to bring Adolf Hitler to power in January 1933 – not in an armed coup but as democratically elected Chancellor.

What surprised the world then and still surprises us today is not that Hitler and the Nazis moved against the Jews but the speed with which they did it. The number of decrees and promulgations depriving Jews of their place in German society passed by the Reichstag in the first months of Hitler's Chancellorship is breathtaking. Clearly the Nazis were well prepared. Even such a minor official as the sinister Achim Gercke, a 'race research specialist' at the Ministry of the Interior, was ready to act. He arrived at his new post armed with a card index containing the names of every Jew in Germany that he had begun a decade earlier while still a student. Yet the Nazis' first priority was not the reckoning with the Jews but the elimination of their old political enemies, the communists. Following the Reichstag fire of 27 February 1933, almost 10,000 party members and sympathizers were arrested and imprisoned, many in the newly opened Dachau concentration camp. Then, with the communists crushed, it was the turn of the Jews. A whole series of restrictions intended to demoralize and humiliate were imposed all over Germany. Yet some Jewish leaders remained optimistic, convinced that Hitler and the Nazis would be a temporary phenomenon and that the good sense of the German people would prevail. Even when, two months later, the boycott of Jewish business began on 1 April, such an important figure in the Jewish community as Rabbi Joachim Prinz declared it unreasonable for Jews to be anti-Nazi. Even as late as September 1933, his co-religionist the Kiel University historian Felix Jacoby, could still proclaim in a lecture, 'As an historian and Jew I have learned not to consider historical events from a private perspective. Since 1927 I have voted for Adolph Hitler . . . Augustus is the only figure of world history whom one can compare him with.'

But others were more realistic, accepting that the Nazi onslaught was but the beginning of a sustained and remorseless campaign against the whole Jewish community. The Jewish director of the Deutsche Bank, Georg Solmssen, wrote prophetically in April 1933, 'I am afraid that we are merely at the beginning of a process aimed purposefully and according to a well-prepared plan at the economic and moral annihilation of all members, without distinction, of the Jewish race living in Germany' (Friedlander, 1997).

Those Jews with intellectual or creative talents and with an established international reputation began planning their escape. The writers Thomas Mann (a Christian anti-Nazi) and Lion Feuchtwanger had substantial foreign earnings from royalties and were able to leave almost immediately and start a new life in exile. But anyone with a business to run found it almost impossible to sell up quickly and move on. However, with the German economy still in a precarious state after the Depression, there was a noticeable, albeit temporary, moderation in Nazi attacks on Jewish businesses in late 1933. Large and important organizations such as the Ullstein publishing empire and the Jewish-owned banks were, for the moment, ignored. Putting the Jewish-owned Tietz department store out of business, for instance, would have cost the economy over 14,000 jobs.

There were other economic considerations for the Nazis to contemplate. Jews had also played a decisive role in capital mobilization and in the development of the Berlin stock market as well as using their international banking connections to promote the German economy. The best-known German bank, Warburgs, had branches in Berlin, London and New York. But Nazi ideology always triumphed over economic expediency, and any high-profile Jew associated with the leading merchant banks had to go. Within a month Max Warburg had been sacked from every financial and industrial company of which he was a director.

Some of the new restrictions astonish by their petty-mindedness: Jews in Cologne were forbidden to use the municipal sports facilities; Jews were expelled from the German Boxing Association; and Yiddish was banned in the Baden cattle market. Then, with greater cultural significance, a bronze statue in Hesse of the poet Heinrich Heine was toppled from its plinth – the rush to de-Judaize the intellectual life of the German nation had begun.

Of all the many decrees and regulations aimed at the Jews none was more devastating than the Restoration of the Professional Civil Service Act of 7 April 1933. At a stroke, every Jew in Germany employed by the government or by state-sponsored local institutions was ordered to be dismissed from his or her post. From university professor to local postmistress, they all had to go. It was an event of the utmost significance for Germany's Jews: for the first time since their emancipation in 1871 the German state had discriminated against them in law. Prominence and reputation shielded no one, as over 1,200 Jewish academics were summarily dismissed. Europe's most famous theatre director, Max Reinhardt, was expelled from the German national theatre and fled the country. Max Lieberman, at eighty-six the best-known German painter of his day and holder of the coveted Pour le Mérite decoration, was forced to resign from the Prussian Academy. His fellow painter Oskar Kokoschka claimed later that none of Lieberman's colleagues expressed the slightest regret and that, when he died two years later, only three Aryans attended his funeral. In all this, the Nazis seem to have had the discreet support of the majority of Germany's non-Jewish teachers and lecturers. Nor must it be forgotten that Hitler's most vociferous supporters throughout his rise to power were the university students and their fraternities which, as early as 1919, had barred Jews from membership. By 1930 the Nazis controlled virtually all German university campuses with barely a murmur of protest from any lecturer in any academic department anywhere in the country.

The dilemma of the German scientists is discussed later in this book; they, too, kept silent and hoped for the best while they watched their

Jewish colleagues dismissed and driven into exile. Their cowardice throughout the whole of the Nazi era was later condemned by the British statesman, Lord Birkenhead, in 1962:

> There is no known instance in which a professor of physics or chemistry without any Jewish family ever made an open protest against Nazi activities. Even in the early years of Nazi power when opposition was not yet suicidal the scientific establishment, led by Planck and Nernst, washed its hands of the growing terror and concentrated on defending its own special privileges. The only notable scientist who was conspicuous in his disapproval of the Nazis was Max von Laue, and even his actions were taken within the physics establishment and not in open criticism of the regime.

Birkenhead claimed that only one non-Jewish scientist, the physicist Otto Hahn, had urged his colleagues to protest against the treatment of their Jewish colleagues at the the Kaiser Wilhelm Institute. Yet even the Jewish-born nuclear physicist Lise Meitner could describe Hitler's installation speech to the Reichstag in 1933 as being 'amicable and dignified'. She also, inexplicably, welcomed the hoisting of the Nazi flag over the Kaiser Wilhelm Institute by the Jewish chemist Fritz Haber (soon to be a Nazi victim himself) as 'a dignified gesture'. Meitner came to regret not leaving Germany at that time and believed that, in staying, she had given tacit support to Hitler. Among the few non-Aryan scientists to resign his post and leave Germany on principle was Erwin Schrödinger, who was immediately declared a traitor by his colleagues. Of those scientists who stayed, only one, the courageous Paul Rosbaud, worked actively against the regime by becoming a British agent and keeping London informed of the progress of German military science throughout the war.

Every academic discipline suffered from the loss of its Jewish members but none more than psychology, for which German medicine was famous. Seven professors and fifteen associate professors, including the heads of four of the five leading psychological institutes in German-speaking universities, were forced to resign. These included William Stern at Hamburg, Max Wertheimer at Frankfurt, David Katz at Rostock and Wilhelm Peters at Jena. Within a year they had all emigrated. Then, after Hitler's annexation of Austria, the Anschluss of 1938, it was the turn of the world-renowned Vienna School of Psychology to suffer the devastating loss of all its Jewish-born psychiatrists including the most celebrated of all, Sigmund Freud, who emigrated to London.

The failure of the German intellectual community to speak out against Hitler was to astonish the world. Why were so many highly educated and supposedly civilized academics supporting what was obviously a brutal totalitarian regime, let alone condoning its vicious anti-Semitism? Some historians have seen their silence as the characteristically German respect for authority – good or bad – that had first been expressed in the teachings of the religious reformer Martin Luther in the early sixteenth century.

Luther's assertion that there were two forms of freedom, inner and outer, was fundamental to his Protestant belief. But he made an important distinction. Outer freedom was subject to the individual's duty to obey authority without dissent, however it be constituted and no matter how brutal or unjust it might be. But a Lutheran's true salvation came from the development of an inner freedom gained by living a virtuous personal life that was totally unconnected to the external duty. Under this uniquely German dichotomy a man could remain 'good' even if he worked in a concentration camp provided he was a good husband, a loving father to his children and led a virtuous personal life. Hitler's own much chronicled kindness to pet dogs and Aryan children is an obvious example of this moral perversion. So fundamental, then, was this German respect for authority that even the few plots that occurred against Hitler appear somewhat half-hearted and show a distinct lack of enthusiasm for the task.

Yet the question still remains why, if Nazi intentions were so obvious, did so few Jews leave the country in those early years of tyranny? In the first year of Nazi rule just 37,000 left. In the next four years the rate of Jewish emigration actually fell, to 23,000 in 1934, 21,000 in 1935, 25,000 in 1936 and 23,000 in 1937. This relatively low rate of departure in the face of what must have been a predictable disaster can only be explained by the fact that the majority of Jews were convinced that the storm would pass or the regime would fall. Throughout their history the Jews had been no strangers to such persecution. As a people they had weathered many storms in many countries, the last being the Russian pogroms at the turn of the century. Given the pattern of the past, there was no reason to think that they would not weather this one, too.

But history itself had set a trap for the Jews. As Austin Stevens has written (1975), 'It offered them nothing to compare with what they were soon to suffer in Germany. Not even the Crusaders had shown the consistency of the Nazis . . . History had no parallel for the Final Solution.'

Yet there was still, before the 5 March Reichstag elections at least, a slim chance that the Nazis might be toppled by a military coup or an even fainter hope of intervention by the other European powers. There was every excuse for holding on, particularly when faced with the difficulties of withdrawing assets from the country. New laws regarding Jewish-owned property meant that it could only be sold at throw-away prices, and the pre-Nazi Brüning government's 'tax on capital flight' on assets of over 200,000 Reichsmarks was now ruthlessly applied. Rigged exchange rates also meant that by 1935 Jews leaving the country could only exchange their marks at 50 per cent of face value. This fell to 30 per cent, then finally, on the eve of war, to a nominal 4 per cent of their real value. Only those low in capital assets but high in intellectual skills could easily make this transition to a different culture in another country.

Meanwhile, uninhibited by moral scruples, many of Germany's academics competed openly for the posts left by their Jewish colleagues and sought to demonstrate their unwavering loyalty to the new regime. On 5 March 1933 the Prussian Academy of Letters had written to its members asking them not to criticize the new government and requesting them to sign a declaration of loyalty to the Führer. Only nine of more than 230 members refused including, to their credit, the novelists Alfred Döblin, Thomas Mann, Jacob Wasserman and Ricarda Huch. It was the first discrete gesture against the new regime by Mann, a Christian married to a Jew, who would later become the accepted moral leader of Germany in exile. Like Einstein, Mann was travelling abroad when Hitler was elected Chancellor. He wrote to the great scientist telling him of his own intention not to return and adding, 'My deepest conviction is that the whole "German Revolution" is indeed wrong and evil.' But Mann was also a realist. To ensure the continuing sale of his books in Germany, he refused to speak out publicly against the Nazi regime for several years more. The silence of Germany's greatest living writer ensured that his books were not included in the notorious auto-da-fé of 10 May 1933.

Other important intellectuals were vociferous in their support for Hitler. Shortly after leaving Germany in the summer of 1933, the Jewish philosopher Hannah Arendt wrote to her lover and professor, Martin Heidegger, complaining of his growing hostility to his Jewish colleagues and students and condemning his open support for National Socialism. Heidegger strenuously denied her accusation, but by 3 November he had withdrawn financial support for the 'Jewish or Marxist' students in his faculty and broken off all contacts with his non-Aryan colleagues. But Heidegger was not alone nor, in this homeland of Kant and Hegel, did a single faculty express shame or opposition when on 10 May 20,000 books by such authors as Karl Marx, Ferdinand Lassalle, Sigmund Freud, Maximilian Harden and Kurt Tucholsky were hurled into the flames as Goebbels ranted outside the Kroll Opera House in Berlin. Thomas Mann's words were an epitaph for that day: 'They were burning', he said, 'books that they were incapable of writing.'

The Nazi intention was to control not only the political life of Germany but the cultural life, too. This meant they must discredit many of the artistic and intellectual achievements of the past and, in particular, those of the Weimar Republic. It was not just the Jews but also the artistic 'degenerates' of the so-called 'modern' movement who must now be purged. Art and thought in the new Germany must be clean, pure and, above all, respectable. The result was an onslaught against a nation's culture that can only be compared to post-revolutionary Soviet Russia or China under the Red Guards. As the historian Helmut Lehmann-Haupt has pointed out, 'Such complete monopolization of the entire creative potential of a people . . . does not exist before the [twentieth] century.'

All aspects of culture and communications were now under Nazi control. To administer the system, a vast bureaucracy, the Reichskultur-kammer (Reich Chamber of Culture), was put in place with the task of turning back the clock and stifling the explosion of freedom and creativity that had characterized German art, literature, film and music in the 1920s. Members of such artistic groups such as Die Brücke (The Bridge) and Der Blaue Reiter (The Blue Rider), Jew or Christian, must be immediately proscribed and all traces of the hated Expressionism, Cubism and Dadaism eradicated. Modern atonal music, recently introduced by the Jewish composer Arnold Schoenberg and his followers Anton Webern and Alban Berg, must also be banned. German artists should realize that they were no longer part of an intellectual or internationalist elite – they were now the servants of the new National Socialist state.

To administer his vast cultural empire Hitler appointed Alfred Rosenberg, who had already founded the Kampfbund für deutsche Kultur (Combat League for German Culture), to control all 'intellectual and ideological training' in the Third Reich, and gave him a rank equal to that of his rival Joseph Goebbels, the Minister of Propaganda and President of the Reichskulturkammer. It was a characteristically Hitlerian appointment, ensuring that both men would compete for ultimate control of German culture and the Führer's approval. Hitler himself, in a speech at Nuremburg soon after his appointment as Chancellor, further clarified his personal opposition to all forms of modernism. He also announced a ban on art criticism, as there could now be only one cultural arbiter in the new Germany – the state. Curiously, he went on to warn his listeners against the potential excesses of even the new, ideologically correct, conservative Völkisch (nationalist) art. Later a manifesto was issued to define exactly what was required. It included the prohibition of all box-like architecture, the removal of all public sculptures not accepted by the German public and the banning of all works of art that showed 'international' or 'Bolshevik' tendencies from museums and collections. Any artists with Marxist or Bolshevik affiliations were to go, as were museum directors who wasted public funds on the purchase of 'un-Germanic' art.

As a form of artistic apartheid the Kulturbund deutscher Juden was established for Jewish artists under the control of the Nazi's chief cultural adviser, Hans Hinkel, now grandly titled Special Commissioner for the Supervision and Monitoring of the Cultural and Intellectual Activity of All Non-Aryans Living in the Territory of the German Reich. Its 180,000 Jewish members were ordered to develop their own culture in total isolation from that of the rest of Germany. In return for this concession Jews were no longer allowed to act in or produce any of the historic German legends nor recite in public traditional literary works from the Middle Ages or the Romantic periods. Schiller was denied them in 1934 and Goethe two years later. Even the English Shakespeare was in part banned because Hamlet's 'to be or not to be' soliloquy contained the subversive words 'the oppressor's wrong, the proud man's contumely'.

The Nazi purge of Jewish influence in music was no less rigorous. On 1 March 1933 the President of the Berlin Hochschüle announced that the Führer had resolved to 'break the Jewish stranglehold on Western music'. By the autumn of 1933 only a handful of Jews remained in academic positions, and such internationally famous soloists as Artur Schnabel and Jascha Heifetz had been banned from performing in Germany. Those who remained were required to join the Kulturbund deutscher Juden. Control of German music was to become a key area of dispute between Rosenberg and Goebbels. Rosenberg's organization had its own music division, the Reichsmusikkammer, which now began vetting musical performances in every German town. Goebbels responded by nationalizing both the Berlin Staatsoper and the Berlin Philharmonic. The Reichsmusikkammer then appointed Richard Strauss as its President, with Paul Graener and Wilhelm Furtwängler as his deputies. Three of the world's greatest composers, Arnold Schoenberg, Paul Hindemith and Béla Bartók, were simply banned from performance, and all of them went into exile in the USA.

The more cautious members of orchestras and choirs and such prominent soloists as the violinist Gustav Havemann, the composer Paul Gracner, the music journalist Fritz Stege and the Wagner scholar Otto Strobel thought it best to join the Nazi Sturmabteilung (SA). Other musicians, if Jewish or modernist, were publicly defamed and their concerts disrupted by Nazi stormtroopers. The eminent conductors Carl Ebert, Fritz Busch, Otto Klemperer, Bruno Walter and Hermann Scherchen were hounded out of Germany, while younger and less principled men such as Herbert von Karajan joined the party and took their place. Those Jews remaining were forbidden to perform any music by Wagner or Richard Strauss. By 1937 this ban had been extended to include the works of Beethoven and, the following year, to those of Mozart. Music by the Jewish composers Mendelssohn, Meyerbeer, Offenbach and Mahler were also banned from performance in Germany. To emphasize the point, Mendelssohn's statue was removed from outside the concert hall in his native Leipzig. Nazi political correctness often reached ludicrous proportions, as when Handel's *Judas Maccabeus* was renamed *The Field Marshal: A War Drama*. Then it was realized that Da Ponte, the librettist of three of Mozart's greatest opera's, *Don Giovanni*, *La Nozze di Figaro* and *Così fan tutte*, had been a Jew. Orders were given that only the German language versions of the libretti were to be used until it was discovered that even these were the work of a Jew, the conductor Hermann Levi. In order to avoid future embarrassment Goebbels ordered two encyclopaedias of Jews and Jewishness in music to be hastily produced. But the greatest problem facing the Nazi censors was the unpalatable fact that German popular and light music was a traditional Jewish preserve. The situation was further complicated by foreign music from Europe and the USA which the Reichsmusikkammer found even more difficult to police. Most embarrassing of all was the strong suspicion that Franz Lehar, the composer of Hitler's favourite operetta the *Merry Widow*, was actually a Jew. Should the Führer be told – and, if so, by whom?

The media, too, came under rigid Nazi control. Newspaper editors were ordered to report daily to the Ministry of Propaganda for official briefings. Radio stations were taken over by Nazi personnel, and a new brand of cheap radios known as 'Goebbels's snouts' was produced for the people to listen to the Nazi diktats. But it was the film industry that attracted Goebbels as the most effective medium of state propaganda. In 1933 German cinema was the most admired in the world for its innovative scripts and technical brilliance, and German film-makers were eagerly sought by studios in Paris, London and Hollywood. Not only were such German studios as UFA hotbeds of socialism but the international comings and goings of its personnel infuriated the Nazis and threatened their concept of a purely German cinema. As strict Nazi controls were imposed, the great days of German cinema came to a sudden end as more than 1,500 people, including its brightest stars, Fritz Lang and G.W. Pabst, fled the country for new careers in Paris, Hollywood and London. Those who remained now jumped to Goebbels's command. The new regulations were severe. No foreign film could be imported without a certificate of government approval, and none could be screened without a similar certificate. All existing German films were now refused a certificate, which at a stroke got rid of the past and created a market for the new Nazi-controlled productions. All films were, naturally, heavily censored both politically and morally by Goebbels's minions. Although shorn of its greatest talents, the German film industry continued to boom under the Nazis. From the beginning of the Third Reich up to 1942 1,100 feature films were produced with party approval, of which only a small percentage contained overt propaganda, the great majority being musicals and light-hearted romances – Goebbels had soon realized that a hard-pressed people needed escapist entertainment.

By 1935 all German culture was in the grasp of the Nazis and most of Germany's Jewish intelligentsia and its leading creative artists were in exile. Those who remained under Nazi rule could never make up for the disappearance of more than 2,000 writers and 4,000 theatre and film technicians and actors, let alone the loss of thousands of scientists, musicians and academics. Germany had been denuded of much of its intellectual and artistic intelligentsia. A nation that, in spite of its political impotence, had enjoyed wide-ranging artistic freedom had been transformed by the Nazis into a conformist, totalitarian state that repressed all intellectual and artistic innovation and comment. Those intellectuals who remained in Germany were faced with the choice of coming out in support of the new regime or simply keeping their mouths shut. Any dissent would provoke immediate dismissal and subsequent investigation by the Gestapo. In reaction, some individuals retreated into what has been called 'inner exile', persuading themselves that their silence was really a form of passive resistance. Others, the Spätexilanten or 'late' emigrants, tried initially to come to some kind of moral accommodation with the new regime but then decided to leave after experiencing at first hand the inflexibility and increasing brutality of the Nazis.

Safe, for the present, from Nazi rule the more optimistic of the cultural refugees contemplated a relatively short exile, little knowing that their 'extended trip abroad' would actually last ten or twelve years. In spite of the common hardship they suffered, they had one distinct advantage over their non-creative fellow exiles. Their talent and, in many cases, reputations meant that they would be able to find work and commissions in their new homes. Many sought to rebuild their careers in German-speaking countries and were drawn to the established émigré communities of Prague, Zurich, Paris and Vienna. The painter Oskar Kokoschka was one of several hundred émigrés who gathered in Prague, once one of the great cities of the Austro-Hungarian Empire, and where a post-First World War liberal Czech government and economic prosperity throughout the 1920s had made it one of the most important cultural centres in Europe. Others chose Budapest, in spite of the growing Hungarian hostility to Jews and a series of right-wing governments that revealed an increasing national sympathy with Nazi ideals and a renewed interest in promoting anti-Semitism. For the majority of exiles German-speaking Austria was the first choice in the first years of Nazi rule. But on 12 March 1938 German troops crossed the border and annexed Austria. The Anschluss ('linking-up') meant that a further 190,000 Jews were under the direct control of the Nazis.

What had begun in Germany was now perfected in Austria. So blatantly aggressive were the initial assaults on the Jews there that even Reinhard Heydrich, the Reichsprotektor of Bohemia, was moved to order the Gestapo to arrest those Austrian Nazis who had carried out the these assaults 'in a totally undisciplined way'. The policy was now to drive as many Jews as possible towards the Austrian border and to push them into Czechoslovakia, Hungary or Switzerland. To expedite this policy, Adolf Eichmann arrived in the wake of the first Wermacht units to advise the local police on Jewish policy. Ominously he informed Gestapo headquarters in Berlin on 8 May that he would shortly have in his possession all the Jewish yearbooks and directories for the neighbouring countries of Czechoslovakia and Hungary. A month later, the world's most famous psychologist, Sigmund Freud, was given permission by the new Nazi regime to leave Vienna, where he had lived for the past seventy-eight years. Having looted his possessions and forced him to pay a heavy emigration tax, the Gestapo agents demanded that he sign a declaration stating that he had not been ill treated. Freud signed the document but added the ironic comment 'I can most highly recommend the Gestapo to anyone.'

Within a year over 100,000 Jews, half of the entire community, and most of Vienna's illustrious Jewish intellectuals had left the country. With the success of the Anschluss Austria's Nazis made sure that their own racial policies were brought into line with those of the Third Reich. Next, in May 1938, it was Hungary's turn to introduce draconian anti-Semitic measures. Hungarian Jews represented 5 per cent of the population, a far larger percentage than in Germany. They, too, were at the centre of a highly cultivated society in Budapest, a city that was reminiscent of Paris with its pavement cafés and vibrant artistic life. But a series of right-wing governments had edged the country ever closer to Nazism, and by 1940 many of Hungary's most gifted Jewish intellectuals had gone into exile. Finally in October 1938 the Fascist Grand Council of Italy introduced its own anti-Jewish laws to the alarm of all but the most committed Italian fascists.

In an attempt to deal with the problem of the Jewish refugees an international conference was held at the instigation of US President

Franklin D. Roosevelt at Evian in France in July 1938. The outcome was a forgone conclusion, as all of the thirty-two participating nations had agreed in advance that none of them would change their existing regulations to accommodate the refugee Jews. The London *Spectator* condemned it as an outrage to the Christian conscience that 'the modern world with all its immense wealth and resources cannot get these exiles a home and food and drink and a secure status'. For those in exile from Nazi Germany it was time to move on. Their ultimate refuge would be the USA or Great Britain, but first they had to find a way through the regulations and restrictions that had been erected to block their path.

2

Clutching at Straws

Dispossessed and dishonoured, rejected by their own nation, Germany's dismissed intellectuals began to leave the country in their thousands. Their initial concern was to find somewhere that would not only admit them but would also provide them with work. The first destination for many was either Austria or Czechoslovakia – where German was spoken – or, for the artists and film-makers, Paris. Often an émigré's destination was determined by the existence of a cousin in Paris, an aunt in Prague, a brother in Vienna or even a well-established business contact in New York. Since many of the refugees were convinced that the Nazi regime would be short-lived, they were loath to move far beyond the German borders. Yet from the beginning of exile there were some who sought to put an expanse of sea between themselves and National Socialism. Their obvious choice was to apply for entry to Britain or make the long voyage across the Atlantic to the USA.

There was much to be said for Britain as a refuge. Culturally distinct from the rest of continental Europe, it had maintained a guarded hostility to Germany for over three decades. The British made it clear that they had little time for Germans – Christian or Jew. But they also maintained a much-admired tradition of fair play that had led to Britain providing an asylum for German and other European political refugees throughout the nineteenth century. For those who remembered the speed of the German advance in the Great War and the close proximity of Calais to Dover, the safest refuge would have been the the USA. Founded by refugees from religious intolerance, it had offered sanctuary to succeeding generations of European dissenters for three centuries. Compared with Britain, it was a large and prosperous country with almost unlimited opportunities for new emigrants to prosper. Yet even this liberal democracy had become increasingly isolationist following the bitter experience of the First World War, the financial trauma of the Wall Street Crash and the subsequent Depression. Times were hard for the American worker; there was a new conservatism in the air and, ominously, a suspicion of all European newcomers and the disruptive socialism that they were rumoured to bring with them.

Times were hard in Britain, too, but political refugees had traditionally been welcomed by all social classes eager to demonstrate the largesse and innate superiority of Britain to other nations. After the abortive uprisings of 1830 and 1848 exiled Germans, including the most famous of all revolutionaries, Karl Marx, had settled in the London districts of Soho, St John's Wood and Camberwell. Others had migrated to the great industrial cities of the north and, like Friedrich Engels in Manchester, had waited in vain for Britain's own, long-predicted revolution to begin. When nothing happened, Engels's friend Carl Hallé abandoned politics and gave his adopted city a famous orchestra, the Hallé, instead. There were few restrictions on immigrants in the nineteenth century, and successive British governments openly welcomed the victims of continental tyranny and were proud that they had the good sense to choose to live in Britain where, as Lord Mansfield had declared a century earlier in freeing a black slave from his master, 'The air in England cannot support a slave.' British support for liberal movements in Europe and the country's readiness to offer asylum to failed revolutionaries persisted. As Lord Malmesbury told Parliament in 1852:

> I can well conceive the pleasure and happiness of a refugee, hunted from his native land, on approaching the shores of England, and the joy with which he first catches sight of them; but they are not greater than the pleasure and happiness every Englishman feels in knowing that his country affords the refugee a home and safety.

But complacency turned to resentment when, at the end of the nine-teenth century, over 200,000 Russian Jews, fleeing the pogroms at home, arrived in Britain provoking a wave of resentment as they crowded together in the slums of London's East End. By 1901 almost a quarter of a million aliens, many of them eastern European Jews, had settled in Britain. Their presence provoked the first organized anti-Semitism since the Middle Ages. During the widespread xenophobia that followed the outbreak of the Boer War in 1899, the newcomers were suspected of supporting the enemy. This public resentment led to the passing of the Aliens Act of 1905, followed by the Aliens Restrictions Bill of 1914, which closed the door on unregulated asylum seekers. By 1920 only those refugees with a work permit or possess-ing substantial financial resources could be admitted. It was these new restrictions that were to prevent Britain from becoming a country of mass refuge in the late 1930s.

This same anti-immigrant mood characterized the USA in 1933. There had been in the preceding two decades an unprecedented influx of refugees from all regions of Europe as part of the phenomenon that led, in the years between 1880 and 1940, to the arrival of half of all the immigrants who ever came there. Most were peasants or unskilled labourers escaping endemic European poverty rather than political or religious oppression. But the sheer weight of numbers produced a predictable backlash among established Americans, who feared that these ethnically diverse newcomers would irreparably alter the national character. Jobs were also scarce as the nation emerged from the Depression and people feared for their own livelihoods. By 1939 *Fortune* magazine found in a survey that 80 per cent of those inter-viewed had grave doubts about admitting more refugees from Europe. Politicians were not slow to respond to this new xenophobia, and a National Origins Act marked a far more rigorous policy of emigration control. When the first of the 100,000 refugees from Nazi Europe arrived, they faced an entry system that was now as strict as anywhere in the world. So restrictive, in fact, that even in the twelve months lead-ing up to the outbreak of war US officials would not even allow the controlled entry quota limit to be reached.

With more excuse, given its size in relation to a large population, Britain, too, tried to stem the tide of European refugees in the mid-1930s. New entry criteria were introduced that favoured those immigrants with an established reputation in the sciences, technology or the arts. The government quite sensibly realized that the country could benefit from a limited influx of such talented and highly trained individuals. Nor had the largesse, so eloquently expressed by Lord Malmesbury eighty years earlier, totally disappeared. A maverick MP, Commander Oliver Locker-Lampson, not only invited the refugee Albert Einstein to Britain in 1933 but also gave him a cottage on his Norfolk estate and two armed farm workers to guard him from Nazi agents. Einstein was in the visitors' gallery of the House of Commons to hear Locker-Lampson win approval for a bill to speed up the naturalization of Jewish refugees after he had stated his own unambiguous support for the great scientist (Hansard, 1933):

> Germany has turned out her most glorious citizen, Albert Einstein. The most eminent men in the world have agreed he is the most eminent. He is beyond any achievement in the realm of science, and stands out as the supreme example of the selfless intellectual. Today Albert Einstein is without a home . . . The Huns have stolen his savings, plundered his place of residence, and even taken his violin . . . How proud this country must be to have offered him shelter.

Meanwhile, businessmen and industrialists with substantial capital resources were also being welcomed at a time when the British economy was, like that of the USA, still recovering from the Depression. Whenever possible they were encouraged to start new businesses in areas of high unemployment such as the north and north-west of England. Less wealthy or talented individuals, 'especially those who appear to be of Jewish or partly Jewish origin', were ordered to be more closely scrutinized. Among those classified for summary rejection were the rank and file of any emigrant group, the small shopkeepers, manual workers, 'ordinary' musicians and commercial artists. Least welcome of all were the émigré lawyers, doctors and dentists who might offer competition to Britain's own established professionals.

An obvious example of professional hostility or, at best, ambiguity towards the refugees was the medical profession. While the Professional Committee of the British Medical Association under Samson Wright gave every assistance to the refugee doctors, their colleagues in the Medical Practitioners' Union strongly opposed them being recognized. Support for their action came, predictably, from the *Daily Express*, which claimed in June 1938 that 'there is a big influx of Jews into Britain. They are over-running the country. They are trying to enter the medical profession in great numbers.' When the Home Secretary proposed giving immediate recognition to graduates of the Austrian medical schools he was vigorously opposed by the whole British medical establishment. As a consequence they were faced with several years' clinical study in Britain before they could be recognized. Even the most experienced and expert practitioners were forced to retrain in a new language. Most suspect of all were the Vienna psychoanalysts, whose rumoured clinical techniques caused consternation among their British colleagues. But when war broke out this intolerable situation changed almost overnight. Now doctors of any sort were desperately needed as British practitioners enlisted in the armed services. By an Emergency Order of 1941 refugee doctors who had failed to requalify were given temporary recognition for the duration of the war, some enlisting in the Royal Army Medical Corps. When the war ended this was made permanent in reward for the loyalty and dedication they had shown to their new country.

But in the mid-1930s an increasingly anti-German mood still united British society. Memories of the terrible and unnecessary losses of First World War caused by German aggression were remained in people's minds. The advent of Hitler had only served to confirm British suspicions that the Germans were still a brutal and unreliable people bent on European, if not world, domination. As one government minister, Robert Vansittart – an open supporter of the movement to exclude all but a few refugees – put it unambiguously to Parliament, 'Eighty per cent of the German race are the moral and political scum of the earth. You cannot reform them by signatures and concessions. They have got to be hamstrung and broken up.'

Nor could the average Briton differentiate between Nazi and Jew – it was enough that they were all Germans. One refugee, newly arrived in Britain, recalled being called a 'Bloody German' in a London street. When he protested that he was not really a German but a Jew his antagonist shouted back, 'Worse still, a bloody German Jew!' The émigré scientist Max Perutz had a similar experience of British ignorance when interned on the Isle of Man. As the camp commander watched a party of new internees with skullcaps and curly side locks arrive at the camp, he turned to Perutz and said, 'I had no idea there were so many Jews among the Nazis.' Perutz remembers distinctly that, like Churchill, he pronounced the word as 'Nazzis'.

Suspicion of the refugees was reflected in hostile articles that appeared in the British press, particularly in the *Daily Express* and *Daily Mail*, whose owner, Lord Rothermere, had applauded the rise of Hitler and Mussolini and given support to the British fascist leader Oswald Mosley. In the USA the press echoed the same sentiments. Under the headline 'Refugees De Luxe', *Life* magazine proclaimed that German refugees were staying in the best American hotels and eating in top-class restaurants at public expense. More responsible journals, however, told the true story and urged their readers to look on the refugees as net contributors to their new country. The *New Yorker* praised the work of the artists, and *Mercury* published a persuasive article entitled 'Hitler's Gift to America'. Anti-Semitism, too, appears to have been more institutionalized in the USA than it was in Britain, particularly in the East Coast schools and colleges where so many of the newcomers hoped to find employment. Some of the Ivy League colleges had for decades maintained a covert policy of limiting the number of Jews appointed to academic posts.

By 1938 the political situation in Europe had further deteriorated, and Britain found that the trickle of refugees applying for admission had become a flood. Until Kristallnacht on 9 November 1938 only 5,500 of the 154,000 refugees who had left Germany had applied to enter Britain. After that night of terror for the Jews, British consuls throughout Germany were inundated by applications for entry visas. Jewish refugee organizations did what they could, and the Society of Friends, the Quakers, with offices in Paris, Prague and Berlin, intervened directly with relevant British government departments on behalf of the Jews. Important work was also done on behalf of the dispossessed scholars and university teachers by the Society for the Protection of Science and Learning, the Federation of University Women in England, the International Student Service and the Jewish Academic Council. The British government's own response to the crisis of Kristallnacht was to relax many of the entry restrictions so that, when war finally came on 3 September 1939, over 55,000 people, almost all of them Jewish, had found asylum in Britain. They were now safe, alongside Britain's Jews in the only sizeable European Jewish community that was to survive the Second World War unscathed.

When Britain declared war on Germany the government was faced with the problem of what to do with its refugees from enemy Europe. Given the British suspicion of all things German, they could not be allowed to wander the country at will, free to carry on acts of sabotage. The collapse of Norway and the work of the infamous, if unproven, 'Fifth Column' of Nazi sympathizers there had alarmed the British public. The press was not slow to suggest that the same treachery might happen in Britain. The *Daily Mail*, as ever, led the campaign with this demand on 20 April 1940:

> Act! Act! Act! Do it now! The rounding up of enemy agents must be taken out of the fumbling hands of local tribunals. All refugees from Austria, Germany and Czechoslovakia, men and women alike, should be drafted without delay to a remote part of the country and kept under strict supervision.

When the Netherlands surrendered to the Germans on 15 May 1940, the British Minister to the Hague, Sir Neville Bland, just managed to escape back to Britain bringing with him reports that a Dutch Fifth Column had assisted German parachutists. On Monday 27 May 1940 the British government, bowing to public and military pressure, ordered the police to begin arresting alien refugees. The story of their internment and eventual release has been well documented elsewhere. Today that policy of internment seems ridiculous for, as the émigré scientist Max Perutz has said, 'They locked us up to stop us, in case we helped our greatest enemies.' But at the time Britain was in a desperate position as France finally collapsed and a German invasion seemed not only inevitable but imminent. There was no time for officials to differentiate between the small group of Nazi sympathizers trapped in Britain by the war and the great majority of Jewish refugees who, had they been allowed, would have willingly taken up arms and joined the British in the fight against their former oppressors.

Internment for the thousands of refugee intellectuals was a bitter and bewildering experience somewhat mitigated by the kindness and good humour shown them by the majority of their British captors.

For many it became a enlightening experience as they met fellow refugees with similar interests to their own and formed friendships that would last a lifetime. Not least of these was the coming together of the first three members of the Amadeus String Quartet. A survey of a single camp on the Isle of Man revealed that, of the 1,500 internees, over three hundred were creative intellectuals or academics. Many had worked before internment in whatever menial jobs they could find in London. According to the publisher George Weidenfeld, some had enterprisingly used their old dinner-jackets to get work as waiters.

As Britain became an armed camp in 1940 the needs of the military became paramount. New training battalions were being raised, and they badly needed the camps occupied by the internees. In desperation the government decided to ship as many internees as possible, like the convicts of old, to Australia or Canada. Then, on 2 July 1940, the liner *Arandora Star* carrying internees to Canada was torpedoed in the Irish Sea by a German U-boat. Of the 1,200 aliens on board, more than six hundred drowned, and the British government was faced with growing opposition both to mass internment and the policy of risking the lives of genuine refugees in long and dangerous voyages. The British press – fickle as ever – having campaigned for internment now called for its abandonment. As swiftly as it had begun it was ended.

Few of its victims were bitter about their captivity. One Austrian psychiatrist said on release, 'We are all grateful for the kindness shown us by the authorities including soldiers whose job it was to guard us. The commandant was very fine.' By the end of 1940 almost 10,000 refugees had been released, some 4,000 into the only section of the British Army open to them, the Pioneer Corps. Most of the refugee intellectuals returned to London, where they settled in the more cosmopolitan areas of north London such as St John's Wood, Swiss Cottage and Hampstead. With so many British men serving in the armed services, jobs were not too hard to find, and even such an esoteric refugee from the world of opera as the Austrian impresario Rudolf Bing found no difficulty in getting a job in a London store. Some spent their evenings as fire-watchers as the Luftwaffe bombed the city. Others, missing the cafés of Berlin and Vienna, congregated every morning in the lobbies of London's Cumberland, Strand and

Regent Palace hotels, easily distinguishable by their dark blazers, long overcoats and large hats. George Weidenfeld, in his 1995 memoirs, gives a vivid picture of refugee life at the time:

> These hotels were the stock exchanges for personal information, business tips and the ratings for small boarding-houses, continental grocery shops and private sales outlets for second-hand clothes . . . above all they served as a centre for information on job prospects. The hotel lobbies were the equivalent of the traditional Viennese café . . . the band played innocuous music ranging from the 'The Teddy Bears' Picnic' to Gilbert and Sullivan.

With their distinctive German accents and continental mannerisms, the refugees were easy to spot in wartime London. Even though they might become naturalized Britons, they could never become 'English' as the American immigrants could become American. This Englishness was hard for a foreigner to comprehend and seemed to depend on an instinctive sympathy for the Church of England, horse-racing, drinking in pubs and an understated affection for the monarchy. Most of all, it depended in some mysterious way on a keen appreciation of that almost inexplicable game, cricket. The great émigré biochemist Sir Ernst Chain always blamed his lack of social success in British academic circles on his total ignorance of the game.

Cultural assimilation was just as difficult. Where continental Europe had respected the intellectual, the British were suspicious of anyone showing a more than discrete interest in ideas for their own sake. Nor were the British much taken with any form of modernism in the arts. With the exception of a small group of aesthetes that included the writers Stephen Spender, W.H. Auden and Christopher Isherwood, who had gathered in Berlin in the 1920s, the new cultural movement was largely ignored. Above all, the British cult of amateurism prevailed. It was considered bad form to be seen to be competing too keenly at anything, even on the sports field. The aspiration of any successful British artist, writer or composer was to be seen more as a country gentleman than as a dedicated exponent of any particular art form. The style had been set by such men as Sir Edward Elgar and Rudyard Kipling with their tweeds and fine country houses. Artistic struggle – like trade – could never be seen to make an appearance in their lives. As the art historian Nikolaus Pevsner, newly arrived from Germany, observed, the British were more interested in portraits of their pets and horses than in paintings with religious or abstract themes. British novelists shared this same obsession with nature and simplicity, setting their plots in the English countryside or in India. The urban novel of ideas held little appeal for writers and even less for the book-buying public. This was a society that had little interest in or understanding of the European urban intellectuals who had arrived in its midst. Yet there was hardly an academic or cultural organization in Britain that would not benefit from their presence and be enlightened by their ideas.

Far beyond the reach of any German invasion, the USA had no need of internment. Only after the crisis that followed the Japanese attack on Pearl Harbor in December 1941 was action taken against aliens, in this case Japanese and Japanese Americans. The USA had, however, witnessed the problems that Britain had experienced in dealing with its own refugees. It simplified the process of admission by appointing an Advisory Committee on Political Refugees in 1940 that produced criteria for admission broadly similar to those operating in Britain. Under the new regulations five hundred creative intellectuals were allowed into the USA, and the final tally was over three thousand. Importantly for the refugees, there was a clause that allowed entry to an unlimited number if they qualified under the National Origins Act as teachers or lecturers in higher education. It was this clause that was to save so many of those trapped in Vichy France in 1940. It was their plight that attracted the sympathy of intellectual America. Eight thousand dismissed academics and 1,500 artists and cultural intellectuals were already safe in the USA, but many more were still at risk. To help their escape an Emergency Rescue Committee was established in New York together with a complementary Emergency Committee for Displaced Foreign Scholars. Its task was to find as many posts as possible for the refugee academics in institutions throughout the USA. It was helped in this work by the Rockefeller Foundation and the Oberlaender Trust, which independently found places for a hundred more.

Individuals helped, too. The educational administrators Abraham Flexner and Alvin Johnson had both travelled extensively in Germany during the rise of the Nazis. They realized that the time might come when the USA could provide a refuge for European scholarship. As director of the Institute for Advanced Studies, Flexner now encouraged American and European scholars to work together at Princeton University. Among the first émigrés to join him there were the art historians Erwin Panofsky and Ernst Herzfeld together with the world's most eminent scientist, Albert Einstein. In New York Alvin Johnson founded his University in Exile where he provided ninety posts for exiled scholars who, like himself, were sympathetic to socialism. From this institution many experienced German administrators and economists went on to join American industrial corporations or found positions with the US government in Washington.

But the most remarkable individual to become involved in this the task of rescuing the endangered scholars was Varian Fry. Although the world knows that Oskar Schindler saved his Jewish workers from the gas chambers, few people have heard of this quiet American hero. But in the chaos that followed the fall of France in 1940 Varian Fry personally rescued over 1,500 of the world's leading artists and intellectuals from under the noses of the Gestapo. Among them were some of the greatest names of twentieth-century culture. Today Fry's achievement is ranked alongside that of the tragic Swedish diplomat Raoul Wallenberg as a saviour of many endangered Jews, and his name is inscribed on the Yad Vasshem memorial at Tel Aviv as one of the righteous among nations.

The plight of the thousands of German-born Jewish refugees trapped in Vichy France had aroused the sympathy of American intellectuals who were appalled by their own government's lack of interest. It was in an attempt to assist them that the Emergency Rescue Committee had been formed in New York. With the fall of France in 1940 the committee decided on positive action and chose as their representative in France an unassuming 32-year-old journalist named Varian Fry. Fry accepted this dangerous mission without hesitation, for on a visit to Germany in 1935 he had seen the Nazis at work. In Berlin he witnessed a pogrom in which Jewish shops were wrecked and their owners beaten up – one frail old man being kicked in the face by Nazi thugs. Fry knew that the refugees trapped in France would now get the same treatment, and his innate sense of decency and commitment to democracy moved him to volunteer his services. He was a most untypical hero, in appearance more like an academic than a man of action. His hobbies were bird-watching and classical literature. The reasons he gave for volunteering to go to Vichy France in his memoir of 1945 reveal an unusual and moving sincerity:

> Among the refugees who were caught in France were many writers and artists whose work I had enjoyed: novelists like Franz Werfel and Lion Feuchtwanger; painters like Marc Chagall and Max Ernst; sculptors like Jacques Lipchitz. For some of these men, although I knew them only through their work, I had a deep love; and to them all I owed a heavy debt of gratitude for the pleasure they had given me. Now that they were in danger, I felt obliged to help them, if I could; just as they, without knowing it, had often in the past helped me.

Fry was given a list of several thousand Jewish intellectuals thought to be under threat in France. The names had been compiled by the Rescue Committee with additional suggestions from exiles already in the USA including Thomas Mann, the French theologian Jacques Maritain, Max Ascoli and Jan Masaryk. The names of endangered artists were provided by Alvin Johnson of the New School for Social Research and Alfred H. Barr Jr of the Museum of Modern Art in New York. Fry's brief was simple – go to Marseilles, find the refugees, give them financial assistance and liaise with the American Consulate to obtain as many entry visas as possible. This, he was told, should take no more than three weeks. But Marseilles was in chaos when Fry arrived with refugees from all over the country who had escaped from German-Occupied France. On his first day in the city, Fry went to the US Consulate only to be appalled by the cynical indifference shown by the officials. He realized that he was clearly on his own. Although he had no experience of either refugee care or of clandestine operations, he set up office in the Hôtel Splendide and began recruiting a team of local helpers as resourceful as himself. Fry soon discovered that he was well equipped for this work and began to display a quiet but unusual tenacity in pestering the Consulate for exit or transit visas for his clients. Within a month the US diplomatic corps in France was urging the State Department in Washington to pressurize the Rescue Committee into recalling him. Fry was not only fighting the Vichy French administration but also his own diplomatic service.

The greatest danger to the refugees' safety was Article XIX, the so-called 'surrender on demand' clause of the Franco-German Armistice. This stated that Vichy France must immediately hand over any named individual requested by the Gestapo in Occupied France. Fry suspected that French compliance would be no more rigorous than any other of their other undertakings to the Germans. Nor was he convinced that Spain and Portugal – the closest neutral countries – would be totally unsympathetic to either the refugees' plight or the Allies' wishes. It was a situation that he set about exploiting with determination. But new anti-Jewish laws in October 1940 led to the arrest of many refugees, among them Marc Chagall – not for being a 'degenerate' painter but simply because he was a Jew. Chagall was one of the first that Fry managed to get released, and by the spring of 1941 his tally of success also included film critic Siegfried Kracauer, the artists Max Ernst and Jacques Lipchitz; Professor Boris Mirkine-Guetzevitch of the Sorbonne, the singer Lotte Leonard; the Romanian historian Valeriu Marcu, the physicist Peter Pringsheim and many more. It was an impressive list.

When Spain, after a visit from Heinrich Himmler, closed its frontier with France, Fry's task became even more difficult. The escape route over the Pyrenees was now blocked, and all visa applications to Spain, Fry suspected, were being checked by Gestapo agents in Madrid. The refugees now ran the risk of being lured into Spain only to be arrested at the border. To add to Fry's problems, only French ships bound for Oran or Algiers were allowed to sail from Marseilles. Throughout his mission Fry had great difficulty in communicating with the Rescue Committee in New York. Departing refugees were sometimes given secret messages to mail from Lisbon or were asked to carry confidential reports secreted in a tube of toothpaste to New York. The Nazis were now openly visiting the Vichy French internment camps searching for named suspects. Nor were Jewish refugees Fry's only concern. With the fall of France groups of British soldiers that had been trapped made their way south to Marseilles. Three hundred were interned at Fort St Jean in the city but were allowed out on parole. Fry managed to provide them with maps and money supplied from Britain by Sir Samuel Hoare which enabled them to escape in small groups across the Pyrenees. These soldiers proved ideal for testing Fry's ever-evolving routes to Syria, North Africa,

Gibraltar, Rabat and Casablanca – even to Dakar in West Africa. He knew that under the Geneva Convention captured British soldiers would be interned by the Germans rather than murdered as the Jewish refugees would have been. Some of the more adventurous soldiers swam ashore as the French ships passed Gibraltar, but the majority stayed on board until they reached a port in either North or West Africa, later to be released by Free French forces.

Fry's most successful escape route, however, was to the French West Indian island of Martinique. Ships departed from Marseilles every four or five days and their passengers did not need transit visas. Among those who escaped by this route were the Parisian photographers Ylla and Lipnitski, the German anti-fascist writer Wilhelm Herzog, the conductor Eduard Fendler, the pianist Erich Itor-Kahn and many survivors of the German and Austrian anti-Nazi underground. Against all the odds, by May 1941 Fry had assisted over 15,000 individuals, of whom 2,000 could be described as refugee artists or intellectuals. Even for those he could not rescue Fry had provided basic support from the fast-depleting $10,000 that Sir Samuel Hoare had given him to aid the British military personnel.

Then came a major setback. A British warship captured one of the Martinique ships as a prize of war and the Vichy government cancelled all sailings on the route. The rescue mission suffered another blow when Harry Bingham, Fry's contact at the US Consulate, was recalled and replaced by a more recalcitrant official who regarded all refugees as troublemakers. Worse was to come – at the end of June the Consulate was ordered to send all future visa applications to Washington for approval. Fry's old enemies at the US Embassy now joined the Vichy police in demanding his recall. When his passport expired the following January the US Consulate in Marseilles refused to renew it. Then, after consulting Washington, it was announced that a two-week passport would be issued to Fry but only if he agreed to return immediately to the USA. At the same time, the Vichy police told him that unless he left France voluntarily he would be arrested. Two days later he was given a one-month passport for westbound travel only, together with a French exit permit and Portuguese and Spanish transit visas. When he still refused to budge Fry was arrested and held incommunicado before being taken to the Spanish frontier and expelled from France. Even with Fry gone, his colleagues in

Marseilles still managed to aid the escape of three hundred more refugees before the office was closed by the police on 2 June 1942. Within weeks thousands of Jews in both the German-Occupied and Vichy areas of France were rounded up and sent in cattle trucks for extermination in Poland. Back in New York Fry continued to plead the refugees' cause by lobbying everyone who had influence in Washington and making a nuisance of himself with his own Rescue Committee until the Japanese attack on Pearl Harbor brought the USA into the war and all contact with Europe ceased.

What Varian Fry had achieved was astonishing. He was an ordinary man who, like a character in a Fritz Lang film, had found the courage to become a great one. An introvert who had failed the army draft board through stress-induced duodenal ulcers, Fry had bribed officials and hired a small army of criminals, forgers, smugglers and black marketeers to work for him. With a hastily recruited team, who were often as inexperienced as himself, he had interviewed over 15,000 people, established an escape network that had rescued British soldiers, gathered intelligence on internment camps and implemented successful and clandestine escapes from Vichy France for more than 2,000 people. What he saved for the world is incalculable – without Varian Fry some of the world's great modern artists including Marc Chagall, Marcel Duchamp, André Breton, André Masson and Max Ernst might not have survived. Nor would the writers Franz Werfel, Heinrich Mann and Lion Feuchtwanger and many others who continued to write in safety. Nor indeed would the USA have gained the services of many European academics and Nobel Prize winners such as the physicist Otto Meyerhof and social philosopher Hannah Arendt.

The arrival of these distinguished representatives of Western culture in their country convinced the American intelligentsia that civilization was indeed under threat from the Nazis. If Britain fell, then the whole of Europe apart from the neutral countries would be under barbarian control. Where the Turks had once been repulsed at the gates of Vienna, the Germans had actually occupied the acknowledged capital of European culture, Paris. With the coming of the émigré intellectuals the torch had passed to the USA, and Europe's creative heritage would have to be kept safe by that country. As the American art critic John Peale Bishop wrote in 1940 (Fleming and Bailyn, 1969):

The future of the arts is in America . . . The presence among us of these European writers, scholars, artists, composers, is a fact. It may be for us as significant a fact as the coming to Italy of the Byzantine scholars, after the capture of their ancient and civilized capital by Turkish hordes . . . the Byzantine exiles did little on their own account after coming to Italy. But for the Italians their presence, the knowledge they brought with them, was enormously fecundating.

3

Fantasy and Film Noir

Who but the British could have made film stars out of Gracie Fields and George Formby? Yet these two working-class comedians from the north of England were the favourites of British cinema audiences in the early 1930s. At the time, British cinema was merely the poor cousin of the American and the German film industries. Hollywood had the big budgets and world-wide distribution, but Germany had the most innovative writers and technicians in the world. Even the Hollywood studio bosses acknowledged that Berlin's UFA studios was the consistent breeding ground for new talent. Each year they attempted to lure the best of the German film-makers to California with offers of lucrative contracts, but few of their talent scouts bothered to visit London. Sadly, British film-making was thought by many to be laughable in everything but its comedies. The trade journal *Kinematograph Weekly* described contemporary British films as 'a collection of old-fashioned hackneyed plots, poorly contrived, badly written, uninspired and dreary tripe'. The film critic of the *Daily Herald* went even further by suggesting that half of all British directors should be immediately banned, half the studios closed and half the producers gracefully retired. The only way to raise the standards of British films, he insisted, was to attract foreign directors and cameramen and to use far more adventurous screenwriters.

Before the arrival in London of the Hungarian Alexander Korda

British films were made purely for domestic consumption. Generally they were poorly made comedies of proletarian life featuring the current stars of British music hall. Social comment or a documentary approach to current events were unknown outside the newsreel. But low-budget productions were needed to meet the conditions of the Film Quota Act of 1927 which stipulated that British cinemas must show a high proportion of British-made films. The British studios were more concerned with quantity than with quality until Alexander Korda showed, with *The Private Life of Henry VIII*, in 1933 that a British film could succeed internationally if it was well enough made. Starring Charles Laughton, this big-budget film was a box office success in both Britain and the USA. But to sustain this progress British film-making desperately needed more skilled technicians – Goebbels's dismissal of so many talented Jewish or left-wing film-makers in 1933 was to help provide them. When the first of these refugees arrived in the mid-1930s, the British film union began complaining about the high salaries being paid to them.

One of the first to bring his skills to London was G.W. Pabst's lighting cameraman, Gunther Krampf, who had photographed *Pandora's Box*, one of the greatest films in cinema history. By 1935 every major British film production company had at least one European lighting cameraman under contract. German art directors, including Alfred Junge, Oskar Werndorff and Erno Metzner, were also working in London. With them came a youthful Ken Adam, later to be an Oscar-winning art director on the James Bond films. Their talent soon led to a marked improvement in the quality of British films. The Hollywood art director Paul Holmes, on a visit in 1935, noticed a new professionalism in British film-making: 'A valuable advance in realism has been attained through the closer co-operation of the director and cameraman with the art director. This essential co-operation has . . . been lacking in this country.'

Even German producers were now attracted by this new spirit in the British film industry. One of the most successful was Rudolph Becker, who had directed at the UFA studio in Berlin. His first British film was a musical entitled *City of Song* shot mainly with an émigré crew. It was remarkable for the high quality of the sound recording – as good, critics thought, as in any contemporary Hollywood musical. Max Schach, another refugee from the Nazi-controlled German film industry, followed Becker to London in 1934. He had been a contract producer at the Emelka Studios in Munich and soon set up a string of London-based production companies including Trafalgar, Buckingham and Cecil Films.

Korda and Schach differed in appearance as much as they did in attitude. Schach was so tiny that it was difficult for his visitors to know if he were standing or sitting behind his enormous desk. But Schach's films were derivative, commercial productions lacking the flair and ambition of Korda's work.

Korda, in spite of his success, constantly balanced on the edge of financial disaster and, having overreached himself yet again in 1939, was only saved from ruin by the outbreak of war. Abandoning his current project, Korda set off to Hollywood, where he made three overtly pro-British films in quick succession, including *That Hamilton Woman*, a celebration of Horatio Nelson. So blatantly pro-British were these productions that Korda was about to be investigated by a Senate committee on the charge of violating US neutrality when the Japanese attacked Pearl Harbor. A close friend of Winston Churchill, Korda is thought to have acted as a secret courier between Churchill and William Stephenson, head of British Intelligence in the USA. Perhaps this explains his knighthood for unspecified services in 1942.

What had characterized German cinema in the 1920s was its dramatic and subtle lighting techniques and the abandonment of realism in pursuit of atmosphere. This style of cinema was unknown in Britain until the emergence of its most influential exponents, the director Michael Powell and the Hungarian-born screenwriter Emeric Pressburger. Together they were to be the most influential and enigmatic figures in British film-making for over thirty years, with a series of films unique both in concept and execution. Their continuing influence even on American film-makers is astonishing. Martin Scorsese and Francis Ford Coppola continue to venerate their work, and another leading US director, Brian de Palma, claims that his career is directly attributable to the inspiration he gained from watching Powell and Pressburger's *Red Shoes* as a child. Scorsese recalls watching their *I Know Where I'm Going* with his crew on the night before he started shooting his own masterpiece, *Raging Bull*, 'I had reached the point of thinking that there were no more masterpieces left for me to discover, until I saw that film on that night on video.

What moved me was its illustration of love laced with mysticism' (Scorsese, 1999).

Emeric Pressburger had been an established screen writer with the UFA studios in Germany when Goebbels announced the dismissal of all Jews working in the German film industry. Arriving in Britain, Pressburger was immediately hired by his fellow Hungarian Alexander Korda and put to work, in spite of his poor English, on current productions. In 1938 Korda introduced Pressburger to the young English director Michael Powell. They struck up an immediate rapport – each was what the other had been looking for. Pressburger recognized Powell as the director best able to translate his ambitious scripts into pictures, and Powell saw Pressburger as a screenwriter with a novelist's imagination who could provide him with the innovative scripts he had been searching for. Their partnership as Archer Films, backed by Alexander Korda, immediately established a new and highly creative force in British film-making. Pressburger was to spend the rest of his life in Britain, always grateful for the refuge and creative opportunity it had given him.

Knowing Churchill's enthusiasm for propaganda, Korda, as the war began, put Powell and Pressburger to work on their first production, *Contraband*, an anti-Nazi film that included – perhaps to amuse Churchill – a scene played in a warehouse full of unsaleable plaster busts of the discredited appeaser Neville Chamberlain. With *Contraband* completed, Pressburger became obsessed with a self-imposed mission to bring the Americans into the war. He wanted to show the isolationists that, even three thousand miles away, they were not immune to the Nazi threat. Unable to film such overt propaganda in the USA, Pressburger chanced, while looking at a map, on the 49th parallel of latitude that separates Canada from the USA. Call a film *The 49th Parallel* but shoot it in Canada and the USA would get the message, he believed. Uniquely, the British Foreign Office decided to back Pressburger's idea and subsidize the film. Pressburger not only wrote the script but personally cast the actors and helped edit the picture. *The 49th Parallel* was the first feature film to deal with the war and became a commercial success on both sides of the Atlantic: it won Pressburger an Oscar for his script and allowed Powell and Pressburger to sever their financial link with Korda. From then on all their films were made by their own production company and feature the familiar end credit 'Written, Produced and Directed by Michael Powell and Emeric Pressburger'.

As 'the Archers' Powell and Pressburger were to make fourteen highly idiosyncratic films over the next thirteen years and create a poetic vision of Britain as seen through foreign eyes. Their productions were British in content but continental in style and execution. Their first independent film was *The Life and Death of Colonel Blimp*, which to many critics remains their masterpiece, revealing its enigmatic and romantic definition of Britishness. Based on a character created by the cartoonist David Low – another refugee from Hitler – Colonel Blimp is a chivalrous relic from the past, much as the British Army was itself in 1939. Pressburger believed that reliance on such men in the face of Nazi ruthlessness would be disastrous. For the nation to survive and Hitler to be defeated, Britain's Blimps must stand aside. The film's dedication, 'to the New Army of Britain, to the new spirit in warfare', is unambiguous. In the climax of the film, Colonel Blimp, now an old man, is dissuaded from making a defeatist wartime broadcast by his lifelong friend and rival, a German officer, now himself a refugee from Nazi Germany. Pressburger clearly saw himself in the character of this honourable German, played in the film by the Austrian actor Anton Walbrook, another refugee.

To many critics the film appears to distort reality in a most un-British way: the one actress, Deborah Kerr, plays all the heroines, and decades pass in a series of quick cuts and ingenious effects, as in the opening sequence when the old Blimp plunges into a swimming pool to come up as his younger self. Winston Churchill, when told of the production, did all he could to stop it, convinced that the portrayal of a British officer as an endearing old buffer would seriously damage national morale. Perhaps Churchill, now in his sixties, even thought himself lampooned by the character of Blimp.

When it was released, the *Observer* described it as 'possibly the most controversial film produced in this country during our entire screen history'. Critics and audiences were equally mystified by its message, but all praised the brilliant use of Technicolor, new to Britain. The *Daily Mail*, fresh from a campaign to deny refuge to Hitler's Jewish victims, predictably complained that it was 'a gross travesty of the intelligence and behaviour of British army officers as a class' and started another of its campaigns, this time to stop the film being shown abroad.

But known government hostility had given the film an almost illicit appeal, and its distributors were quick to exploit this with advertisements urging audiences to 'See the banned film!' A heavily cut version was eventually released in the USA, but not until 1983 was it restored to its original uncut version by the British Film Institute. When it was reissued that year it was recognized by the critics as a lost masterpiece and arguably the finest British film of the century. The respected American critic Andrew Sarris dubbed it 'the British *Citizen Kane* – but with a deeper understanding of women'. Everyone agreed that it had not, unlike its realistic contemporaries, dated and that its extraordinary combination of humanity and caricature, satire and fantasy is unique in the history of the cinema.

Emeric Pressburger's next two films were more explorations, this time in black and white, of the peculiarities of the British character. *A Canterbury Tale* and *I Know Where I'm Going* are both about personal struggles to find meaning in life. The war was at its height and the refugee Pressburger was concerned more than most to find out just what the British were fighting for. Was it merely to restore the past or was it to bring about a new society that would make the rise of men like Hitler impossible? Pressburger, a non-practising Jew, was fascinated by the traditional values of Christianity and the sense of continuity that he had lost in Hungary but rediscovered in Britain. In *A Canterbury Tale* – the story of three people, modern pilgrims united by the war, who meet up in Canterbury on the eve of the Normandy invasions – Pressburger's fascination for Britain is seen in the inquiring character of the American sergeant. Perhaps the film was too personal a vision, for the critics found it whimsical and the public virtually ignored it.

Their next film, *I Know Where I'm Going*, in spite of Martin Scorsese's later adulation, was also a critical failure. It follows a headstrong young woman to Scotland where she is to marry a rich businessman. Delayed by bad weather from reaching his island, she succumbs both to the attractive but impoverished local laird and to the spirit of the place in finding true, romantic love. This tale of the triumph of heart over head caught the imagination of the war-battered British public in 1943 and the film was a box office success. At a time when more than 30 million people went to the cinema each week, *I Know Where I'm Going* recouped its production cost from the British market alone. To other, non-British film-makers it has always retained a strange appeal. When Pressburger visited Hollywood in 1947, he was told by Anatole Litvak of Paramount that the studio used its own print of the film to show its trainee writers what a perfect film script should be. Unknown to themselves, Powell and Pressburger had become cult figures in Hollywood. Billy Wilder, another admirer, described their films as having colour even when they were in black and white. He made a point, he said, of seeing them as soon as they were released because they were so different to anything that was being made in the USA.

Perhaps it was this acclaim that gave Pressburger the confidence to explore an ambitious and almost mythic plot in his next screenplay, *A Matter of Life and Death*. As a crashed Royal Air Force pilot battles for life, the hospital where he lies is linked to heaven by a huge symbolic escalator above which the gods debate his fate. Heaven is shot in monochrome and earth in Technicolor. Love, in the person of a young American nurse, eventually saves the pilot's life by offering to take his place in the next world. The heavenly judges finally decide that nothing in the universe is stronger than love itself. Some have seen Pressburger's script as an appeal to Britain and the USA to put aside their petty differences and together build a new and better post-war world. Again, an Archers' film had baffled the critics, even though they admired the courage and ambition of its creators.

Pressburger's urge to confront the contemporary tide of British realism and the plethora of realistic war films that flooded Britain now found its most dramatic expression in the Archers' next production, *The Red Shoes*. To many Powell and Pressburger admirers, this film is their true masterpiece. Its release, as well as transforming a generation of small girls into aspiring ballet dancers, earned Powell and Pressburger undivided critical acclaim in both Britain and the USA. Not only did *The Red Shoes* inspire Brian de Palma to become a film director but Gene Kelly claims it led him to make *An American in Paris*. When Emeric Pressburger, in old age, visited the Drury Lane Theatre in London to see the musical *A Chorus Line*, its choreographer asked a young performer in his presence what inspired her to become a dancer. 'I saw *The Red Shoes*,' she replied. Successful in Britain, it was a smash hit when released in America, playing continuously at the Bijou cinema in New York for over two years. Up to the 1990s it remained the biggest-grossing British film ever shown in America.

With the *Red Shoes* on release Powell and Pressburger were at the height of their fortunes, but all was to change when they agreed to rejoin Alexander Korda in his new enterprise, London Films. The artistic freedom they had enjoyed as independent producers financed by the Rank Group – they were allowed to go twice over budget on *The Red Shoes* – now ended. Their next film, *The Small Back Room*, a grim, factual story shot in black and white about a bomb disposal expert with a drink problem, was the start of their misfortunes. The British film critics were delighted, declaring it a welcome return to traditional British realism. But the public, still entranced by *The Red Shoes*, virtually ignored it. Worse was to come, as Korda's London Films was now in serious financial trouble. To redeem the situation Pressburger proposed making another musical in the style of *The Red Shoes*. This ambitious production, based on Offenbach's *The Tales of Hoffmann*, was shot in Technicolor and used a combination of song, dance and drama to spectacular effect. It was a box office disaster, failing to recover the production costs and playing only in art-house cinemas in Britain and America. Yet it did provoke the following letter to Emeric Pressburger from the most formidable of all Hollywood moguls:

> Your production of *Tales of Hoffmann* has proven that you can have everything. For the first time in my life I was treated to Grand Opera where the beauty, power and scope of the music was equally matched by the visual presentation. I thank you for your outstanding courage and artistry in bringing to us Grand Opera as it existed until now, only in the minds of those who created it.
>
> Sincerely,
> Cecil B. de Mille

The last film that Powell and Pressburger made together was a further attempt at recapturing the popular success of *The Red Shoes*. Their 1954 film of the Strauss operetta *Die Fledermaus*, retitled as *Oh Rosalinda*, was their attempt to match a big-budget Hollywood musical. When it, too, failed at the box office the partnership fell apart and Powell and Pressburger went their separate ways. Powell later directed the critically acclaimed *Black Narcissus* and the controversial *Peeping*

Tom, but Pressburger's career faded into relative obscurity. Today their work is seen as being of fundamental importance in freeing British film from the dominance of documentary realism and Pressburger's scripts as revealing the more enigmatic aspects of the British character. His were the eyes of the outsider seeing merit and interest where few others had bothered to look. Just as the art historian Nikolaus Pevsner showed the British the glories of their architectural heritage, so Emeric Pressburger had shown them the virtues and eccentricities of their national character.

Refugees from Nazi Europe also had as important, if less dramatic, an effect on the US film industry. But Hollywood was far less desperate for skilled technicians in the 1930s than Britain. What it needed was ideas men – producers, writers and directors – who could give MGM, Paramount or Warners the competitive edge. Since the 1920s the Hollywood studios, locked in mutual competition, had sent talent scouts each year to sign up the most promising Europeans. Germany had them in plenty because of the creative freedom that the Berlin studios allowed their film-makers. Not surprisingly, the gifted film-maker Fritz Lang was inundated with offers almost from the start of his career in Berlin. But many of Germany's brightest stars were either Jews, left-wing sympathizers or both, and joined the refugee diaspora after 1933.

At first the free German film industry appeared to have moved to Paris. Fritz Lang arrived to find his old colleagues from UFA – Erich Pommer, G.W. Pabst, Robert and Curt Siodmak and Billy Wilder – already there. All had left in haste, Robert Siodmak having just completed his film *Menschen am Sonntag* in the month that Hitler came to power. Both the writer and director were Jews, and the film was premièred on the day following the Reichstag fire. Not surprisingly it was the last Jewish-made film ever to appear in Nazi Germany. Within a few weeks Goebbels had it banned and Siodmak was in exile, denounced as a 'corrupter of the German family'. But Paris provided only a temporary refuge for the German film-makers. Even the buoyant French film industry could not provide them with sufficient work, and the call of Hollywood became ever stronger. As Alfred Hitchcock had said, American films played to the world – and had the budgets to match.

Fritz Lang was the first to succumb. He had been spotted years earlier by the Hollywood producer David O. Selznick, who had left him an open invitation to join the MGM studio. Lang took the long sea journey to New York, then crossed America by train to arrive in Hollywood with high hopes but no specific project agreed. At least he was known in the USA as the director of the sensational *Metropolis*. When the film had first opened in New York in August 1927 ten thousand people queued to see it, as much for the visionary Bauhaus architecture as for the story. But now Lang was just one of many contract directors with nothing to do. For a whole year he wandered about the MGM lots watching the filming and getting to know the ordinary technicians on the set. Lang spent the rest of his time reading the daily newspapers, particularly the comic strips, for insights into the national character and to master the use of American slang. He found it all refreshingly different from Germany. The American tradition of personal freedom and the individual's traditional suspicion of central government were in marked contrast to Lang's experience of Germany – there, Lang claimed, even a corpse must obey the state. Lang's German films such as *Die Nibelungen* and *Metropolis* had portrayed the hero as a superman, a creation far different from that of the ordinary man. Hitler himself aspired to the same mythic status. Perhaps as a reaction to all this, Lang was to create his American heroes as ordinary citizens who were capable, when challenged by fate, of noble and self-sacrificing actions. It was the same hero that the nation saw in the character of the average GI who was soon to cross the Atlantic, free Europe from the Nazis and then return to his home, family – and obscurity.

But for the present Lang was almost a forgotten man at risk of losing his contract because the studio could find nothing for him to do. In desperation, he pleaded with Louis B. Mayer's assistant Eddie Mannix for an opportunity to demonstrate his talents. Reluctantly he was given a scenario about a mob lynching in the South and told to get on with it. But Hollywood studios could never avoid interfering, and Lang was soon ordered to change the black victim to white and the hero from a lawyer to an ordinary worker. The completed film *Fury* could easily have been shelved without distribution if the film critic of the *Hollywood Reporter* had not seen a review print and praised it so enthusiastically that MGM was forced to release the film for public showing. The audiences in 1936 loved it, and *Fury* was an unexpected box office hit. It was also the first time that a refugee film-maker from Nazi Europe had achieved a major commercial success in the USA with an American film. What delighted both critics and audiences were the stylish techniques that Lang used to tell the story – as in one famous scene where gossiping women are intercut with clucking hens. But it was Lang's use of atmospheric lighting, a technique he had perfected at the UFA studios, that seemed so innovative. Traditionally in American films a woman would be lit from the direction that best enhanced her beauty, but Lang introduced the German technique of lighting the whole scene from just one side. The resulting effect gave a more dramatic atmosphere and endowed the characters with a new authenticity. By using such techniques in *Fury* Lang had inaugurated a new style of film-making that was to evolve into the highly distinctive American *film noir* genre of the 1940s.

Attempting, as always, to repeat a formulaic success, MGM gave Lang another thriller to film. But when *You Only Live Once* failed at the box office, the studio switched tactics and teamed Lang with his fellow refugee Kurt Weill to shoot a comedy entitled *You and Me*. When that, too, failed with the American audience, MGM, perhaps in desperation, offered the German émigré Lang the unlikely vehicle of an American Western, *The Return of Frank James*. But Lang had long been fascinated by the Western and thought it as valid a myth as any Wagnerian legend. The resulting film delighted both critics and audiences with its subtle use of the new Technicolor and Lang's sympathetic handling of the characters. The studio, of course, offered him a similar production, *Western Union*. This time Lang managed to repeat his success, and the film was accepted as a powerful new addition to the Western genre. One group of old-timers in Arizona even wrote to Lang telling him that he had captured the atmosphere of true West far more accurately than any American director. Lang's unique mastery of the Western was later to be demonstrated in one of the most famous of them all, the Marlene Dietrich vehicle *Rancho Notorious*.

But with war imminent Lang naturally became involved in Hollywood's propaganda campaign against Nazi Germany. The first wartime project he was offered was an adaptation of the Geoffrey Household novel *Rogue Male*. Retitled *Man Hunt*, it told the story of an attempt on Hitler's life by a maverick Englishman. Lang was given a free hand provided he did not show too many swastikas, and the result is an effective attack on Nazi tyranny. As the USA became drawn into the European conflict, three more anti-Nazi films followed, *Hangmen Also Die, The Ministry of Fear* and finally *Cloak and Dagger* in 1945. When the war ended, Lang, now an established Hollywood director, returned to specifically American themes with *The Woman in the Window* and *Scarlet Street*. Both are dark, brooding studies of sexual obsession, jealousy and ultimate degradation in the manner of Josef von Sterberg's *Blue Angel*.

Lang continued working into the early 1950s with undiminished powers on such films as *Clash by Night*. But suddenly and mysteriously all production offers from the studios ceased – Lang soon discovered the reason why. As he wrote in 1965, 'I was in the dog house and didn't even know why. For a year I didn't know what was going on. Finally I found out there were lists made by somebody and, because of my affiliation with certain people, I had been put on one' (Bogdanovich, 1997).

Lang had become another victim of the anti-communist hysteria that swept Hollywood in the early 1950s. He had been photographed by the FBI leaving a fund-raising meeting for a local left-wing activist. When the studios were informed they blacklisted him as a communist sympathizer. Lang denied any political affiliation other than being a liberal, but he pointed out that at the time of appeasement the only group prepared to take on the Nazis were the communists. Like many of the German refugees, he had openly supported the Hollywood Anti-Nazi League and used his films to get their message across. What Lang experienced reveals how insidious the whole business was. The American Legion had called Lang's studio and hinted that he might soon be under investigation for un-American activities. That was enough for the studio bosses, terrified of bad publicity, to drop him from their production lists. Ironically, Lang had once been suspected by his fellow refugees of being a closet Nazi when he first arrived in Hollywood, looking like a typical Prussian with cropped hair and a monocle. Not only did he ignore his part-Jewish ancestry but he openly declared himself a Catholic. Moreover, everyone in Hollywood knew that Goebbels had once offered him control of the Nazi film industry. Finally, after a year and a half in the wilderness, the political climate in Hollywood changed and Harry Cohn gave Lang a job again. But his enforced idleness had left its mark, and Lang was now less idealistic about the USA as he showed in his savage treatment of contemporary society in *The Blue Gardenia* and *While the City Sleeps*. In the latter film the journalists are portrayed as being even more degraded and corrupt than the psychopath they are hunting. During his years in the USA Lang gradually abandoned his early symbolism, but he never lost his preoccupation with the individual's struggle 'against destiny, against fate', nor did his skills as film-maker ever decline. The care with which Lang composed each scene in every film places him in the highest rank of directors for, as he often said, it is not the dialogue of a film that the audience remembers, but the images.

Lang's career in the USA was unique; only Billy Wilder ever approached the critical success of his old colleague, although he more than matched his success at the box office. Others found Hollywood success far more difficult to achieve. Even the producer Erich Pommer, who had been successful in France and Germany, met disaster with his first Hollywood project, *Music in the Air*, a film version of the Jerome Kern and Oscar Hammerstein musical. As there were few second chances in Hollywood, Pommer was forced to retreat to London, where he spent the war working on low-budget productions for Alexander Korda and Charles Laughton.

Few arrived in California with a higher reputation than G. W. Pabst, perhaps the greatest German director of them all, but his poor understanding of English and almost total ignorance of American society led to his first project, *A Modern Hero*, being a disappointment and the second being cancelled by the studio. Disillusioned and disappointed by Hollywood, Pabst returned to France where he saw out the war in virtual obscurity.

More celebrated in Europe than even Pabst was the Austrian Max Reinhardt, the most successful theatre director of his age. His reputation as a master of spectacle led in 1934 to an invitation to recreate his production of *A Midsummer Night's Dream* at the Hollywood Bowl. It was a brilliant success, and Warner Brothers immediately offered him a huge budget to make a film version using Warner's star contract players. Reinhardt cast James Cagney as an unlikely Bottom, Dick Powell as Lysander, Olivia de Havilland as Hermia and Mickey Rooney as Puck. Reinhardt's old colleague and fellow exile William Dieterle was hired to co-direct. Dieterle was to go on to establish a niche himself in Hollywood as a director of biographical films of such worthies as Louis Pasteur and Emile Zola. *A Midsummer Night's Dream* was an ambitious project, and the critics were impressed with the result, but it proved yet another box office disaster, returning little of the $1.3 million invested in it. Not even the great Max Reinhardt could survive that, and no more offers came to him from the studios. In desperation, he established a drama school on Sunset Boulevard, calling it grandly 'the Max Reinhardt Workshop of Stage, Screen and Radio'. All his lecturers were famous in the film world and included Erich Korngold who taught music, Paul Muni and Basil Rathbone (acting), Rudolph Maté (camerawork and lighting) and the young John Huston (script-writing). Aspiring young Californian film-makers rushed to join, delighted at the opportunity to learn from such luminaries.

But Reinhardt missed the live theatre, and in spite of the success of his academy he attempted to revive his stage career by accepting an offer to direct Thornton Wilder's *The Merchant of Yonkers* in New York. To Reinhardt's disappointment the production folded within a month, and he was forced to return to California a defeated man. Ironically *The Merchant of Yonkers* was later revived as the stage hit *The Matchmaker* before being transformed into the musical *Hello Dolly!*. Reinhardt now concentrated on passing his theatrical skills to the next generation, but he never lost his ambition to succeed as a theatrical director in the USA. When yet another scheme for establishing a repertory theatre in Los Angeles fell through, he took off again to New York to stage the Strauss operetta *Die Fledermaus* in New York with Erich Korngold as musical director. At last his luck had changed, and when it opened in October 1942, now entitled *Oh Rosalinda*, it was a great success and later became the basis of the Powell and Pressburger film of the same title. Reinhardt had at last found the genre that best suited his skills, and he was not slow to capitalize upon it with another adaptation of operetta entitled *Helen Goes to Troy*, based on Offenbach's *La Belle Hélène*.

Many of Reinhardt's old colleagues from Vienna had made their way to California, too, among them Otto Preminger, who was offered a contract by Twentieth Century Fox in 1934. Like Fritz Lang and Billy Wilder, Preminger had little to do at first other than learn English and watch the productions at Fox. The studio boss, Darryl Zanuck, admired his enthusiasm, however, and soon gave him a chance with a low-budget production, *Under Your Spell*. Zanuck liked the result and Preminger's Hollywood career appeared to have taken off. Another success followed, the comedy *Danger, Love at Work*, and then Preminger was offered a golden opportunity, the chance to direct a big-budget version of Robert Louis Stevenson's *Kidnapped*. Knowing nothing about either Scotland or Stevenson, Preminger hesitated to accept the production, but, not wishing to cross Zanuck, he agreed reluctantly to do it. It was an unwise decision. When previewed, *Kidnapped* was a fiasco, and Zanuck fired him on the spot. Never a man to panic, Preminger sat out the rest of his contract in 1937 and then moved to New York. When he returned to Hollywood a few years later he was careful never again to overreach himself and built a steady, if unspectacular, career with such films as *Laura, Fallen Angel, Where the Sidewalk Ends* and *Angel Face*. In 1952 Preminger was successful enough to leave the studios and become an independent producer-director. Preminger had quietly achieved far more than his fellow European directors Henry Koster, Curtis Bernhardt, Douglas Sirk or Anatole Litvak, who all lacked both his luck and his patience.

Of all the film-makers who took refuge in Hollywood only Billy Wilder matched the critical and popular success of Fritz Lang. Arriving there with even less English than Lang, Wilder spent his early years cooped up in a tiny flat and struggling to pick up the language from the radio every night. By day he hawked script ideas round the studios. Then in 1938 Paramount gave him a contract to write for Ernst Lubitsch, Hollywood's longest-serving German exile. The film was *Bluebeard's Eighth Wife*, and Wilder was given a partner to work with, the ex-Broadway writer Charles Brackett. They worked so well together that they were commissioned to write the script for Lubitsch's next film, *Ninotchka*, starring Greta Garbo. When Howard Hawks saw the result he immediately hired them both for his next production, *Ball of Fire*. Then in 1942, now an established Hollywood screen-writer, Wilder got his first chance to direct. It was Hawks's new comedy *The Major and the Minor*. From now on Wilder both wrote and directed and used his outgoing personality to establish an impress-ive network of contacts throughout the Hollywood studios. His own contribution to the war effort was *Five Graves to Cairo* starring Erich von Stroheim as Rommel. His next film showed how far he had come in adapting to the USA. In *Double Indemnity* Wilder used his mastery of expressionist lighting to produce a dark and sinister film. He captured the same brooding atmosphere in his next production, *The Lost Weekend*. But his masterpiece of *film noir* was to be a portrait of Hollywood itself, *Sunset Boulevard*. In a long career Wilder showed that he was capable of changing with the times and able to switch from realism to the escapism of *The Emperor Waltz* or the satirical comedy of diplomacy in the Cold War, *A Foreign Affair*.

Not all the émigré film-makers in Hollywood were German or Austrian. As the German armies approached Paris the French government had asked the directors René Clair and Julien Duvivier and the producer Jean Lévy-Strauss to set up a French film industry in exile. Arriving in Hollywood they were reunited with Jean Renoir, who had shared a cabin *en route* from Lisbon with the writer and aviator Antoine de Saint-Exupéry, whose book *Wind, Sand and Stars* he had planned to film for Fox. René Clair, director of *The Ghost Goes West*, started work immediately on a Marlene Dietrich vehicle, *The Flame of New Orleans*. But yet again an émigré's first production in the USA died at the box office. Clair's career was saved by a chance encounter with Preston Sturges of Paramount, who offered him the opportunity to direct *The Passionate Witch* starring Veronica Lake, followed by the highly successful *I Married a Witch*.

Julien Duvivier, who had made the highly acclaimed *Pépé le Moko* and *Un Carnet de Bal* in the early 1930s, arrived in 1938 with a contract from MGM, and he went to work on *Marie Antoinette*, followed by the highly successful musical drama *The Great Waltz*. Before leaving Paris Duvivier had shot a patriotic film for the government entitled *Un tel Père et Fils*, which he now edited in New York as his contribution to the Free French Government in London. A chance meeting with Alexander Korda led him to direct a remake of *Carnet de Bal*, now called *Lydia*, starring Korda's wife Merle Oberon. Although the film was only a modest success, Duvivier was offered similar projects, such as *Tales of Manhattan* and *Flesh and Fantasy*, both starring Charles Boyer and Edward G. Robinson. Duvivier's last film in the USA was a French Resistance story, *The Impostor*, starring another refugee actor, Jean Gabin. When the war ended, Duvivier, now without work, sailed for France as soon as he could and attempted to revive his career there.

While some of the exiled film-makers achieved little in Hollywood, none had a more disastrous experience than the Spanish Surrealist Luis Buñuel, who arrived in 1937 as a virtual unknown. His only useful contact in America was his old Surrealist colleague the painter Salvador Dalí, who suggested to his new friend Cecil B. de Mille, who had expressed an interest in finding out what Surrealism was about, that he see Buñuel's film *Un Chien andalou*, 'a wonderful, beautiful film' he was assured. The viewing was a disaster for Buñuel. One of de Mille's cohorts staggered vomiting from the room at such shocking images as a human eyeball being sliced in half, and the rest sat stunned. When the lights went up, de Mille, ashen-faced, left the room without a word. Buñuel's Hollywood career was over before it had even begun.

For the next two years he lived in virtual penury, unable to secure any consistent work from the studios and reduced to writing begging letters to the immensely successful Dalí. In desperation Buñuel took the train to New York where he had no better luck and was reduced to washing dishes in a hotel. Then an old friend introduced him to Iris Barry of the Museum of Modern Art film department. One of the few New Yorkers who knew his work, she obtained him a job supervising the editing and dubbing of US art films intended for South America. But Hollywood, having lost its own European markets, now sought to oust New York and get to control the South American film market for itself. Both Buñuel and Barry were attacked by this powerful lobby, and the *Motion Picture Herald* ran an ominous headline, 'Senate Unit to Weed out Meddlers in US Films'. Buñuel's virulent anti-clericalism that, as expressed in *L'Age d'or*, was now used by such journals as the *Catholic Herald* to portray Buñuel as an anti-Catholic with communist leanings, and in June 1943 he was forced to resign his post at the Museum of Modern Art. He headed south to Mexico, where he revived his career with a series of brilliant films including *Los Olivadados* in 1950 and, when he returned to Europe, *Belle de jour*. Had he remained in New York the world would have forgotten about Luis Buñuel.

The most important single contribution to American film by the exiles from Nazi Europe was undoubtedly their influence in establishing *film noir*. All the most celebrated examples of these atmospheric films were directed by German-born film-makers. Robert Siodmak's *Phantom Lady* is a classic example. Set in New York at night, this low-budget film uses key lighting in the German manner to enhance the drama of a quest to find the vital witness to a crime. As ever, Siodmak was asked by the studio to repeat the success with *The Suspect*, which starred Charles Laughton as a Dr Crippen character. But Siodmak's most lasting success was *The Spiral Staircase*, thought by many to be the best suspense thriller of all time. *Film noir* is now considered, after the Western, the most archetypical Hollywood creation, but it would never have been possible without the technical skills and visual ambition of the Europeans.

4

Art Blooms in Exile

Had Adolf Hitler been allowed to study art, as he desperately wished to as a young man, the world might well have been spared his political career. Rejected by the Kunstgewerbeschule, Vienna's leading art school, Hitler sank into depression and resentment against a society that had refused to recognize his creativity. His obsession with art now became channelled into politics. If he been allowed to join the school he would have studied alongside the young Oskar Kokoschka, soon to become the most famous Austrian painter of his generation and a man who represented everything that Hitler loathed about modern art. As with all the arts, the Nazis established a rigid control over painting and sculpture when they came to power. Their position was made clear by their chief cultural adviser, Hans Hinkel, who after attending an exhibition of modernist art in 1934 declared, 'Hand any of these paintings to an ordinary worker and he couldn't tell the top from the bottom . . . but if some expert told him this was the art of the future, the poor chap would believe him and think himself stupid . . . art for the experts is not art . . . a new German art must be created for the people.'

What Hinkel, Rosenberg, Goebbels and the Nazi establishment referred to as 'real' art was no more than the idealized portraits and sentimental landscapes overlaid with the neoclassicism that had characterized German nineteenth-century art. The first step in creating, or rather re-creating, a new German art was to get rid of the current modernism. A vast bureaucracy was now put in place to impose and regulate a traditional culture that was by definition economically and politically unthreatening to the Nazis. Only Soviet Russia, at that time, had ever attempted anything as ambitious as this Nazi takeover of a nation's artistic life. The new arbiters of culture went about their business with vigour, ridiculing and persecuting the so-called 'degenerate artists' and driving them from the country in an act of cultural purgation unparalleled in modern history. Those who wished to stay must not only accept political tyranny but also produce work that conformed to the personal taste of Adolf Hitler. This Nazi crusade against modernism culminated in their 1937 'Entartete Kunst' (Degenerate Art) exhibition, which opened in Munich and then toured every major German city. It contained what Hinkel considered the worst examples of un-German and degenerate art, much of it confiscated from public collections. Beside each painting or sculpture appeared a lengthy written condemnation comparing it to the art of primitive peoples and with accompanying photographs of deformed or insane people. Interestingly, only six of the one hundred and twelve artists pilloried in 'Entartete Kunst' were in fact Jews.

Yet the Nazis' opinion of modern art was shared by many ordinary Germans, and the exhibition was a popular success, attracting over two million visitors in Munich alone. It is an extraordinary fact that the popularity of 'Entartete Kunst' has never since been matched in attendance by any exhibition of modern art. Five times as many people saw it as visited the complementary exhibition, 'Grosse Deutsche Kunstausstellung' of Nazi-approved art. To many ordinary Germans, the Nazis were merely calling the bluff of so-called 'modern' art and of its arrogant artists and critics. Few complained when this 'degenerate' work was banned and removed from German galleries and museums. Goebbels decided that the most provocative examples must be taken to Berlin and ceremoniously burned by the city fire brigade, the recent immolators of so many German books. The remainder was sent off to the Theodor Fischer Gallery in Lucerne, Switzerland, where it was sold at knock-down prices to Swiss and American collectors and institutions. In all, over sixteen thousand works of art – paintings, prints and sculptures – were confiscated and their creators vilified.

Not surprisingly, one of the first artists investigated by the Nazis was Oskar Kokoschka. An inquiry into his racial background failed to find a single drop of Jewish blood, and he was allowed to remain, for the time being, at his teaching post. But Jewishness was not the only reason for an artist to be persecuted. As Kandinsky, Klee, Grosz – even the Nazi party member, Nolde himself – were to discover. To be a modernist like Kokoschka was to be part of an international movement that was, by Nazi definition, un-German. Kokoschka responded to this Nazi attention with the enterprise that characterized all his actions in the coming years. His ability to stay ahead of events that engulfed others saved both his career and his life. With Hitler in power in neighbouring Germany, he left Austria for Czechoslovakia. Refugees from Germany or Austria required neither visa nor work permit, and even anti-Nazi propaganda was permitted by the liberal Czech government. Kokoschka was a welcome guest, recognized by the intellectual community of Prague as the leading German artist then resident in Czechoslovakia. Even the organization set up to promote German art in exile was called the 'Oskar Kokoschka Association'. But Kokoschka's sojourn in Czechoslovakia was to be short-lived. When the 'Entartete Kunst' exhibition opened in Munich it included nine of his canvases hung alongside the daubings of a confined lunatic. Kokoschka responded by painting his *Self-portrait as a Degenerate Artist*. Now a marked man, Kokoschka was informed that all of his work remaining in Germany would be either burned or sold in Switzerland. Today, even Dresden, where Kokoschka spent five of his most formative years, has only one of his paintings on display.

As German forces mobilized on the Czech border in September 1938 Kokoschka decided to move on. He had considered going to the USA where he had been offered a teaching post at Mills College but, as with many of the exiles, he was loath to abandon his European roots. His decision finally to seek refuge in Britain can be attributed to the enthusiastic response that his work had received when exhibited in London in 1937 and again in the following year when he was one of the most prominent artists featured in Herbert Read's and Roland Penrose's 'Modern German Art' exhibition, their hastily assembled counterblast to 'Entartete Kunst'. But the London art world had given the exhibition a mixed reception, with the critic of *Apollo* magazine expressing a robust contempt for all things German. One of the members of the exhibition committee was Kokoschka's fellow exile painter Fred Uhlman, who was told at the exhibition by an angry critic, 'I paid 2s. 6d to see it and would willingly have paid 5s. not to have.' Other spectators seem to have agreed with Hitler that the modernists were indeed degenerates.

Kokoschka, with his customary foresight, had realized that the exhibition might well be counter-productive and tried, at the last minute, to withdraw his work. He was also enraged by the catalogue that described him as having been influenced by Art Nouveau, Expressionism and French Impressionism. Always the individualist, he considered himself as an artist without a school. Luckily his work continued to impress the influential critic Herbert Read, who had the job of recommending refugee artists for residence permits. Kokoschka, never one to forgo a useful contact, wrote to Read from Czechoslovakia on 17 May 1938, adding a bitter postscript, 'I have to start at the beginning again and therefore need powerful protection and if possible permission to work in England. Otherwise I am lost – since your Lords have generously handed over my homeland Austria to the Nazis as a present.'

Summer found him still trapped in Prague and hesitating to take the final step in leaving until his wife, Olda, decided to get the visas and tickets to Britain herself. With Czechoslovakia cut off by land, the only way out was by air, and on 17 October 1938 the Kokoschkas took off from Prague with just £10 in currency and a small painting to sell in London. Granted a one-month visitor's permit by the British authorities, Kokoschka wasted no time in tracking down anyone who could help him. His first stop was the National Gallery to see the influential director Kenneth Clarke. He then went on to the Tate Gallery where John Rothenstein, oblivious to his plight, offered him a cup of tea and asked him to donate a picture. Later that same day Kokoschka arrived at the Courtauld Institute to plead his case. Unfamiliar with the national character, he had mistaken English politeness for a firm offer of help. As it turned out, his fellow refugees gave him more help than the London art establishment ever did.

What few commissions he managed to obtain came from his new English friends the collectors Michael Croft and Edward Beddington Behrens. He did, however, produce a series of multi-figure allegorical paintings that showed a new influence on his work, that of the great English caricaturists Hogarth and Gillray. Although less dependent on language than the émigré writers, the refugee artists had none the less to compromise their work in an attempt to find a patron or buyer. Martin Bloch, less renowned than Kokoschka, later painfully recalled the demands made on him to tone down both his colours and his expressionism:

As much as I have an accent in my language I have an accent in my painting. In German art of our century, expression and feeling comes into it
a lot. Whereas mainstream art in Britain is more good taste and playing
down feelings. The majority of English people find my paintings too
emotive, too direct. English art is a refined understatement.

In spite of the frustrations, Kokoschka enjoyed life in London as
Britain prepared for war. He joined the Freier Deutscher Kulturbund
and mixed with fellow members, including the writer and critic Alfred
Kerr, the film producer Berthold Viertel (soon to move on to Hollywood)
and Austria's most famous novelist Stefan Zweig. The Kulturbund was,
at that time, keenly supported by Britain's radical intellectual establishment, and Kokoschka was able to make contact with such eminent figures
as Ralph Vaughan Williams, Julian Huxley, J.B. Priestley and Gilbert
Murray. Part of the organization's work was to obtain visas for artists
and their families still trapped in Germany and Austria. As there was
now a scarcity of domestic servants in England, many of these highly
educated and distinguished exiles were amused to find themselves
reclassified as cooks, cleaners and housemaids when they arrived in
Britain. In all this, Kokoschka played his part, but the nagging insecurity that had compelled him to leave Austria and Czechoslovakia now
led him to abandon the refugee community of London in the last days
of peace for the isolation of Polperro in Cornwall. Here he began experimenting with new media, using coloured crayons to produce work
with the transparency of watercolours and producing four important
oil paintings, including the famous *Crab*, now in Tate Modern.

As a Czech citizen, Kokoschka, unlike the majority of his friends, was
not interned when war broke out but ordered to move away from the
British coast. In spite of the danger, Kokoschka decided to return to
London and endure the worst of the Blitz. He managed to find a studio
in a half-deserted Mayfair, where he embarked upon a series of pictures
with a political theme combining these with a series of portrait commissions. Once, when painting an aristocratic lady there, a bomb fell on
a nearby house and they were both covered in dust. His subject neither
moved nor even referred to the bomb, and Kokoschka was much
impressed with this example of British phlegm. But the British class system
both annoyed and perplexed him, as did the British belief in their own
natural superiority and their general lack of interest in modern art. Yet

Britain had given him refuge, and he was proud to gain a British passport in 1945 and loyally retained it in spite of the blandishments of the Austrian government later when they bombarded their greatest living painter with offers of academic posts, a generous pension and honorary citizenship.

With his new British passport Kokoschka was able to visit his family in Prague and Vienna after the war. When his first post-war exhibition was held at the Kunsthalle in Basle in 1947, Kokoschka realized that his reputation had survived intact. He also discovered, to his delight, that many of his paintings still survived. One of the best known, *The Tempest*, had been rescued by the Kunsthalle itself and was now a permanent exhibit. Kokoschka was given important shows in Washington, New York and San Francisco. Although many of his paintings were in private American collections, this was the first public recognition of his work outside Europe. As with other artists who had survived the tyranny, Kokoschka's reputation was enhanced by public esteem for anything unsullied by the Nazis. Only in Britain, where the Kokoschkas maintained a home, was real fame denied him.

For the rest of his life classical themes dominated his work, and he became convinced that only classical humanism could save the world from more barbarity. His hostility towards Austria finally mellowed, and in 1953 he returned to open a summer art school in Salzburg Castle. He called it his 'School of Seeing' and based its teachings on his belief that anyone could paint if they opened their eyes to the world around them. In 1956, the year of his seventieth birthday, he was awarded Germany's highest honour, the Pour le Mérite. Not everyone was pleased by this: his old rival George Grosz wrote to a friend that Kokoschka had become 'the semi-official painter of the Federal Republic' and likened his later work to that of J.M.W. Turner in his dotage. Kokoschka was also honoured in Britain, but the recognition that pleased him most was the major retrospective of his work at the Tate Gallery in 1962. Public and critical reaction was one of astonishment that such a major artist had lived, virtually unknown, amongst them for so many years. Kokoschka's final years were celebrated by exhibitions throughout Europe, and his family house at Pochlarn in Czechoslovakia became the Kokoschka Museum and Archive. In 1980, the year that he died, *The Tigon*, one of his greatest works, painted at London Zoo while he was in exile, came up for sale in New York. The Austrian Chancellor Bruno Kreisky ordered that it be purchased for the nation whatever the cost.

No such honours awaited the German artist Kurt Schwitters, today seen as one of the most important of the age. Schwitters died in exile and in virtual obscurity in Britain, but his influence on the evolution of twentieth-century art was to be fundamental. Born in Hanover, a city that would experience in full the turmoil and excitement of the Weimar Republic, Schwitters returned from army service in 1918 and decided to dedicate the rest of his life to art. 'The past', he declared, 'has collapsed . . . we must build anew from its fragments.' Schwitters was to do this symbolically by incorporating fragments of rubbish into his pieces; as his work evolved he became the world's leading collagist. By July 1919 he had gathered enough work to exhibit at the fashionable Sturm gallery. Schwitters chose the word 'Merz', or rubbish, as the description of his style of collage. Although both Picasso and Braque had used similar techniques, Schwitters was the first to involve material objects in his work. This put him at issue with his former friends the Berlin Dadaists, who found Schwitters's 'Merz' far too frivolous. For them, it lacked the political commitment and the fundamental rejection of traditional laws of beauty and order that their own work displayed. But Schwitters was now recognized not only as an important German artist but as one with a growing international reputation, too. His incredible energy produced an avalanche of art, theatre designs, typography and photography. A leading exhibitor at the 'Abstract and Surrealist' exhibition in Zurich in 1929, a few months later he was in Paris at the avant-garde 'Cercle et Carré' exhibition. Nor were his talent and energy confined to pure art. He launched his own *Merz* magazine and even set up an advertising agency: in one advertising collage he combined pages from the *Koran* with Camel cigarette packets. Nor did he confine his interests to the visual arts – poetry was equally important to him, and he was much in demand as a writer and lecturer. He was, in fact, a one-man art movement driven by neurosis and insecurity.

Naturally, Schwitters was the kind of person that the Nazis detested, and as early as 1925 they had begun barracking his lectures. As with Kokoschka, storm troopers looted his work for the 'Degenerate Art' exhibition in Munich. Although not a Jew, Schwitters was an avant-garde artist and an outspoken anti-Nazi. Nor did they forget that when attending an exhibition of Nazi portraits he had openly joked to his friends, 'Shall we hang them or just put them up against a wall?' Warned that he faced imminent arrest, Schwitters escaped to Norway in January

1937. He never saw his wife again and lived the rest of his life in exile. The Norwegian authorities, wary of giving offence to the Nazi regime, badgered him to move on to America – or anywhere. But again, like Kokoschka, he was reluctant to leave Europe.

Rejecting all things German, including the language, he found solace in the wild beauty of the Norwegian landscape and began involving its flowers, pebbles and leaves in his collages. However, in April 1940 the Germans invaded and Schwitters became a fugitive again. Fortunately, three days before they arrived in Oslo he managed to get aboard a fishing boat to Tromsø, then on to a Norwegian icebreaker with his fellow painter Max Ernst, bound for Scotland. On arrival they were both arrested and interned on the Isle of Man. With his customary energy Schwitters threw himself into camp life, lecturing on art, reciting his poetry and writing for the camp newspaper. But all this frenetic activity and extrovert behaviour disguised an inner sadness and despair. His fellow internees thought him, if not mad, then an irrelevant footnote to Dadaism. Schwitters created over two hundred works of art in the tiny garret studio given him by the kindly camp commandant. Many were bizarre statues made out of such materials as stale porridge surrounded by *objets trouvés* and scraps of painted linoleum.

When Schwitters was released in October 1941 he went to London where he was, like Kokoschka, taken up by the critics Roland Penrose and Herbert Read. Yet no one wanted to buy his collages and as a non-Jew he was reluctant to seek aid from any of the German refugee organizations. Fate continued to deal harshly with Kurt Schwitters. He was isolated, poor and virtually unknown in Britain, his house and office in Hanover were bombed, and his wife died of cancer. He then suffered a stroke and was partially paralysed. His only comfort in all this tragedy was a woman, Edith Thomas, who befriended him and nursed him back to health at his new home in the Lake District in 1945. Here, in Ambleside, he survived by selling paintings to the summer tourists and on the £5 sent to him each month by a friend in London. In spite of the poverty, Schwitters was not unhappy and, like past visitors to the Lake District, had become entranced by the dramatic landscape. With his growing sense of place he began once again involving in his collages *objets trouvés* that he gathered on the fells.

Today, when incongruous artefacts are central to many works of art, Schwitters is seen as a true iconoclast. Schwitters's achievement was to have combined the Cubist structure of his assemblages with Impressionist painted elements. It has been said that his great contribution to technique was to fuse the 'wet' processes of oil painting with the 'dry' medium of assemblage. The day before he died, on 8 January 1948 at the age of sixty, Schwitters heard that he had been granted British nationality. Two weeks after his death an exhibition that would have restored his fortunes opened in New York. Other retrospective exhibitions followed, together with tributes from friends and critics. Although Schwitters was not forgotten he had been neglected; one of the most individual and pioneering artists of the twentieth century had been allowed to die largely unrecognized in poverty and exile. Not until 1956, at a time of renewed interest in Dada, was a full-scale retrospective exhibition of his work mounted. Today his reputation is secure, and he is seen as a modern master whose work is a bridge between the pioneering modernists of the 1920s and the new generation of post-Second World War artists. Perhaps his tragedy was that he did not join his avant-garde colleagues in the USA but remained in Europe in a country that gave him refuge but ignored him.

Would Schwitters have been better appreciated in the USA? Certainly American dealers and critics were more receptive to innovation and there had been nothing more radical than the short-lived American Dada when it began in 1915. Known as 'the skyscraper primitives', Francis Picabia and Marcel Duchamp launched this anarchic movement in New York with Duchamp's notorious painting *Nude Descending a Staircase*. Although fascinated by machines and skyscrapers, the protagonists of American Dada had decamped to Paris by the early 1920s. The New York art scene then returned to its relative conservatism until the arrival of the Nazis led many of Europe's most radical painters to seek refuge in the USA. In the 1940s they were to help transform New York into the new world capital of art. But before their arrival American picture-buying was controlled by the agents of Paris dealers, who encouraged their clients to buy from Europe rather than support the work of American artists. All this was to change as the cultural links to Europe were cut by the war. The USA had now to subsist on its native culture and on the work of the European painters in exile, the great majority of them Surrealists. The art critic James Thrall Soby wrote prophetically about the presence of the newcomers in 1942 (Boyers, 1988):

It can mean the beginning of a period during which the American traditions of freedom and generosity may implement a new internationalism, centered in this country; it can mean that American artists and patrons may form a xenophobic circle and wait for such men to go away leaving our art as it was before. Meanwhile, the arts are the only currency left which cannot be counterfeited and which may be passed from nation to nation and from people to people . . . These . . . artists have brought us art in high denomination. Let us therefore say to them, for their sakes but also for ours: Welcome, and welcome again.

Nevertheless life was tough at first for the exiles in spite of the belief among many New Yorkers that a dealer mafia existed to promote their work at the expense of local artists. A number of German gallery owners from Berlin had already set up in New York, among them Karl Nierendorf and Curt Valentin. They, along with other émigré dealers, were helping popularize modern German painting. While some critics attacked the 'Surrealist Circus' in particular, the heiress Peggy Guggenheim supported them in the most practical of ways. Even when in France on the eve of the German invasion she had honoured a pledge to buy one picture every day from a refugee artist. These works of art became the basis for her future New York collection. Her generosity also included paying André Breton's fare to New York and supporting him with $200 a month until he found a job broadcasting propaganda in French to Occupied Europe from the Voice of America. Guggenheim had originally planned to establish a gallery for her rescued collection in London, but the speed of the German advance in Europe persuaded her to return to the safety of New York. With Breton as her adviser she opened Art of This Century as a showcase for the art of the refugees that she had helped to rescue. Her gallery was important in giving status and commercial recognition to their work, even though it was still difficult for American institutions to be seen buying émigré art rather than supporting American-born artists.

Max Ernst had the least problem establishing himself, having married his patron Peggy Guggenheim, but even he missed Paris and the fellowship of the other Surrealists. With the help of Varian Fry, Ernst had escaped from France without a visa. Arriving at the Spanish border, he was forbidden entry and ordered to return to Pau. As he turned to leave, the senior customs official asked him what was in the bundle he was carrying. Unrolling his canvases, Ernst spread them out on the platform in an extraordinary private exhibition as his fellow passengers gathered round. All were amazed by the contorted shapes and brilliant colours of Ernst's fantastic landscapes. The only silent observer was the official who had refused Ernst entry to Spain. After gazing at the pictures for several minutes he turned to Ernst, obviously moved, and said, 'Sir, I adore your talent. You have a great talent. But I must send you back to Pau. There is the train for Pau. Here on the left is the train for Madrid. Here is your passport. Don't take the wrong train.'

Nor did he. When Ernst arrived in New York with Guggenheim on a Pan-Am Clipper from Lisbon he was immediately taken to Ellis Island and kept for three days as an illegal immigrant. However, once he had settled down, Ernst became fascinated by the American landscape, especially the monumental valleys of the far south-west with their rugged rock faces. He painted these in a series that revealed his new decalcomania technique, which involved transferring designs from paper on to glass. The resulting images are strangely reminiscent of today's computer-generated art and were described by one critic as 'rocks and trees which crawl with half-human forms, so numerous and strange that their very precision makes them hard to see'.

Wild America was to entrance many of the exiled painters. Fernand Léger, one of the founders of Cubism, travelled the country keeping a pictorial diary of his journey from the New York skyline to the Rockies. For him, it was the duty of the newcomer to absorb himself in this atmosphere and to 'hold fast in this luminous, electric intensity; in America life is burned up'. Léger learned much from his American exile; his last project before returning to France after the war was a vibrantly coloured abstraction entitled *Adieu New York*. But it is the work of Josef Albers that best shows the effect of the American land-scape on the exiles. From hard-edged, urban and formalized sandblasted glass paintings he turned to the pre-Columbian abstract style of the south-west. Perhaps its simplicity reminded him of the folk art of his homeland. But Léger's old Parisian colleague, Marc Chagall, was less taken with the USA. Arriving in November 1941 with enough material to hold an immediate exhibition in New York, Chagall became convinced that the American art world was not for him, and American references did not appear in his work.

The Surrealist Marcel Duchamp, in spite of his earlier dramatic impact on the American art scene, produced little of significance during his wartime years in New York. He did, however, fall in love with the city and its network of apartments and the low cost of living. He produced cover design for magazines, including one for *Vogue* that was rejected as too scandalous: George Washington's face was replaced by the Stars and Stripes in sagging sackcloth. André Breton arrived as the undisputed leader and theorist of European Surrealism but found it almost impossible to continue the intimacy and easy communications that had held the group together in Paris.

While Breton remained in relative obscurity, the career of the most notorious of all the Surrealists, Salvador Dalí, blossomed. Arriving from Lisbon in August 1940, this supreme self-publicist took whatever project he was offered from fashion designs to film sets. His 'Surrealistic Night in an Enchanted Forest', at the Hotel Del Monte in Oakland, California, the following year caused a sensation. One thousand guests appeared wearing costumes illustrating 'their own worst dream'. Dalí, the showman, had already recognized the power of the American mass media, and he became its arch-manipulator. But his capacity to alienate the critics and to enrage his fellow Surrealists isolated him from the influential art world. In the USA Dalí assumed a new persona as a money-driven clown and manipulator described by his fellow Surrealist André Breton as 'Avida Dollars' (an anagram of his name). As Dalí himself wrote, 'I began to look around me, and from then on I regarded most of the people I met solely and exclusively as creatures I could use as porters on my voyages of ambition.'

Soon everyone had heard of Dalí, but few realized that Breton was the real leader of Surrealism. Since his appearance in a diving suit at Surrealist exhibition in London in 1937 Dalí's principal concern was for notoriety. In the USA he found it in full as the public and outrageous face of Surrealism. The product and the presenter had become one. As much as Breton deplored his vulgarities, even he had to admit that Dalí had brought a remarkable awareness of art to a huge public, having hijacked Surrealism in the process. Dalí's legacy was to be, as the critic Leslie Fiedler put it in 1955:

> The transformation of Surrealist gallows humour into commercial entertainment . . . an extraordinary process which begins for literature in the columns of the *New Yorker* and for art in the cartoons of the same magazine, as well as in certain shop-windows decorated by Salvador

Dalí . . . The avant-garde images of twenty-five years ago . . . have become now the common property of gifte shoppes and greeting card racks, [and they] fall as stereotypes from the mouths of twelve-year-olds.

Dalí returned to Europe in 1948 having achieved little of any lasting worth in America but with an enhanced reputation as being his own worst enemy. In contrast to Dalí, Piet Mondrian arrived quietly, celebrating his exile in October 1940 with a series of paintings that attempted to capture the atmosphere and rhythm of New York. Famous for the geometric regularity of his compositions, Mondrian introduced a new vitality into his American paintings and worked in a style he termed Neoplasticism. This was abstract without any references to natural forms. Mondrian claimed a new artistic purity for this Neoplasticism saying, 'Plastic art is a free aspect of life . . . its only function is to "show". It is up to us to see what it reveals.'

Other émigré artists working in New York were the sculptor Jacques Lipchitz who, after a temporary return to France, spent the next three years in the USA and the photographers Andreas Feininger and André Kertész. Within three weeks of arriving in New York in 1937 Feininger was working for the Black Star Picture Agency. His arrival at *Life* magazine the next year marked the beginning of the new genre of the picture story in the USA: Feininger is credited with being the leading innovator of this new photo-journalism through the medium of the mass-produced American weekly magazine. His work was to elevate photography into the cultural mainstream in the USA, and he was to influence a whole generation of photographers.

Kertész came with a more established reputation as an artist with a Surrealist vision. Within a few weeks of his arrival his work was featured in the 'History of Photography, 1839–1937' exhibition. However, Feininger was unable to get him a post as a photo-journalist at *Life*, his work being thought too artistic and European for a news magazine. As they told him, 'You're talking too much with your pictures. We only need documents. We have editors to write the text.' But later, in the 1960s, as photography became more recognized as an art form, Kertész was seen as an important modern artist, and he was honoured with a solo exhibition at the Museum of Modern Art in New York.

George Grosz had been one of the most incisive critics of German society in the 1920s, whose decadence he believed had led to the rise of Hitler. Loathed by the Nazis, he was already safe in the USA when they came to power. In exile he tried to reject Germany, but he could never shake off the memories and responsibilities of the past. At first he devoted himself to a series of watercolours of American landscapes with dark and cloudy skies. When he found that his friend the writer Erich Muhsam had been murdered in a concentration camp, Grosz turned to gloomy, symbolic paintings, in the manner of Goya's *Disasters of War*. Grosz never recaptured the verve of his early work, having convinced himself that satire was an inferior form of art. This negative approach had little appeal for the American critics: *Parnassus* magazine dismissed his work ironically as 'decadent art, an art which is permeated by a deep-rooted bitterness, which sees in landscape decay and obscenity'. In the late 1950s Grosz returned to Berlin, no more at home there than he had been in New York, and died in a drunken fall.

Perhaps the greatest contribution of a refugee artist to the USA was that of Hans Hofmann and his art school on East 57th Street, New York. Through this academy passed some of the next generation of important American painters: Larry Rivers, Alan Kaprow, Louise Nevelson and Helen Frankenthaler. Hofmann was closely involved in the emergence of New York's Abstract Expressionists, and his free-hand painting foreshadows that of Jackson Pollock. The effect of the twenty or so leading European artists on East Coast painting and on Abstract Expressionism in particular was dramatic. As one art critic put it, 'to see, occasionally to talk with, Mondrian, Masson, Ernst, Tanguy, Léger, Lipchitz, Duchamp, among others, was, so to speak, to join the School of Paris, to join, that is, the central creative tradition of twentieth-century art'. One of the emerging young American artists, Robert Motherwell, also recalled walking the streets with one or other of them and joining in their discussions at the French Canteen in New York. He found their willingness to debate ideas a refreshing change from the innate conservatism of established American artists. The result, for the young Americans, was a growing confidence in their own art and abilities so that, by the late 1940s, their work had made New York the new capital of world art. American art had been transformed, with the help of the Europeans, from regional to international and, finally, to universal art.

5

Losing a Tongue But Finding a Voice

Not the least of Nazi victims was German literature. As so many of the nation's finest writers were driven into exile, the German language itself came under the direct control of Joseph Goebbels and the Reichskulturkammer. For over a decade nothing of any literary significance was produced in Germany. At first exiled German writers struggled to rebuild their lives and retain their native language in the neighbouring countries of Austria and Switzerland. Both were German-speaking or, more importantly, German-reading, as was the Czecho-slovakian Sudetenland. German-language publishing houses also flourished in Paris, Amsterdam, Prague and Zurich – but for how long? Stefan Zweig, one of the three best-known German writers of the period, expressed the pessimism of his colleagues when he wrote, 'It's practically all over for German books; if the Sudetenland goes then German language publishing (in exile) is finished. One million Swiss do not make a big enough market.' From now on Zweig, a world-wide best-seller, could publish his work only in translation. The Nazis, he said, had successfully robbed him of his own language. In 1934 the playwright Ernst Toller put it even more succinctly, 'We have lost our people, our market, our publishers, newspapers, theatres, homes, bank-accounts, passports, papers, our manuscripts and our friends' (Toller, 1936).

Fortunately Stefan Zweig was successful enough to be able to live in comfort on the income from translations alone, but he was one of only ten living German authors who could. As with the artists Vienna and Prague were to provide no more than a temporary refuge for the exiled writers. Few of them had initially considered seeking refuge in Britain – that strange cultural backwater with no German-language theatre and only a minuscule readership for German books. Even educated Englishmen and women in the 1930s virtually ignored the whole of German culture. European culture, for the British, began and ended in Paris. With the greatest language in the world and a vast empire to share it with, the English had little need of German or any other continental language for that matter. At most, the average British reader might occasionally consider a translation of a book by that oddly named German novelist Lion Feuchtwanger.

For the German writer exiled in an English-speaking country there was a simple choice: continue writing in German or make the bold attempt to master English. Many were tempted to try – given the difficulties of finding an exiled German publishing house – but very few succeeded. Less than a dozen of the writers who settled in Britain managed to complete a novel in English. The best known are Ernst Bornemann, Hermynia zur Muhlen, Anna Sebastian, Anna Gmeyner, Robert Neumann and, most notably, the Hungarian Arthur Koestler. As a journalist, Koestler had an distinct advantage over the others. His articles for British newspapers in the late 1920s had given him an unusual facility in written English that he was later able to develop into the sustained narrative needed for a novel. Few others found it as easy. Peter de Mendelssohn and his wife Hilde Spiel devised their own crash course in English by reading every article in the newspapers each day before plodding through the London literary magazines. They completed their day by reading passages from the great English stylists Hazlitt, Lamb and Pater to each other.

One exiled writer, the Austrian Robert Neumann, did produce a significant novel written in English. Neumann had arrived in 1933 with a reputation based on the overnight success of his parody *Mit fremden Federn* (*With a Foreign Pen*). At first he continued to write in German and publish in translation, but while interned on the Isle of Man in 1940 he attempted his first novel in English, *Scene in Passing*. It impressed the literary critic Philip Toynbee, who described it as 'heroic – linguistically on a par with Conrad'; no higher praise for a foreigner writing in English.

Exiled poets found English even more difficult to write in. The Viennese Erich Fried, who had seen his father beaten to death by the Gestapo, wrote only in German, refusing, as he said, to give Hitler the satisfaction of robbing him of his native language. During his British exile he continued to write some of the finest modern German poetry.

Another interned writer, Richard Friedenthal, in his post-war novel *Die Welt in der Nusschale*, described life on the Isle of Man and wrote amusingly in German about the foibles of his British hosts. Friedenthal was so taken with London that he stayed on after the war and completed highly successful biographies of Goethe and Luther in German.

The Italian exile Elias Canetti also felt at home in Britain, where he completed a major work of European literature, *Die Blendung*, which appeared in English as *Auto-da-fé*. He is also credited with encouraging Iris Murdoch to publish her own first novel *Under the Net*.

With the exceptions of Arthur Koestler and Robert Neumann, the impact of exiled writers' work on British literature was minimal. Of far greater consequence was the great contribution that the exiled publishers made to the resurgence of British publishing after the war. Their most spectacular achievement was to bring the art book to Britain. Picture-led books of high quality were virtually unknown in Britain until introduced by the Phaidon Press and Thames and Hudson – both founded by expatriates. Phaidon Press moved with its founders Ludwig Goldscheider and Béla Horowitz from Vienna to London and soon became renowned for the superb picture research and beautiful typography of its books. Thames and Hudson, named after rivers of London and New York – a symbolic union of the old world and the new – was a partnership of Walter and Eva Neurath, who had fled to Britain after the Anschluss in 1938. Both began in London by working for another émigré, Wolfgang Foges, who had founded Adprint, the pioneers of this new art book format in Britain. Walter Neurath had been released from internment to become production director at Adprint. His skills were seen by the Ministry of Information as being essential for the production of a morale-boosting work of propaganda entitled *Britain in Pictures*. This publication, with its stylish blend of high-quality pictures and bold typography, was the forerunner of Thames and Hudson's successful series of World of Art books. These books began to appear on British coffee tables during the late 1950s, providing a well-illustrated and reasonably priced introduction to culture for a new readership.

Other émigrés became part of British mainstream publishing, bring-ing a new vitality to a profession that had become characterized by a gentlemanly nonchalance. Ernest Hecht, Max Reinhardt, Bruno Cassirer, Oswald Wolff, Peter Owen, Paul Hamlyn, André Deutsch and the buccaneering George Weidenfeld – who introduced a new competi-tiveness to the sedate world of British publishing – all became familiar names in the London literary and publishing worlds.

If one cause united the émigré writers, it was the need to bear testa-ment to what had happened in Germany and to warn the British against the Nazi threat. They had seen the power of Goebbels's propaganda machine and now attempted to create one of their own in exile. The leaders of this group were Rudolf Olden, an early biographer of Hitler, and Otto Lehmann-Russbueldt, whose book *Germany's Air Force* had first exposed the facts of Germany's illegal rearmament in violation of the terms of the Treaty of Versailles of 1919. Both were recruited by British Intelligence to write the scripts for broadcasting to Germany even before hostilities began. German speakers were then in short supply, as the Foreign Office found when they tried to broadcast Chamberlain's statement on the Munich Agreement. When no suit-able German-speaking diplomat could be found, the BBC had to persuade Walter Goetz, a refugee cartoonist with the *Daily Express*, to read the speech. This fiasco prompted British Intelligence to set up a competent propaganda service with native German speakers under the direction of the bilingual British journalist Sefton Delmer. A true maverick, Delmer frequently ignored Foreign Office guidelines in favour of his own opinions, as when he broadcast, without consulting any government department, a personal rejection of Hitler's offer of a truce if Churchill would resign as Prime Minister.

Under Delmer and his boss Hugh Carleton Greene a team of talented German exiles began to assemble at the BBC. With their expert knowl-edge of the country and their understanding of the German character they were able to play an important role in undermining enemy morale. The most prolific of the scriptwriters was Karl Otten, who wrote over 125 scripts for transmission during the war. In collaboration with the British poet Louis MacNeice, Otten devised a weekly programme based on the supposed bizarre personal habits of the Nazi leaders. To counter-act any British complacency about Nazi intentions, Otten then created a chilling series that described in graphic detail just what would happen if the Germans ever invaded. Otten, a committed pacifist, also devised a series that told the British how the refugees were playing their part in the fight for freedom. But Otten's most telling contribution was a series, 'Black Gallery', in which he unmasked those who had betrayed the German people and brought Hitler to power. Even by Goebbels's standards it was impressive propaganda and all the more effective as the Reichsminister's own efforts became increasingly strident and unbelievable.

What began to give the BBC broadcasts the edge was their combination of traditional British humour and the biting, satirical wit of Berlin cabaret that the exiles had brought with them. So famous did the broadcasts become that even Germany's most distinguished novelist, Thomas Mann, began contributing a weekly newsletter in the manner of Alastair Cooke. Recorded in California, Mann's recordings were flown to London for transmission to Germany by the BBC. Less eminent contributors to the broadcasts included the Austrian writers Bruno Adler, Julius Braunthal, Hans Flesch-Brunningen, Robert Neumann and Martin Esslin – later a pioneering Head of Drama at the BBC's Third Programme. Emigrés as diverse in character and profession as the publisher George Weidenfeld and the art historian Ernst Gombrich also played their part. Curious to find out how well they had done, the BBC conducted a survey after the war and was amazed to discover that 10 million Germans had been regular listeners in spite of persistent jamming by the Nazis and the dire penalties that awaited anyone caught listening.

As Arthur Koestler's career began to flourish in exile, that of his contemporary, Germany's world-renowned historical novelist Stefan Zweig, declined. By a bizarre coincidence both were to die by their own hands in a suicide pact with their wives; But here any similarity ends: Koestler was a man of action and Zweig a passive victim of fate. When Arthur Koestler first joined the Communist Party in Hungary, Stefan Zweig was already at the height of his fame. Invited to lecture in Florence, he was enchanted by Italy and captivated by Mussolini. So confident was Zweig of this new friendship that he wrote to the Italian dictator pleading for the life of the condemned Doctor Germani, a colleague of the murdered socialist leader, Matteotti. When Germani was promptly released, a delighted Zweig declared that his letter to Mussolini had been more important than his Nobel Prize for Literature. As a man of principle who had opposed the rise of the Nazis, Zweig's position became increasingly tenuous as they tightened their grip on his native Austria.

From his home near the German border Zweig could see Hitler's base at Berchtesgaden and the steady stream of refugees beginning to trek into Austria. Dismayed by the withdrawal of German citizenship from Thomas Mann and by the book burnings in Berlin, Zweig moved to neutral Switzerland where his fellow exiles berated him for failing to speak out against the Nazis. Their criticism prompted a move to London, where he intended to complete his biography of Erasmus.

At first he liked the British, these polite but distant people, as he called them. New friends included George Bernard Shaw, H.G. Wells and Shalom Asch. Zweig was both happy and productive in London and had no hesitation in rejecting a lucrative offer from Hollywood. On a brief return visit to Austria he became caught up in a riot by socialist workers and witnessed the Dollfuss government's brutal reponse. The peril of remaining in Austria was made even more apparent to Zweig when the police arrived to search his house for arms. Relieved to be back in London, he wrote to a friend, 'It is wonderful to walk the streets without anyone checking what party badge you have in your lapel.' But he had not escaped his critics. Their new accusation was that he was allowing Richard Strauss, still working in Germany with Nazi permission, to use his libretto for the new opera *Die scheigsame Frau*. Strauss, often accused of ambiguity towards the Nazis, insisted, however, that Zweig must clearly be billed as the librettist, so provoking a row with Goebbels and Rosenberg. Goaded by his fellow exiles, Zweig declared that he had, indeed, attempted to withdraw his permission for the libretto to be used but was overridden by his lawyers. All his royalties, he announced, would be donated to refugee charities instead.

But his romance with Britain had begun to wane. Zweig now realized that what he took for British reserve was, in fact, cool indifference and that apparent sympathy for the refugee was merely politeness. His growing disenchantment with Britain led him to accept an invitation to lecture in the USA alongside Toscanini and Shalom Asch. When he arrived in New York the ordeal began again as journalists repeatedly asked him, with little success, for his response to events in Europe. He delivered his lecture on Mary, Queen of Scots and spent the following days promoting his idea for an international magazine that would be a showcase for refugee Jewish writers and artists. This, he considered, would be far more effective than the Jews having to descend to the polemics of their Nazi opponents. Three weeks later Zweig was back in London for the publication of *Maria Stuart*. Condemned in Germany as the work of a Jew, it was a best-seller throughout the rest of the world.

As Zweig hesitated in London, Arthur Koestler was working as a communist agent in Spain. He had been sent to Madrid to investigate German and Italian backing for Franco's Nationalist forces in the civil war but with a commission from the London *News Chronicle* as his cover. As the city fell to Franco, Koestler managed to escape with suitcases full of incriminating documents. A few months later he was besieged in Málaga as the Nationalist army invested the city. Here he accepted the protection of an expatriate Englishman who, unknown to Koestler, was a target for the Nationalists. As the city fell, Koestler attempted escape by car then, inexplicably, changed his mind and returned to his host's villa, where he calmly awaited his fate reading in a deckchair. Both Koestler and his host were arrested and taken to the local police station, where he watched as captured Republicans were brought in and beaten to death. He had hidden a syringe and sufficient morphine tablets to commit suicide but was unable to find enough water to dissolve them.

Over 4,000 captured Republicans were summarily shot over the next weeks, and Koestler had no reason to believe that he would not be one of them. But his predicament was known to the *News Chronicle*, and it began a campaign to save him. Koestler spent the next four months in solitary confinement, an experience he would later utilize in his most famous novel *Darkness at Noon*, until a three-week hunger strike persuaded his captors to ameliorate his conditions. Asked to make a statement praising Franco's leniency, he courageously refused. After considerable British diplomatic pressure, Koestler was finally released and handed over to the British authorities at the Gibraltar frontier in May 1937.

While Koestler languished in a Spanish gaol, Stefan Zweig was contemplating a move to Brazil, where he was the best-known European author, a fact that he had discovered when attending a PEN conference at which the Brazilians had treated him royally. He found the people exotic and delightful, and Brazil's multi-racial society made it a paradise on earth. Here, he believed, the European cultural tradition could be revivified by the vitality of the new world. But Zweig was now fifty-five and appeared, to his friends in London, a broken man. Yet he continued to work ceaselessly and completed a novel,

Ungeduld des Herzers ('The Impatient Heart'), set in the heyday of the Austro-Hungarian Empire. His only political gesture in London was to join the Freier Deutscher Kulturbund and give an oration at Ernst Toller's memorial service. In July 1939 he moved to Bath and announced, uncharacteristically, that every Jew of military age should join the fight against Hitler. In the event of a German invasion of Britain, he declared, the Nazis would not find him alive.

When Arthur Koestler arrived at Tilbury on the cruiser HMS *Derbyshire* on 21 May 1937, his adventures in Spain had already made him a celebrity. His experiences were published that autumn as *A Spanish Testament*, and launched his new career as a serious writer. The book captured the terror and impotence felt by the individual when faced with a cruel and implacable system. It was Koestler's under-standing of these emotions that was to make *Darkness at Noon*, a devastating exposure of Stalinism, such a powerful and seminal work. Koestler would live in Britain for the rest of his life, becoming a major figure in the literary and intellectual world. But he did not, at first, abandon journalism. His new celebrity won him assignments in Greece, the Balkans and Palestine, where he gained first-hand experience of the Arab–Jewish conflict.

Koestler was trapped in France when war broke out in September 1939. Interned, then released, he characteristically enlisted in the French Foreign Legion as one Albert Dubert, a Swiss taxi-driver. Ignoring orders to report to Angers, he headed south to Vichy, sleeping in barns and blending in with the rag-tag of the defeated French army. Reaching Marseilles he was officially discharged and found his way to Varian Fry, who put him on a ship bound for Oran and then on to Lisbon. But only after a seven-week delay and strenuous efforts on his behalf by such eminent figures as Harold Nicholson was he given an entry visa and flown to Britain. Still officially classified as an enemy alien, Koestler was arrested and was still in Pentonville Prison when *Darkness at Noon* was published. Its effect on a generation who had become increasingly disillusioned with communism was extraordinary. Decades after its publication the Labour politician Michael Foot remembered the effect it had on him (Foot, 1986):

> Who will ever forget the first moment he read *Darkness at Noon*? For socialists especially, the experience was indelible. I can recall reading

it right through one night, horror-struck, over-powered, enthralled. If this was the true revelation of what had happened at the great Stalin show trials . . . a terrifying shaft of darkness was cast over the future no less than the past.

In 1940, the same year that *Darkness at Noon* appeared, Stefan Zweig left London *en route* to Rio de Janeiro with his second wife, Lotte. This time his welcome in Brazil was far more muted and his Brazilian friends distinctly less warm. Even his new book, *Brasil – Paîs do Futuro*, received poor reviews in the Brazilian press. Nevertheless, Zweig stuck with his plan to buy a house there near the provincial town of Petropolis. As ever, he was happy at first, enjoying the wonderful views and the quality of the local coffee. But the old melancholy returned in this unreal world. He began to be overwhelmed by a sense of guilt that he had abandoned all that made him the writer he was. 'It is not only plants that cannot live without roots,' he wrote. His last great project, a biography of Balzac, was almost impossible to research in Brazil, and without the focus of work Zweig was never in control of his emotions. His quest for solitude had led him, he believed, to this terrible fate – buried alive in Brazil. News of what was happening to the Jews had now reached there, and this added to Zweig's guilt and despair. When the USA entered the war, Zweig became convinced that even Brazil would soon become involved. Perhaps he had already decided to take his life when he wrote on 4 February 1942, 'I leave behind a document [his autobiography] which will show what we wanted, attempted and experienced, we, the generation of writers who bore perhaps the heaviest burden of fate for centuries.'

By this time a British citizen, Arthur Koestler had, like many of the refugees of military age, joined the Army Pioneer Corps. The future Labour government minister John Stratchey was amused at seeing the rumpled, battle-dressed figure of Private Koestler, 'Surely', he wrote, 'one of the oddest men ever to dig a British latrine.' At weekends Koestler travelled up to London to attend literary parties and intellectual soirées with friends such as Cyril Connolly and the future Viscount Astor. In the rough khaki uniform of a private soldier and with his dark hair cut short in military fashion, Koestler cut a bizarre figure in the London salons. By 1942 he had abandoned latrines in favour of writing scripts for the BBC's Europe in Revolt series, as well as contributing articles to the London *Evening Standard*, the *Observer* and Cyril Connolly's literary magazine *Horizon*. In 1943, his new novel *Arrival and Departure* earned further praise from Michael Foot, who praised him as 'the greatest foreign novelist since Joseph Conrad paid us the compliment of writing in the English tongue'.

Cut off from the events in Europe and wracked with guilt and depression, Stefan Zweig was nearing the end of his life. On 14 February 1943 he went, totally out of character, to the Carnival in Rio. The following Saturday smoke was seen coming from a bonfire in the Zweig's garden. When a visiting writer telephoned to ask for an interview, Zweig claimed he was too busy. That evening the Zweigs entertained their closest friends at what was to be a last supper and returned the books that they had borrowed. When his guests had gone, Zweig wrote letters putting his affairs in order. To one friend he wrote, 'Excuse me if I cause you trouble and work, but I was at the end of my strength because of my nomadic life and the bad state of health of my dear wife.' His last letter was an open declaration to the world (Prater, 1972); after thanking Brazil for its hospitality, he continued:

> After one's sixtieth year unusual powers are needed in order to make another wholly new beginning. Those that I possess have been exhausted by the long years of homeless wandering. So I hold it better to conclude in good time and with erect bearing a life for which intellectual labour was always the purest joy and personal freedom the highest good on earth. I salute all my friends! May it be granted them to see the dawn after the long night! I, all too impatient, go on before.

The following morning the Zweigs' bedroom remained locked until the servants, in late afternoon, broke open the door to find them dead from a massive dose of veronal. Outside the bedroom door their small dog lay waiting for his evening walk. The literary world mourned his loss. *The Times* of London described him a sad exile from the twentieth century and his death as marking the end of his wanderings. Yet throughout his life Zweig had been haunted by depression only relieved by complete immersion in his writing or by moving on to a new home. But Petropolis was the end of the line where he had, perhaps deliberately, marooned himself. His biographer Donald Prater describes Zweig's dilemma of exile perfectly (Prater, 1972):

The ideal of personal freedom, the 'connecting thread' of his life's work, had, in fact, meant for him nothing more than freedom to move and to exchange one ambience for another, to still his inner restlessness with new scenes and new people. Without such change he could not maintain his extraordinary application to the work which was his whole life.

When the war ended Arthur Koestler became an even more prolific writer. He completed a novel, *The Age of Longing*, and a volume of autobiography, *The God That Failed*, in which he again traced his disillusionment with, and subsequent hostility to, communism. But Koestler was never at peace, constantly seeking controversy and maintaining a personal life that was famously priapic. By the 1960s Koestler had developed an obsession with science and, above all, with a mission to disprove the tenets of behaviourism. This quest led to a fascination with the workings of the brain and he flirted with the effects of hallucinogenic drugs. The culmination of all this was *The Ghost in the Machine*, published in 1967, in which he advocated the use of drugs to control human behaviour. In later years Koestler trod a fine line between quasi-science and orthodox science before gravitating towards a wholehearted belief in the existence of the paranormal. In 1976 Koestler was diagnosed as having Parkinson's disease. Stoically, he prepared for his own death by writing suicide advice for the Euthanasia Society. The manner of his death was almost identical to that of Stefan Zweig in Brazil. A maid arrived at the Koestlers' London home one morning in March 1983 to find the bedroom locked and a note telling her to call the police. Koestler was dead in an armchair, an empty whisky glass still in his hand. His wife, Cynthia, who had been in perfect health, lay dead beside him on a sofa. They had swallowed the barbiturate Tuinal. But no dog waited outside; their terrier had been quietly put down the day before. To the chagrin of their friends both Koestler and Cynthia had left a will bequeathing his fortune amounting to almost a million pounds to paranormal research.

In many ways Stefan Zweig was a man of the past who died mourning a lost world of European cultural unity that Nazi barbarism had swept away. Essentially a pacifist, he had found it almost impossible to comprehend the political conflicts of his time and felt powerless in the face of events that he could neither control nor influence. His vast body of work reveals where his heart lay – in the past. Zweig wrote about the great figures of history, Dostoevsky, Tolstoy, Marie Antoinette, Magellan, Dickens and Erasmus, but he failed to draw the lessons of the past and see their relevance to contemporary Europe. His response to the challenges of his time was to run as far away as possible to the edge of the Brazilian jungle. Yet even there he could not escape the survivor's guilt that he undoubtedly felt about the fate of the Jews. Today Zweig is little more than a footnote in twentieth-century literary history. Arthur Koestler, however, with his restless, inquiring mind, was very much a man of his age. He took on the challenges of the times and acted decisively, first as a communist agent, then as an important novelist writing in a new language and finally as interrogator of scientific advance. That he was able to envisage a future where the spiritual and the inexplicable have a relevance shows him as a true visionary.

Stefan Zweig had been one of only three German writers whose names were known throughout the world in 1933. The others, Thomas Mann and Lion Feuchtwanger, friends and colleagues in Germany, chose exile in America. They settled in the same suburb of Los Angeles, drawn there by the Californian climate and the company of fellow exiles rather than by the lure of a Hollywood contract. Both continued writing in German and publishing in translation, their American work continuing to enhance their reputation as Germany's leading writers. Mann was without question the greater of the two and was the most eminent representative of German culture in exile. So greatly was he respected by the émigré community and by the American government that it was suggested that he should become head of state of the new Germany when the war ended. The admiration was mutual. Mann declared his enthusiasm for the American system in general and President Roosevelt in particular. Later, the rise of McCarthyism and the USA's increasing illiberalism led to disillusionment and provoked his eventual return to Europe. Lion Feuchtwanger, too, would have returned to Europe with him had not the House Committee on Un-American Activities, ironically, deprived him of an American passport so forcing him to stay in the country until his death in 1958.

Thomas Mann's problem with the Nazis began in 1933, when he gave a lecture in Munich on 'The Sorrows and Grandeur of Richard Wagner': his proposition was that Wagner was not the militant German nationalist that he appeared to be. A month later Mann was astonished to read a letter in a Munich newspaper accusing him of a 'calumny' against Wagner in his lecture and of posing abroad as a 'representative of German culture'. There were forty-five signatories to this letter including Hitler's publisher, Max Amann, and, to Mann's horror, the composer Richard Strauss. Mann's dignified reply refuted the accusations and reiterated his admiration for both Wagner and German culture. But Mann was now a marked man. Marooned without a passport in Paris, he wisely accepted an invitation from his American publisher Knopf to visit New York. Mann made the journey by travelling on a French Certificate of Identity. On his return in 1936 Mann spoke out against the Nazis for the first time, warning the world that it was not just the Jews but the whole Christian and classical tradition of European culture that they hated (Prater, 1995):

> This conviction has led me to avoid the country in whose intellectual tradition I am more deeply rooted than those who have been hesitating for three years whether to dare openly to withdraw my citizenship . . . I am sure that I have acted rightly, towards my contemporaries and before posterity.

With so many of the great names of German culture already gone, the Nazis hesitated finally to strip Thomas Mann of his citizenship. But in December 1936 he was informed that his continued membership of 'Jewish controlled' international organizations and his 'violent insults to the Reich' had disqualified him from German citizenship. When Bonn University withdrew his honorary doctorate, he acknowledged their decision with pleasure. Having seen the disgraceful role of German universities in the nation's moral decline, he told them, he would henceforth treasure only his honorary degree from Harvard. His duty now, he declared, was to help 'preserve the lofty dignity of German culture'. He completed the letter to Bonn with the words, 'God help our darkened and misused country, and teach it to make peace with the world and with itself!' From now on, he wrote, 'Where I am, is Germany.' This letter, published as a pamphlet in Zurich, was widely circulated throughout Germany in 1937 as an important declaration of resistance by Germany's most respected writer, now the moral leader of German culture in exile.

Lion Feuchtwanger had also fallen foul of the Nazis with his novel *Success*, set in Bavaria and containing a thinly disguised attack on Hitler.

When the Munich press denounced it as a work of hatred by a Jewish traitor, Nazi storm troopers wrecked and looted Feuchtwanger's empty villa in Berlin while he was in Switzerland. What particularly infuriated them was a portrait of Eleanor Roosevelt, one of Feuchtwanger's keenest admirers. A few days later Joseph Goebbels himself denounced Feuchtwanger on German radio as an enemy of the people. None of this affected Feuchtwanger's reputation as one of Europe's most celebrated historical novelists, however. His most famous work *Jud Süss* (*Jew Suss*; entitled *Power* in the American edition), published in 1925, tells the story of the rise and fall of a Jew at the Court of Wurtenburg. Thomas Mann, on a visit to London, noted that the fashionable compliment in literary circles at the time was to say of a book, 'It's almost like Feuchtwanger.' The *The Times* even credited *Jud Süss* with reviving the popularity of the historical novel, and the *New Statesman* thought Feuchtwanger 'a major star in the firmament of modern European literature'. Unusually for a German, Feuchtwanger was popular in Britain and received invitations to meet both King George V and the Prime Minister Ramsay MacDonald. Asked at a literary reception to name his favourite British author, Feuchtwanger delighted everyone by replying without hesitation, 'Rudyard Kipling'.

Given Feuchtwanger's celebrity in Britain, it seems strange that he later preferred exile in the USA. But it was to Sanary in the South of France that he went first in 1933 to complete his novel *The Oppermanns*. This was the first anti-Nazi novel written by a German writer in exile. It tells of the malevolent pressure exerted on the German-Jewish Oppermann family from November 1932 to summer 1933. Described by Klaus Mann as a brilliant and accurate depiction of the rise of the Nazis, it made Feuchtwanger even more enemies among Germany's new rulers. When war came and France swiftly capitulated, Sanary came under Vichy French control. Feuchtwanger, as an alien, was immediately interned at a camp at Les Milles near Marseilles. A prime target for the Nazis under the so-called 'surrender on demand' clause of the Franco-German Armistice agreement, Feuchtwanger faced deportation to Germany and inevitable death.

His account of his experiences at Les Milles, published later in the USA as *The Devil in France*, tells of the hardships he endured and of the irony of being interned by the French while the RAF were dropping leaflets on the Germans that contained quotations from his writings and the Americans were freezing his bank accounts in New York. When news of his arrest reached Washington, orders were given at the behest of Mrs Roosevelt to rescue him. Miles Standish of the American Consulate in Marseilles was sent to the camp and discovered that the prisoners were allowed to bathe in a local river every day. One afternoon Standish drove to the river and picked up Feuchtwanger without the guards noticing. Feuchtwanger was given a woman's coat, headscarf and dark glasses and then, disguised as Standish's mother-in-law, driven through numerous checkpoints to safety in Marseilles. There, hidden in the villa of another American diplomat, Hiram Bingham, Feuchtwanger was reunited with his wife and waited until Varian Fry was able to get them out of the country. It was too dangerous, given Feuchtwanger's notoriety, for them to cross the Pyrenees into Spain with the next party of Fry's refugees, so they were taken by train to the border town of Cerbère and crossed separately into Spain before going on to Portugal, where they were put on board a ship for New York.

Feuchtwanger arrived in America to find Thomas Mann already installed as the doyen of the émigrés and the voice of German conscience in exile. The *New York Post* said that the USA was enriched by Mann's presence. His acceptance by almost the entire American nation meant that even the highest political circles were open to him. Mann, like most of the exiles, deeply admired President Roosevelt, 'this wheelchair Caesar', as he called him. When Roosevelt was re-elected for a third term Mann was delighted, convinced that it was the turning point in the struggle against Hitler: with the USA united under Roosevelt and Britain under Winston Churchill, Mann felt that Europe would soon, at last, be free. His telegram of congratulations to the President produced an immediate invitation to stay at the White House.

Both writers now had a living to make. Feuchtwanger could live in opulence on his American royalties alone, but Thomas Mann badly needed financial support. Early in 1940 Princeton University came to his rescue with an offer of a part-time post at a salary of $3,000 a year. Then his friends added to his security by obtaining for him a sinecure at the Library of Congress as 'Consultant in Germanic Literature'. In his letter of acceptance Mann wrote of his honour at being involved in the cultural life of his new homeland. Now with an adequate, if modest, income, Mann devoted himself to his writing. He completed *Lotte in Weimar* and then, in just five months, wrote *The Transposed Heads*. In

January 1943 *Joseph* was published and sold nearly a quarter of a million copies in the first six months alone. The character of Joseph was based on Roosevelt, seen an as an American Hermes, whose New Deal will revive the fortunes of his people. Mann had already started work on his great novel *Doctor Faustus*, but his his work on behalf of his fellow refugees and against the Nazi regime continued in spite of his prolific writing. When the truth about the concentration camps became known, Mann berated the Germans in his weekly broadcasts transmitted by the BBC. Only by supporting the oncoming Allied armies, he told them, could they find even a modicum of salvation.

Feuchtwanger, too, found California a sympathetic place to work. Within a year of his arrival he had completed both his life of Josephus, the first-century Jewish historian, and *The Devil in France*. There were seven novels still to come with subjects as varied as the Crusades, Joan of Arc and Marie Antoinette. Feuchtwanger admired the vigour of American writing and was a keen reader of the younger American novelists, although he never risked writing in English himself. His interest in his new homeland prompted two novels with American themes, *Proud Destiny* and *The Devil in Boston*. Of all the exiled writers, Feuchtwanger alone had, with these, attempted the American novel. Socially, Feuchtwanger was liked by almost the entire émigré community, but his closest friend was Bertolt Brecht. When Brecht had arrived in Los Angeles in July 1941 Feuchtwanger was there to meet him. Soon he was involved with Brecht, the arch-collaborator, in his latest passion, a play about Joan of Arc set in contemporary France. But they could not agree on the character of Joan, and it was decided that Brecht would complete the play, now called *The Visions of Simone Machard*, while Feuchtwanger would write it as a novel. It was an amicable arrangement, and when Feuchtwanger sold the film rights of the novel *Simone* in 1942 he generously shared the advance with Brecht. Brecht's play was eventually produced in 1957, but Feuchtwanger's novel was abandoned as a film project.

As the war neared its end, the liberal political climate of the USA began to change. Roosevelt was gone and suspicions of Russian motives were paramount. Thomas Mann did not like this new America, but in spite of repeated invitations from Germany he refused to return. It had been a twelve-year ordeal of exile, of which he wrote, in 1945, that 'all of you who swore loyalty to the "charismatic Führer" . . . and pursued culture under Goebbels had never experienced . . . the asthma of exile, the uprooting, the nervous terrors of homelessness'.

By 1949 he was prepared to visit Germany briefly and address the audience at the Goethe Anniversary celebration. Before leaving Germany he made a short visit to the East that was monitored by the Federal Bureau of Investigation. The consequence was that when he returned to the USA he found himself banned from lecturing at the Library of Congress's hundred-and-fiftieth anniversary celebration. Mann was outraged, given his openly declared and constantly repeated opposition to totalitarianism and Soviet communism, yet he made no public comment on the Mundt–Nixon bill that was before Congress. This act required all communists and communist organizations to be officially registered, and party members to be interned during a national emergency. If the bill was passed, Mann declared, he would leave America. In April the House Committee on Un-American Activities listed him as one of those 'affiliated with various peace organizations or communist fronts'. On the same list were the names of Einstein, Marlon Brando, Norman Mailer, Frank Lloyd Wright and Lion Feuchtwanger.

Feuchtwanger had just completed *The Devil in Boston*, his novel about about Cotton Mather and the seventeenth-century Boston witch-hunts, when the House Committee on Un-American Activities began its sittings in 1946. His attitude to the Soviet Union had now changed, and he had come to realize that Stalin was indeed a brutal tyrant. But his change of mind had obviously not impressed the American author-ities. When he applied for final citizenship papers in January 1948 his loyalty was questioned and he was subjected to constant interrogation and rejections until his death in 1958. Even Richard Nixon appealed on his behalf, but Feuchtwanger's was seen as an important test case that the state could not give way on. All manner of excuses were produced to deny him citizenship, including the suggestion that he had sent telegrams of congratulation to the Soviet Union each year on the anniversary of the Bolshevik Revolution, that he was a member of the Committee for Friendship with the Soviet Union and that he had accepted a literary prize from the East German government. When they failed to prove his communism, the investigators accused him of being a dirty old man who bedded young actresses. In all this his constant defender was Thomas Mann, who appealed not only for

Feuchtwanger to be left alone but also for the lives of the communist spies the Rosenbergs. Mann was dismayed by what he saw as the USA's new cultural arrogance and the increasing repression of the individual. He thought again of returning to a Europe that could be an honest broker between East and West and to what would be 'not a German Europe, but a European Germany'.

Mann's final testament was his late masterpiece *Doctor Faustus: The Life of the German Composer Adrian Leverkuhn as Told by a Friend*. It is the most important work on Germany and the Nazi phenomenon written by an exile in America. The story of twentieth-century Germany is told through the experiences of the main character, Adrian Leverkuhn. This Nietzschean composer in the twelve-tone musical system sells his soul to the devil in return for professional success. In researching the background of the novel Mann had needed to consult Bruno Walter and Theodor Adorno. When the book appeared, the doyen of the exiled composers, Arnold Schoenberg, saw the character of Leverkuhn as an attack on himself. A famous quarrel broke out between himself and Mann. When the book was released in German in 1948 it met a hostile reception, but when published in the USA it was chosen as the Book of the Month Club selection.

Mann finally left America in 1952. He did not return to Germany; what had happened there made it impossible, for, as he wrote, 'I have no desire to rest my bones in this soulless soil to which I owe nothing, and which knows nothing of me.' He chose instead to live again in Switzerland, considering himself neither American nor German but simply a European. His life had witnessed the truth of Goethe's assertion that the Germans were prey to 'any ecstatic rogue who arouses their basest qualities, reinforces their vices, and teaches them to see nationality as isolation and brutality'. His fear was that the Germans 'have learned nothing, understand nothing, regretted nothing' and that Europe must be eternally wary of German nationalism.

6

Berlin to Broadway

German theatre had never been more buoyant than in the decade before the Nazis came to power. Bertolt Brecht and Erwin Piscator were acknowledged as the most innovative playwrights in the world, and the Austrian Max Reinhardt was acclaimed as Europe's finest theatrical director. Nazi storm troopers may have controlled the streets, but German audiences still packed the theatres. German drama was bold, experimental and skilfully presented, with imaginative lighting techniques and innovative audience participation. Even Hollywood was fascinated by it.

Compared with the fireworks of Berlin, London theatre in the early 1930s remained depressingly unadventurous and formulaic. All that was available to London audiences were repetitive musicals and comedies of manners. So little was new on the London stage that the two most successful productions, Ivor Novello's *Careless Rapture* and Terence Rattigan's *French Without Tears*, had opened in the 1920s and were still running a decade later. If this interminable round of light entertainment was occasionally interrupted by a foreign play, it was almost certain to be by Henrik Ibsen. German Expressionism meant little to British audiences, and the names of Ernst Toller and Bruno Frank were unknown outside the tiny circle of the London avant-garde. Virtually no London theatre-goer had even heard of the Nobel Prize-winning dramatist Gerhart Hauptmann.

Even Bertolt Brecht, a sensation in continental Europe and the USA, was known in Britain only as the librettist of Weill's *Threepenny Opera*. Trying to interest the British in any of the new European developments in art, music or writing was a thankless task. Content with the greatest literary language in the world and with a comfortable, if unchallenging, art, the British appeared to have little need of modernism. So it was a strange cultural backwater that awaited the many hundreds of German actors, stage technicians, writers and directors who sought refuge in Britain after the cataclysmic events of 1933.

What shocked them most of all was the amateurish nature of British stage production when compared to the professionalism that characterized their own German and Austrian theatres. Going to a play in London in the 1930s was more a social than a cultural event; choice of drama was of far less significance than choice of companion. No wonder Bertolt Brecht was shocked by what he saw on the London stage in 1934. Why, he demanded, in this land of Shakespeare was there nothing that challenged or stimulated the mind? The great Viennese director Max Reinhardt, a frequent visitor to London in the 1930s, asked the same question. Although every other nation in Europe was clamouring for Reinhardt's services, the British merely offered him the opportunity to direct an amateur production of *A Midsummer Night's Dream* at the Oxford University Dramatic Society. Surprisingly he accepted and inspired his student actors to give a performance that one awe-struck spectator described as a 'true eye-opener'. All of this was to change after the war, when the British theatre began to reflect the great social changes that had occurred in the country so that, by the late 1950s, even Brecht's highly cerebral Berliner Ensemble season could be received with rapture by a London audience.

But, for the time, being the newcomers had to take British theatre much as they found it: poorly subsidized and subject to the most basic commercial pressures. With the paramount need to recoup their money, managements were fearful of experiment and would only back productions that promised long and profitable runs. Consequently only anodyne and universally appealing productions were offered to the public. As the Austrian-born actress Amy Frank recalled, 'If you were lucky and the play you were in was a success . . . you had the doubtful pleasure of playing it nine hundred times without a break, Sundays excepted!'

Another exile, the director Friedrich Richter, was amazed to find that the Oxford Playhouse managed to put on a new play every week. This was only possible, he believed, by staging light conversation pieces that needed little rehearsal and even less directorial input. With such a production schedule there was simply not enough time for a director to get involved. What also irritated foreign actors was the famous British tea break that disrupted the action and destroyed the actor's concentration. This British obsession with refreshments even featured in their plays. The exiled German playwright Julius Berstl sarcastically described the plot of a typical British drama as 'Act One – tea is served. Act Two – cocktails are served. Act Three – whisky is served'. No wonder British provincial theatre bore no comparison to that on the Continent. Berstl heartily endorsed Kurt Schwitters's judgement on the arts in Britain, 'Nobody in London cares about good art except for a few foreigners.' But the British did recognize a good play and appreciate a fine actor when they saw one. As the theatre critic of the communist *Daily Worker* wrote of Julius Gellner's Old Vic production of *Macbeth*, starring Frederick Valk, 'It is a sad commentary on the state of our drama that . . . the best production of Shakespeare has been by a foreign director with a foreign lead.'

The partnership of Gellner and Valk, both exiled from Germany in the late 1930s, was one of the most important ever seen on the London stage. The zest and professionalism that they brought to the English classics at the Old Vic was to influence a whole generation of young British actors and directors. With so many actors in the armed services, Gellner and Valk virtually dominated the serious London theatre in the war years. Each year they led the Old Vic on a tour of provincial England with their bold and dynamic interpretations of Shakespeare. Gellner was a master of modern stage techniques and in particular of the atmospheric lighting that had characterized both German theatre and film in the 1920s. A typical review of his *Othello* praises both the 'cultured production' and the dramatic use of lighting to enhance the action. Not since the great days of the maverick Edwardian director Edward Gordon Craig had the British stage seen such boldness and imagination in presentation. Valk's success as an actor is even more remarkable given the difficulties he had in mastering the English language. Occasionally he could turn this to good account by utilizing his foreign accent to give a convincing portrayal of Shakespeare's most famous aliens, Shylock and Othello. At a time when a more effete style of acting dominated the London stage Valk's virile and forceful performances impressed his wartime audience, with his powerful and well-modulated voice presaging that of Richard Burton at the Old Vic in the late 1950s. Paradoxically, Valk's style had been criticized in his native Germany by the experimentalists Brecht and Piscator as being old-fashioned and histrionic. But his London audience admired the force and conviction of his performances; this, to them, was what Stanislavsky had meant by 'truthful acting'. Today the work of Valk and Gellner can be seen as heralding a renaissance of classical British theatre rather than as a footnote to stage history. Their tenure of the London theatre left it in good order for the return of Olivier, Richardson and Redgrave after the war.

Frederick Valk's problems with the English language were common to all the refugee actors who appeared in the late 1930s. The London stage, according to Salka Viertel, wife of the film director Berthold Viertel, seemed full of them. The best-known, Adolf Wohlbrück, opted for a quick name change before moving on to Hollywood as Anton Walbrook. Other popular Austrian and German actors appearing in London included Albert Lieven, Lucie Mannheim, Grete Mosheim, Oskar Homolka, Fritz Kortner, Conrad Veidt, Paul Gratz, Ernst Deutsch and the beautiful Elisabeth Bergner. One young unknown German actor, Herbert Lom, stayed on to become a much-loved British film star. Yet all of them had one great advantage over the local talent: they were ideal for casting as foreigners. So, when not playing Nazi villains, they entertained the British with their charm and sophistication in the settings of Parisian nightclubs and Viennese bars.

Together with the actors, writers and directors arriving in the West End came Germany's most eminent and respected theatre critic Alfred Kerr. His biography of Walther Rathenau, the first martyr to the Nazis in 1922, had made him an immediate target. Kerr was one of the bitterest critics of his own people and his presence in London polarized the exile community. Whatever had happened to the German people, Kerr could see no historic or economic excuse for them to support Hitler, nor could he detect any trace of serious resistance to Nazi rule. Rejecting everything German, he encouraged his son to join the RAF and fight against his native country. When his London home was bombed, Kerr was relieved – now he could now share the dangers and discomforts of the Blitz with his new British neighbours. In the prospect of exile he gained the same consolation that his colleague Egon Schwarz had found, 'It led me away from the insularity, provincialism, and narrow-mindedness of my middle-European existence,' he wrote. Kerr's greatest problem was that, like so many of his fellow exiles, he felt too old to master the nuances of the English language and so was condemned to near-isolation in Britain, writing only for other refugees.

Another writer who struggled with English was Ernst Toller, who arrived in February 1934. He found it so difficult to learn that he continued to write in German throughout his four-year domicile in Britain. Toller was then Germany's leading Expressionist playwright and even more celebrated than Bertolt Brecht. So great was his fame that even London theatre management had heard of him. Toller's celebrity and his links with international socialism gave him a unique access to the London literati. His intellectual friends included Henry Wickham Steed, editor of *The Times*, Harold Laski and Lady Oxford. They encouraged his involvement in the British anti-Nazi movement, and he took to addressing political meetings with such vehemence that the authorities, alarmed at his attacks on the Appeasement lobby, even considered deporting him.

All was forgiven in 1939 when Churchill and his fellow rearmers triumphed at Westminster, and Toller was praised for his bold stand. But none of this political involvement appears to have helped him get his work staged in London. The commercial theatre largely ignored him, although many of the smaller drama clubs were eager to stage his plays. London's Gate Theatre, in particular, was much taken with him and by 1936 had produced four of his major work: *Masses and Man*, *Hinkemann*, *Miracle in America* and *Draw the Fires*. That same year the Gate staged his first British play, an anti-fascist comedy entitled *No More Peace!* with lyrics by the English poet W.H. Auden. The subtlety of what Toller described as this 'thoughtful comedy' was, however, lost on his London audience. The critic of the *Manchester Guardian*, although sympathetic to the writer, concluded that 'the play itself never quite made up its mind whether to be funny, sad, or just pathetic'. Toller's last attempt to win the British audience was *Pastor Hall*, produced at the Manchester Repertory Theatre in 1938. Disillusioned and depressed by the insularity of British audiences, Toller finally gave up and set off to try his luck in the USA.

Better suited to the contemporary London stage than Toller's heavy Expressionist dramas were the light, social comedies of Bruno Frank. His best-known play in Germany had been *Sturm im Wasserglas* (translated as *Storm in a Teacup*). The plot concerns a dog and how its treatment by a group of people reveals their own hidden rivalries and petty jealousies. When produced in London, with the action transposed to Scotland and with additional dialogue by James Bridie, it was a great success. That the play was politically non-controversial – the Foreign Office was still anxious not to offend Hitler – was confirmed by an investigator from the Lord Chamberlain's Office who could find 'no trace of foreign origin in this play'. Frank followed this modest triumph with *Young Madame Conti*, produced at the Savoy Theatre in November 1936. Frank again recruited a well-established British dramatist, Benn W. Levy, the author of many successful West End farces, to provide additional dialogue and to direct the play. This story of an Austrian prostitute (played by the young Constance Cummings) who shoots her lover so excited the drama critic of *The Times* that he completely forgot to mention the author's name in his review. Perhaps in reaction to this affront Frank decided to refuse the British citizenship he had been offered and left for the USA immediately.

Lesser dramatists found it even harder to get their work performed in London, particularly if it did not appear in an English translation. Fortunately there were émigré theatre clubs where the exiles could meet and discuss their work and, with luck, even get it produced in its original German. The best-known of all was the Freier Deutscher Kulturbund in Hampstead, north London, which offered support and companionship to all the cultural exiles. Others of particular interest to exiled dramatists were the Laterndl, the Österreichische Bühne and the Blue Danube. These German language clubs offered the exiled actors, directors and stage designers an invaluable outlet for their talents. Between 1933 and 1945 they staged over eight hundred new productions. Even British theatre-goers, particularly those with a smattering of German, despairing of the poor fare being served in West End theatres, began attending performances. One visitor, the theatre critic of the *Spectator*, was deeply impressed by what he saw at the the Laterndl:

Austria's loss has been our gain . . . I hope that the Lantern will find imitators and create a tradition here before they leave us again. We have no form of theatre so intimate, so direct, as this; it has all the charm of amateur theatricals without the amateurishness.

But the exiles also brought something unique with them: Berlin cabaret. London critics were fascinated by their first experience of this bold combination of song, dance and political satire. To a London audience cabaret meant only an innocuous after-dinner entertainment, not a provocative challenge on social issues. Berlin cabaret was meant to shock and inform as well as entertain, unlike the broad comedy of traditional British music hall. But the Laterndl, and the other clubs where it flourished, did not attract enough of an audience for this style of theatre to migrate to the London stage. Nor did it help that the exiles' isolated position in British society and their obsession with the struggle against Hitler burdened productions with remorseless and repetitive propaganda. Not until the 1960s and *Beyond the Fringe* would London see anything like this style of theatre again.

The limited resources of the clubs also made large-scale productions of longer plays more difficult to stage. It was far more economical to put on short plays and cabarets that needed simple sets and small casts. What the theatre clubs did achieve, apart from entertaining their members, was to become a major irritant to Goebbels's Reichskulturkammer in Berlin. Through the German embassy in London it complained to the British government that the clubs were slandering the German nation and should be suppressed. When this protest was ignored, Goebbels ordered the Reichskulturkammer to form its own touring company to show the rest of Europe that German theatre was flourishing even better without the dissidents.

Luckily the British intellectual establishment had much in common with the exiled playwrights and actors and gave them great support. H.G. Wells, J.B. Priestley, Sybil Thorndike and the Huxleys were frequent visitors to the theatre clubs and the Bishop of Chichester helped raise funds to help the *Freier Deutscher Kulturbund* build its own theatre in Hampstead. British actors and directors, too, played their part in helping the exiles. Laurence Olivier was a regular visitor, Peggy Ashcroft starred in a club production of Zuckmayer's *The Golden Toy*, John Gielgud even made his directorial début with a production of Hasenclever's *Scandal in Assyria* in 1939 and Michael Redgrave both directed and starred in Franz Werfel's *Jacobowsky and the Colonel*.

Yet many of the exiled playwrights remained unperformed in Britain. Hans Jose Rehfisch, one of the most active German dramatists in exile, had only two productions of his many plays produced before being interned on the Isle of Man. Fortunately, he teamed up with another interned writer, Max Zimmering, to write the first of many anti-Nazi revue sketches that were later broadcast to Germany. This kind of political revue, like cabaret, was virtually unknown in Britain at the time. To a London audience revue was more a light-hearted modish entertainment full of tuneful songs and pretty girls than a challenging dramatic experience. Only the communist Unity Theatre ever attempted anything remotely like it with a Brechtian, agit-prop version of the traditional pantomime *Babes in the Wood*, in which Austria and Czechoslovakia appeared as the babes and Neville Chamberlain as the Wicked Uncle.

If Berlin cabaret had little appeal to London audiences, epic theatre had even less. Few had seen the work of the genre's greatest exponents, Bertolt Brecht and Erwin Piscator. Brecht had seen at first hand what little interest his play *Senora Carrar's Rifles* had aroused in London when he attended its première at the Unity Theatre in 1938. Brecht was an exponent of dramatic techniques developed in collaboration with Piscator that the Berlin critics had named 'epic theatre' and its subject matter as 'agitprop'. What made it so challenging was its polemical blend of speech, mime and dance. The theatre, so Brecht and Piscator believed, was not just a place of entertainment but a crucible for ideas and propaganda. Audiences should not remain passive spectators but be drawn by the action into participating themselves. It was all too much for London theatre-goers at the time, who were more at ease with a C.B. Cochrane revue. Nor had epic theatre been any more appealing to the Nazis, who had targeted Piscator as a dangerous opponent long before they came to power. But Piscator, ahead of events, had left Berlin in 1931 and moved to the Soviet Union, where both his politics and his directorial skills were much admired.

Then, in 1939, on the eve of war, Piscator, perhaps as a result of the Nazi–Soviet Pact, turned his back on the Soviet experiment and accepted an offer to direct the Dramatic Workshop in the very heart of capitalism, New York. It was a move that was to have a radical influence on American theatre, as Piscator's experimental style of presentation and direction was greatly to influence the next generation of American dramatists. Both of the leading American playwrights of the late twentieth century, Tennessee Williams and Arthur Miller, became his students, and among the young actors he worked with and inspired were Marlon Brando, Tony Curtis, Harry Belafonte, Rod Steiger, Shelley Winters and Ben Gazzara, all later associated with the Actors' Studio in New York. A man of unblemished integrity, Piscator was later described by the playwright Rolf Hochhuth as the 'last surviving champion of the truly clean, sermon-on-the-mount type of socialism of the twenties'. Although he came to love the USA, Piscator never lost his early socialist principles, which made him an obvious target for the House Committee on Un-American Activities, and he was summoned to join many of his colleagues from film and theatre at a Senate hearing.

While few outside the theatrical world and the arts knew much about Erwin Piscator, the name of Bertolt Brecht was known throughout the world. Today Brecht is recognized as the most influential figure in the development of twentieth-century theatre. He was a most unusual and charismatic person, loved or hated wherever he went. A loner in most things, Brecht could not bear to work in isolation. With his lean, angular figure and cropped hair, piercing eyes, high cheekbones and Roman nose, he looked to some like a modern Savonarola; to others a cigar-chewing Julius Caesar. Badly shaven, with dirty fingernails and crooked teeth and perennially dressed in baggy trousers and a high-collared working-man's jacket, Brecht took great pains to affect a proletarian look and to distance himself from the despised bourgeoisie. But his odd appearance disguised a brilliant intellect and forceful character. He was, according to his friend and collaborator the writer Eric Bentley, quite simply 'the most fascinating man I have ever met'.

As a young man Bertolt Brecht, in spite of his socialist leanings, was intrigued by the whole idea of America; he thought it much like himself: tough, pragmatic and dynamic. The chance to see it at first hand came with an invitation to direct his play *Mother* at the Marxist New York Theater Union in 1935. Brecht arrived with a reputation based upon his authorship of the sensational *Threepenny Opera*. Yet to the unfortunate members of the Theater Union he appeared to have more in common with Hitler than with Sophocles. Brecht began by taking an instant dislike to the young director of the play, immediately countermanding everything that he had done so far. Within a fortnight the whole company was so outraged by Brecht that they physically threw him out of the theatre, one stage-hand promising to break every bone in his body if he ever returned. No production could survive this chaos, and when it opened without him it was, predictably, a failure. Nor were the New York critics any more sympathetic to epic theatre than their London colleagues. The *New York Times* bluntly described *Mother* as 'an animated lecture on the theme of revolution, which may have an educational value, but which is desultory theatre'.

While in New York Brecht cleverly renewed his passport at the German Embassy – he had no chance of getting another in Germany – and returned to Copenhagen. When the Germans invaded Denmark on 17 April 1940 Brecht escaped with his family to Finland, where he managed to get tickets to the USA on a ship leaving from Vladivostok. After a ten-day journey across the Soviet Union on the trans-Siberian railway, the Brechts arrived in time to catch the last ship to cross the Pacific before the attack on Pearl Harbor stopped all such traffic. Arriving in California in July 1941, Brecht found his enthusiasm for the USA had evaporated. He hated everything about him, the houses that looked like garages, the bread that was awful and the Californian sun that was too hot. Worst of all, he found the English language more difficult to master than he had expected. But Brecht was always a malcontent. Elsa Lanchester said perceptively of him, 'Brecht was anti-everything, so that the moment he became part of a country, he was "anti" that country.' What most shocked him about the USA was that he found a society in which everything, even good ideas, needed to be sold. There were other disappointments too – an important production of the *Threepenny Opera* that opened at New York's Empire Theater just six weeks after his arrival closed after only twelve performances. It was a major setback to Brecht's American career, and for the next fourteen years he fought to regain the lost ground and make a successful comeback on Broadway – on his own terms, of course.

Naturally Brecht, like all the expatriate writers in California, looked to Hollywood to restore his fortunes. What he needed was a script idea with which to tempt one of the studios into giving him a contract. He thought he had found it in a back copy of *Life* magazine. It contained a true story about a married couple and their children who had won a contest to find the perfect family. Put on display at the Ohio State Fair, they immediately quarrelled and the family split up. Brecht thought it would make an amusing satire on the illusion of all-American domestic bliss. But when he told his idea to Gottfried Reinhardt, son of the exiled stage director, Reinhardt advised him to forget it, as there was as much chance of selling it to MGM as the Berliner Ensemble had of putting on *Gone With the Wind*. This was merely a setback for the resolute Brecht, who persisted with even greater vigour to attempt his break into films. A clever networker, he began making useful contacts throughout the Hollywood film industry and canvassing anyone he thought might be of use. But every attempt floundered because of Brecht's stubborn refusal to compromise himself by producing ideas that paid lip-service to Hollywood conventions or to recognize the need for box-office success.

Brecht was determined to succeed on his own terms or not at all. Not for him the fate of other writers whose brains had been, so he claimed, shrivelled by the Californian sun. Now he tried a different tack. What he needed was a partner who knew the film business intimately, and Fritz Lang was the obvious choice. Not only had they been friends in Germany but Brecht knew that Lang had long respected his work and shared his contempt for Hollywood. Lang took little persuasion to agree to collaborate on a script based on the assassination of Reinhard Heydrich, the Reichsprotektor of Bohemia, by Czech patriots. For ten weeks Brecht and Lang worked well together until a German-speaking American writer, John Wexley, was brought in to help with the dialogue. Brecht took umbrage at Wexley's involvement and insisted that his own name be removed from the credits. This proved to be a great mistake: eventually appearing as *Hangmen Also Die*, the film was a great box office success in both the USA and Britain. At a time, early in the war, when Hollywood was still churning out comedies and escapist musicals, *Hangmen Also Die* had a veracity that caught the public imagination. Today it is recognized as one of the best anti-Nazi films ever made. At least the fee that Brecht received enabled him to stay on in California for another four years in pursuit of elusive success.

Brecht's endless quest for collaborators now brought him into contact with with his fellow exiles Salka Viertel and Vladimir Pozner. Little came of these associations other than to increase Brecht's growing sense of frustration with Hollywood. Finally he approached Lion Feuchtwanger, who immediately succumbed to the Brecht charisma, and they worked together on *The Visions of Simone Machard*. Although never produced, the film script earned both writers a very large fee from MGM – Brecht invested part of his $20,000 in a new pair of trousers. Even though he now had the financial resources to pursue other projects, Brecht continued his obsession with Hollywood success. What drove him was not just the appeal of the money he imagined he could earn but the prospect of the vast audiences that could be reached with a film. What better way of bringing epic theatre to a huge worldwide audience, for, as Alfred Hitchcock had said, if one made films in Hollywood one made them for the world. Epic theatre, as some critics have noted, is after all nothing more than a drama produced using the techniques of film-making.

Brecht was nothing if not persistent in pursuit of a Hollywood career. In all, he wrote more than fifty film scenarios during his time in California. If knowing the right people alone could have brought success, Brecht would certainly have found it. By 1942 he knew everyone who mattered in the industry, from humble screen-writers to such leading actors as Charles Laughton and Charlie Chaplin, his most powerful champions in Hollywood. His inner circle of friends included the writers Clifford Odets, Ben Hecht, Donald Ogden Stewart, Lester Cole and Henry Mankiewicz. Among the producers and directors he cultivated were George Auerbach, William Dieterle, Lewis Milestone, Orson Welles, Mike Todd, Jean Renoir, Elia Kazan, Joseph Losey, John Huston and Billy Wilder. In spite of his accepted failure in Hollywood, many later directors including Joseph Losey and Jean-Luc Godard claimed that Brecht had been an important influence on their own work, and some critics believed that his 'alienation method' had influenced films as disparate as *Citizen Kane* and *Alfie*.

Brecht's inability to compromise not only doomed his Hollywood career to failure but denied him the influence he should have had on American theatre in general. After the fiasco at the Theater Union, few companies would risk working with him, admired and respected as he was. One of this many collaborators, John Houseman, described him in 1988 as 'an absolute devil at rehearsals, caused by his unshakeable belief in his own greatness and a principled stubbornness about his views and his works. The word "compromise" was not in the vocabulary.'

Eric Bentley recalled 'his quickness to damn, a penchant for calling those who disagreed with him on theatrical matters a "criminal" (*Verbrecher*) or a "Nazi" '. But, even if Brecht had presented himself as a more agreeable and flexible personality, the USA in the 1940s was just not ready for his epic theatre. Moreover, his plays had more in common with traditional American burlesque, vaudeville and musicals than they did with straight theatre. For him it was ideas not characters that really mattered As Bentley observed, 'Brecht was not really interested in people as individuals – he found them boring.' Certainly the characters in his plays generally lack the depth and complexity which Shakespeare or Chekhov gave to theirs. That he was not concerned with the individual was also apparent at rehearsals, which were more like committee meetings with no small talk or banter allowed and with Brecht as the presiding genius. The world for Brecht consisted of good and evil, and the characters in his plays reflect this uncompromising simplicity.

As success in the USA continued to elude him, Brecht finally attempted to adapt his concept of epic theatre to better suit an American audience, perhaps with the early disappointment of *Mother* in mind. Two of his plays written in the USA, *Galileo* and *The Private Life of the Master Race*, show more concern with characterization, but the latter still managed to antagonize the critics by its length and the slow pace of the action. *Master Race* was the only Brecht work staged in the USA during his time there – too often disagreements led to other projects being abandoned in the planning stage. Even his friend Erwin Piscator walked out on a production of *The Good Woman of Setzuan* because of Brecht's persistent interference in his direction. Sadly, Brecht's masterpiece, *The Caucasian Chalk Circle*, although specifically written for Broadway, had to wait twenty years for its New York première, long after Brecht had returned to what was now East Germany.

All of this may give the impression that Brecht was a cold and distant man, but he was capable of deep and lasting friendships. Since Peter Lorre had appeared in his 1931 production of *A Man's a Man* in Berlin he had been one of Brecht's favourite actors, and Lorre had come almost to worship Brecht in return. Brecht saw beneath this highly intelligent and well-read man's exterior a capacity for mayhem and menace that suited his own maverick idea of what acting should be. Lorre, increasingly typecast as a pathetic clown by the Hollywood studios, was sustained by Brecht's appreciation of his worth as an actor. When, in 1946, Warner Brothers refused to renew Lorre's contract he became seriously depressed and sank into morphine addiction. Brecht's genuine concern and support for another friend, Charles Laughton, had earlier restored that actor's self-confidence when Hollywood had also condemned him as bad box office; now he gave almost unconditional support to Lorre by involving him in current ideas and projects and acting, almost, as a self-appointed therapist. He even expressed his feelings for Lorre and contempt for Hollywood in a 1944 poem:

> I saw many friends
> And the friend I loved most
> Among them helplessly sunk
> Into the swamp.
> I pass by daily.
> And a drowning was not over in a single morning.
> This made it more terrible.

His concern for Lorre continued long after he had returned to Europe. Brecht cabled repeated invitations for Lorre to join him in playing a leading role in the theatrical ensemble he was creating in East Germany. The role of Schweyk, Brecht wrote, was there, just waiting for him. But Lorre's drug addiction was now too powerful and life in the USA too sybaritic for him to abandon it and risk the rigours of a communist state in winter. They never met again. Such friendships were important to Brecht, and his gravitation to ensemble theatre demonstrates how important it was for him to work with others, no matter what arguments and mayhem it produced. In spite of his insistence on dominating, Brecht loved to be surrounded by people. He could only flourish in a theatrical collective where he could draw on other opinions, even if he later ignored them as he did in the Berliner Ensemble. Those who worked with him over the years appreciated this, and in spite of the heated discussions and outbursts of the famous Brecht temper few took it personally or lost respect for him.

Throughout his time in the USA Brecht had doggedly maintained his exile status and never applied for citizenship. He saw his future in the new Europe that would evolve after the war rather than in contemporary American society. 'The exile's trade is hoping,' he once wrote. The state of exile, of almost temporary being, appealed to him much as it did to the Irish writer James Joyce. Unlike Thomas Mann or Stefan Zweig, Brecht had not taken Germany into exile with him, nor was he concerned with his own Jewishness, considering the topic of anti-Semitism unworthy of discussion. Brecht, by and large, avoided refugee activities in the USA, but most of all he avoided Thomas Mann. Brecht loathed Mann and all that he represented, but primarily he was scornful of the role that Mann had assumed as the dignified guardian of the intellectual traditions of Germany. Nor could Brecht, in spite of all appearances, be described as an orthodox communist. He never even joined the party, and when he returned to East Berlin in 1949 he, surprisingly, took Austrian rather than East German citizenship. When he won the Stalin Peace Prize in 1955 he deposited the money in a Swiss rather than a Russian bank. By then he was the most famous and most eagerly sought-after figure in world theatre, bombarded with requests to direct his own work personally in every major European city.

Before he left the USA Brecht had one last problem to deal with. Throughout his time there he had been a model guest avoiding political issues and meticulously obeying all the regulations that applied to enemy aliens. This did nothing to persuade the FBI that he was not a dangerous left-wing revolutionary and a threat to US security. In March 1943 the FBI concluded in a report that 'the subject's writings . . . advocate the overthrow of Capitalism, establishment of Communist State and use of sabotage by labour to attain its ends'. By 1946 Brecht's phone was being tapped and, when he was just about to depart for Europe on 19 September 1947, he was served a subpoena to appear before the House Committee on Un-American Activities. Brecht found that he was in good company. On 22 September the West Coast edition of *Variety* and the *Hollywood Reporter* carried lists of more than forty persons summoned to appear with him. Among them were his old friends Charlie Chaplin, Clifford Odets and Donald Ogden Stewart. Brecht, however, was ready for his interrogators. He bought time by making a vague and enigmatic statement and then, during an adjournment, slipped quietly out of the country before he could be called before a full hearing of the committee. American democracy was no longer his problem.

7

The Music Begins Again

Forbidden by law to perform the music of Mozart, Beethoven, Richard Strauss or Wagner, Germany's Jewish musicians were among the most deprived of the nation's cultural intellectuals in the mid-1930s. German music was now rigidly controlled by the Reichskulturkammer, whose Unterhaltungsmusiker section controlled music performance throughout Germany from concert hall to café. Even owners of music shops and manufacturers of musical instruments came under its control. Folk and traditional music, of particular interest to the Nazis, was given generous financial support as the whole canon was systematically stripped of all 'un-German' music.

Soon the great German conductors Bruno Walter and Otto Klemperer had left the country and emigrated to the USA. Even such non-Jewish liberals as Fritz Busch were hounded from their posts. That most charismatic of all conductors, Arturo Toscanini, also chose exile from fascist Italy, and sailed to the USA in 1937. The National Broadcasting Company of America responded by providing him with his own orchestra, and for the next seventeen years he brought symphonic music weekly to an enormous radio audience across the USA. At the age of eighty, Toscanini appeared on television for the first time. No other exile in the USA was more respected than this brilliant and highly principled man. Almost as popular in California was the French conductor Pierre Monteux, who had arrived by invitation in

1936 when the San Francisco Symphony Orchestra was in a parlous state. Under Monteux it became one of the finest ensembles in the USA, helping to popularize French music and that of Monteux's friend Darius Milhaud in particular.

Three of the world's greatest composers, Arnold Schoenberg, Paul Hindemith and Béla Bartók, were banned from performance in Germany and went into exile in the USA with Darius Milhaud and the Russian-born Igor Stravinsky. Their influence as teachers on the next generation of young American composers, such as John Cage, would be of enormous importance and comparable to that of the Bauhaus trio of Gropius, Breuer and Mies van der Rohe on the resurgence of American architecture. But with the exception of the brilliant trio of Carl Ebert, Fritz Busch and Rudolf Bing – who were to revitalize British opera production at Glyndebourne – the composers Roberto Gerhard and Matyas Seiber and the future members of the Amadeus Quartet, few European musicians of international significance settled in Britain. To many, Arnold Schoenberg was the future of music, but as the originator of the infamous and dissonant twelve-tone music system he was as antipathetic to the Nazis as he was to music traditionalists throughout the world.

An Austrian-born Jew, Schoenberg had a foretaste of the Nazis in 1922 when he had rented a holiday villa at Maltsee, near Salzburg. A deputation from the local council knocked on the door and told him that Jews were not welcome there. Schoenberg, a baptized Christian, quietly packed his bags and returned to Vienna. In spite of this insult Schoenberg remained loyal to German culture, believing that his discovery of the twelve-tone system would give German music world dominance for the next hundred years. The Viennese press, which had in the past conducted a vigorous anti-Semitic campaign against Gustav Mahler, now attacked Schoenberg as a Jew and a dangerous modernist influence. The Nazi party portrayed him more sinisterly as a Sophoclean figure who was leading young German composers astray. Certainly he was admired and respected by the two most promising young composers in Austria, Anton Webern and Alban Berg. Even Britain had recognized Schoenberg's importance, and the BBC had invited him to conduct the British premières of his *Gurrelieder* and *Erwartung* in London. The British composer Havergal Brian, who met him there in the early 1930s, was struck by his dramatic appearance and remarked, 'Schoenberg's merry black eyes pierce like an eagle – they are mirrors of his mind. He misses nothing in his vast orchestral apparatus at rehearsal.'

Schoenberg, who had arrived in Paris in 1933, became a practising Jew again and, despairing of Europe, looked to the USA as his final place of refuge as France moved towards war with Germany. His friends in America managed to obtain him a teaching post at the Malkin Conservatoire in Boston. When he arrived in the USA Schoenberg was quickly disillusioned to find the Malkin a small and relatively insignificant academy and the climate of Boston both cold and damp. Although pursued by the famous Julliard School of Music in New York, he decided that he could not face a second East Coast winter and, rejecting the offer, set off for California instead. Now based in Hollywood, he was to write some of his finest music and spend the rest of his life in the sunshine at his home in Pacific Pallisades. But his first year in Los Angeles proved to be an ordeal, as he struggled to support his family on a minuscule income from a part-time lectureship at the University of Southern California and by taking private pupils. The pressure eased when the University of California at Los Angeles appointed him a full-time Professor of Music. After Vienna, being in Los Angeles seemed to Schoenberg like living in musical obscurity. He found his pupils lacked an adequate knowledge of musical history and a grasp of basic musical technique. This, he thought, must be attributable to the disproportionate cost of musical scores in the USA and the high price of concert tickets.

Yet, in spite of his poor opinion of the system and his forbidding appearance, Schoenberg proved to be an approachable and inspiring teacher to pupils of all abilities from those merely studying 'musical appreciation' to the students of advanced composition, such as his most famous pupil John Cage. So convinced was Schoenberg of Cage's great potential that he offered to teach him without fees if Cage promised to devote his life to music. Like all the eminent composers now domiciled in California, Schoenberg was approached by a Hollywood studio eager for the great man to write a film score for them. It was a brief and curious experience for both parties. Irving Thalberg of MGM invited him to write the music for *The Good Earth*. But the supposedly unworldly Schoenberg demanded an enormous fee of $50,000 dollars and a written guarantee that not a single note of his composition would be altered. Not surprisingly he never heard another word.

A gregarious man, Schoenberg struck up a close friendship with the Broadway composer George Gershwin, and they played tennis together and socialized with the Hollywood community until Gershwin's sudden death in 1937. As a tribute to his friend, Schoenberg broadcast a moving oration comparing Gershwin to Johann Strauss and Offenbach. Other Hollywood friendships were more fraught. Thomas Mann had consulted Schoenberg on musical composition for his novel *Doktor Faustus*, but, when it was published, Schoenberg was outraged to discover that Mann had credited his character Leverkuhn with discovering twelve-tone music while suffering the mental delusions caused by syphilis and, adding insult to injury, after making a pact with the devil. It was many years before they were reconciled.

In spite of his teaching commitments Schoenberg continued to compose prolifically in California, completing the Violin Concerto and String Quartet No. 4 in 1936. Yet he, like all the exiles, could not escape the memories and the constant reminders of the current horrors of Europe. He suffered acute depression when he discovered that his brother had been murdered in a Nazi hospital and that a cousin had perished in a concentration camp. Then, at the end of the war, when all the horrors seemed to be over, he was told that his most gifted pupil, Anton Webern, had been randomly shot by an American soldier in occupied Vienna. These experiences were the impetus for *A Survivor from Warsaw*, which reflects his continuing interest in Judaism, and his last work, a setting of the Psalms. Unlike the majority of his fellow refugees Schoenberg was never attracted to communism, believing that all fundamental political ideologies disregard the rights of the individual and invariably lead to human misery. For such a revolutionary figure in the history of music, he was, at heart, a traditionalist who would have preferred to remain in Vienna.

Schoenberg's fellow composer Paul Hindemith should not, theoretically, have fallen out with the Nazis. Although he insisted on continuing to play chamber music in public with his Jewish colleagues after the Nazi accession, he was neither a Jew nor involved in politics. Moreover, his latest work, the *Mathis der Maler* symphony, was based on an ancient German legend fully approved by Nazi ideologues. But Hindemith had, while on a visit to Switzerland, made the mistake of publicly criticizing Adolf Hitler. He was to find out, as did Thomas Mann, that nothing infuriated the Nazis more than public criticism of the Führer by Germans when abroad. Just as *Mathis* was about to be broadcast on Frankfurt Radio, the conductor was informed by Goebbels that the work was now banned. The conductor, Wilhelm Furtwängler, still walking a tightrope of approval with the Nazis, was refused permission to play it at the Berlin State Opera. When he protested, he was told that only the Führer himself could revoke the ban. Furtwängler then discovered that what had really infuriated Hitler was not Hindemith's criticism of him but the acute embarrassment he had felt when attending an earlier performance of Hindemith's *Neus vom Tage* at seeing a naked soprano singing in her bath.

Furtwängler wrote to Hitler, as Max Planck did on behalf of German scientists, pointing out the loss to the nation if such an important artist as Paul Hindemith were forced to leave. But as the party newspaper, the *Volkischer Beobachter*, replied on Hitler's behalf in December 1934, it was Germany's new rulers who now decided artistic policy, and there could be no appeal against their decisions. In protest Furtwängler resigned from his posts at the Reichsmusikkammer, the Staatsoper and the Berlin Philharmonic. But it was Hindemith who was the greater victim of the dispute: in September 1937 he left Germany for ever and sailed to the USA to lecture at the Tanglewood summer festival.

Yet again, the USA responded to the presence of a world cultural figure by finding a secure teaching position for Hindemith at a leading university. As Visiting Professor of the Theory of Music at Yale, he was a great success over the coming years, working long hours and enthusing his students by his music and his idiosyncratic ideas on composition. So great was Hindemith's involvement with Yale that he almost ceased performing and even gave his teaching commitments priority over composition time. Yet he still managed to complete his Symphony in E flat and the Cello Concerto by 1940. In spite of a lucrative offer from Chicago University, in 1944 Hindemith stayed loyal to Yale. His love for the place and his affection for the American nation were the inspiration for his requiem, *When Lilacs Last in the Door-Yard Bloom'd*, which he dedicated to that great protector of the

European exiles Franklin Delano Roosevelt and to the American dead of the Second World War.

In 1947 he returned to Germany to attend a performance of this work but felt little sympathy for the new Germany; nor were the Germans much interested in him. However, when he retired from Yale in 1953 he decided to spend more time on composition and chose to live, like Thomas Mann, in Switzerland. The USA, loath to see this great musician depart, awarded him honorary citizenship and the freedom to return whenever he wished. Never a follower of Schoenberg's twelve-tone system, Hindemith was not a radical, but in the USA he had continued to evolve as a great and influential composer, scoring his work to suit the large-scale symphony orchestras that are part of the American tradition.

If Schoenberg and Hindemith suffered from German anti-Semitism and artistic intolerance, the composer Béla Bartók suffered equally from persecution by Hungarian fascism. As a Jew he opposed the growing anti-Semitism in his own country, which reached a climax under the regime of Admiral Horthy. In a gesture of open support to his fellow Jews, Bartók refused to perform in either Germany or fascist Italy, and, despairing of events in Europe, he began planning his move to the USA as soon as he had completed his Violin Concerto. He had received a commission from the jazz clarinettist Benny Goodman that became the grandly titled *Contrasts for Violin, Clarinet and Piano*, which he recorded on a trip to New York early in 1940. Returning to Budapest for a last time, he gave a farewell concert for his friends and then, realizing that his name would be for ever linked with Hungarian music, he warned his fellow countrymen that 'as long as there are any squares or streets in Hungary named after Hitler or Mussolini let there be no public memorials to commemorate me'.

On his arrival in the USA he received a more muted welcome than Schoenberg and Hindemith but was offered a similar teaching post at Columbia University, where he was invited to catalogue over two thousand recordings of Serbo-Croatian folk songs in the university archives. Bartók found it a fascinating project but was less enamoured of the distracting noise and bustle of New York. More than his émigré colleagues, he found his early years in the USA a constant struggle for survival. His European royalties had been seized by the Nazis, and he earned little from concert performances. Since his arrival he had written little new music, and when his contract at Columbia ended he was saved from ruin only by being offered a series of lectures at Harvard. So desperate was his plight that he even considered returning to Hungary.

Depressed and in ill health, he needed all the practical support that his American friends, including Eugene Ormandy and Benny Goodman, could give him. Then the National Institute of Arts and Letters made him a donation in the guise of an award. The wealthy conductor Serge Koussevitzky visited Bartók in hospital and, after pressing a cheque for a thousand dollars into his hand, commissioned him to write a new work, the Concerto for Orchestra. Other commissions followed, including a violin sonata for the young Yehudi Menuhin, who had recently added Bartók's Violin Concerto to his own repertoire. Bartók now had the resources to move to the warmth of Ashville, North Carolina, where he completed both a Piano and a Viola Concerto, but his health never recovered and within a year he was dead. Bartók had lived a solitary life in the USA, failing to achieve the celebrity of his fellow émigré composers, but to many he had become, with his Concerto for Orchestra and Third Piano Concerto, the most American of all. Bartók's roots remained in the folk music of Hungary, which he brought to a worldwide audience but, as his music publisher wrote of him, 'It was his misfortune to have been born and to live in such troubled times; for ultimately they overwhelmed him.'

No such problems troubled the American exile of the exuberant French composer Darius Milhaud, who flourished even more in the sunshine of California than he had done in his native Provence. So happy was Milhaud teaching at Mills College, Oakland, that he stayed on long after the war ended, in spite of his enduring devotion to his family, friends, religion and to his birthplace, Aix-en-Provence. Milhaud loved the USA. 'I am very happy here,' he wrote; 'I work well in this calm atmosphere, a place of trees – giant eucalyptus, pines, and acacias – of quiet walkways, ponds, and flowing streams.' Easy-going and the least pompous of men, Milhaud found the relaxed atmosphere at Mills suited him ideally. His daily routine never varied: in the mornings he taught (remarkably Milhaud had no teaching experience before coming to Mills) and in the afternoons he composed.

With his southern French ebullience, Milhaud was a welcome

addition to the Mills campus and to the community of musicians domiciled in nearby San Francisco. Among the many old friends he was reacquainted with there was his fellow Provençal and Jew the conductor Pierre Monteux, who, like Milhaud, found American audiences the best in the world because, as he said in 1942:

> Americans come to hear music and to enjoy it. They feel it is a privilege to attend the première performance of any musical composition. In Paris every new composition is received as an unnecessary intruder, and the musical audience eagerly anticipates tearing it to pieces.
>
> (Collaer, 1998)

The USA was equally delighted by Milhaud. A natural teacher and communicator, his enthusiasm for music was passed on to his pupils, many of whom were inspired to became teachers themselves. Perhaps Milhaud's greatest contribution, together with that of Stravinsky, was to show the USA that Germany and Austria alone did not have a monopoly of innovative modern music.

Igor Stravinsky was no stranger to exile, having abandoned revolutionary Russia for Paris twenty years earlier. An internationally famous composer but a Jew – a fact that the Nazi press had not been slow to point out – Stravinsky decided at the outbreak of war to accept an offer of a visiting professorship at Harvard University. The best known of all the European composers, he none the less encountered the same initial financial difficulties that afflicted them all. Like Brecht he soon succumbed to the lure of Hollywood and spent his early years in the USA in a vain attempt to secure commissions for film scores. In the meantime, he supported himself with a myriad of small projects that included a writing a tango for Benny Goodman, a polka for a parade of circus elephants and ballet music for a Broadway revue. None of this stopped him completing his Symphony in C and his first serious American work, the Symphony in Three Movements. Never one to waste a good musical idea, Stravinsky based the slow movement of the symphony on his abortive score for the Franz Werfel film *The Song of Bernardette*. Now firmly established in California, Stravinsky had no further need to seek out commissions – they came to him. For the jazz clarinettist Woody Herman he wrote *The Ebony Concerto* and for another band leader, Paul Whiteman, the *Scherzo à la Russe*. With a wide circle of expatriate friends, Stravinsky enjoyed life in California and developed such a fierce loyalty to his adopted country that he would permit no criticism of the USA in his presence, even at the time of the House Committee on Un-American Activities hearings.

Beside the many instrumental works he composed in the 1940s and 1950s, Stravinsky became increasingly interested in opera. At an exhibition of English art in Chicago in 1949 he had seen Hogarth's series of paintings *The Rake's Progress*, which he thought would make an ideal theme for an opera in the manner of *Don Giovanni* or *Così fan tutte*. With W.H. Auden as his librettist, Stravinsky completed *The Rake's Progress* in the summer of 1951, and it was premièred at La Fenice in Venice that September. But Stravinsky was fast approaching an artistic crisis as he became increasingly disillusioned with the neoclassicism of his work. In an attempt to find a new direction, he leaned heavily on his assistant and amanuensis, the young American Robert Craft. A keen admirer of twelve-tone music, Craft encouraged Stravinsky to reappraise his own work in the light of Schoenberg's innovations. Gradually, to the dismay of fellow musicians such as Ernest Ansermet, Stravinsky's work began to incorporate much of Schoenberg's twelve-tone system. It was an extraordinary intellectual metamorphosis for a composer of Stravinsky's maturity to have changed his style so radically. Perhaps it was a transformation made easier by the ever-changing and evolving society that surrounded Stravinsky in California. As Pierre Boulez said of him, 'Where a host of others have continued to stammer and to pontificate, to chatter and to prejudge, to mince round issues or to skimp them, to rage, to threaten, to mock and to torpedo, Stravinsky has simply acted.'

The émigré musicians mentioned so far were either ignored or rejected by Hollywood, but the Austrian composer Erich Korngold was positively embraced by it. Korngold had been a child prodigy under the tutelage of his music critic father and had developed into one of Austria's most promising young classical composers. But, in 1934, he made the mistake of basing his first opera on a story written by a Jewish novelist about a German girl's romance with a foreign soldier. Naturally it attracted the attention of the Nazis, and Korngold was immediately vilified as a Jew and a defiler of the Austrian people. He was saved from imprisonment by Max Reinhardt, who invited him to join him in Hollywood where he was filming his celebrated production of *A Midsummer Night's Dream* for Warner Brothers. Reinhardt had decided that Mendelssohn's incidental music, critical to the success of the production, needed a completely new arrangement. Korngold arrived in Hollywood looking and acting like every American's idea of a Viennese composer. When asked about Hitler, he told reporters in his heavy Viennese accent that Felix Mendelssohn's music would still be played when Hitler was long forgotten.

Immediately he began work at Warners, Korngold discovered his strange affinity with the complicated business of producing music for film. His first question to the head of the sound department was, 'How long does it take a foot of film to pass through the projector?' When told that it took two-thirds of a second Korngold needed little else explained to him. From that moment he demonstrated a complete and idiosyncratic understanding of the relationship between picture and music. Throughout his time in Hollywood he used neither a cue sheet nor a pulsed track as a timing device. Warner Brothers were delighted with what he produced, and Paramount attempted to poach him by offering an even better contract, which Korngold, fortunately, put to one side without giving an outright rejection.

Loath to abandon his career as a serious composer in Europe, Korngold returned to Vienna in July 1934 only to find that the Nazis were even closer to power. The chancellor, Dollfuss, had been assassinated and Austria was in a state of crisis. With his escape ticket, the offer from Paramount, in his pocket Korngold completed his last work in Europe, the opera *Die Kathrin*, and left Austria for good. Back in Hollywood, his first project for Paramount was the musical *Give Us This Night* with lyrics by Oscar Hammerstein. With it Korngold began to create a new genre of film music written to a much higher standard and tailored specifically to the action. No longer would simple adaptations of existing scores be considered good enough for major Hollywood productions.

With Korngold, film music came of age and could now be taken almost as seriously as more formal classical pieces. Lured back to Warners by an even more lucrative offer, Korngold began work on one of his most famous scores, that for the film *Captain Blood* starring Errol Flynn. Working round the clock, he completed it in record time with the help of a young assistant, Hugo Friedhofer, who in 1948 described their work pattern (Duchen, 1996):

> We would sit together at the piano with the sequences to be orchestrated, and he would play them through, with me filling in the occasional notes that were outside the capacities of ten fingers . . . he had the most extraordinary way of making a piano sound like an orchestra that I have ever encountered.

The score of *Captain Blood* won an Oscar for the entire sound department of Warners and confirmed Korngold's triumph in Hollywood. He had devised a technique by which the music discreetly underscored the actors' voices, so adding dramatic emphasis to each scene. This was completely new to Hollywood, where talkies were still in their infancy and sound departments had found it difficult to move on from the loud and continuous musical accompaniments that characterized the silent film. Because of his classical background, Korngold also knew the value of the Wagnerian leitmotif and the subtle use of musical colour in key passages of a film.

Korngold's success meant that he was now able to extract better working conditions from the studios, beginning with a new contract that limited him to no more than two productions a year and gave him the right to refuse any unsuitable project. Korngold was now fully in control of his work, protected by contract from the whims of the studio bosses and never revealing his score until it appeared as part of the finished production. For the first time in the USA the film score became noticed by the public, and Korngold fan clubs sprang up across the country. Some enthusiasts claimed to have seen a film up to sixty times just to hear Korngold's music. Of all the musicians exiled in the USA, Korngold alone achieved a glittering financial success if not the critical acclaim he desired. He was also the only composer at the time to understand fully the demands of the medium. Igor Stravinsky, in contrast, when asked to write music for a film, did not bother to find out what was required and turned up at the studio ten days later with a completed score before filming had even started.

Korngold's Hollywood success continued with scores for *Elizabeth and Essex* and *Devotion*, but he was also composing classical music, often – perhaps fatally as far as the critics were concerned – using familiar melodies from his film scores. His Violin Concerto of 1947, first played by Jascha Heifetz, was given short shrift by the critics who thought it mere Hollywood film music. The *New York Times* wrote, 'The melodies are ordinary and sentimental in character, the facility of the writing is matched by the mediocrity of the ideas.' Korngold ignored the criticisms and, as if in defiance, produced a Cello Concerto almost identical to the music he had written for Bette Davis to play in the film *Deception*. Even his later Symphony in F sharp major was clearly a recycled version of the score he had written for the film *Anthony Adverse*. Korngold was now in a creative limbo, rejected by the classical world and finding the rewards from film music merely financial. He identified himself completely with the melodic tradition of music and openly condemned atonalism.

A last attempt to revive his career as an opera composer while on a visit back to Vienna after the war ended in disaster. *Die Kathrin* was given a minimalist set by the producer and his light classical music, according to Korngold, was treated with contempt by the orchestra. After six performances it closed – it was his classical nemesis. But when Korngold died in November 1957 he was remembered with affection not only in the USA but in Europe, too. There had been renewed interest in Korngold's classical music, but his true legacy remains the Hollywood film scores now more popular than ever and issued as collections in their own right. Uniquely he used the melodic tradition of Brahms and Mahler to create a new and popular art form that brought symphonic music to cinema audiences throughout the world. Perhaps, as one critic put it in an obituary, 'Korngold had always written for Warner Brothers without knowing it.'

What Erich Korngold achieved in Hollywood, Kurt Weill attempted to emulate on Broadway. He arrived in New York far more famous than Erich Korngold as the composer, with Bertolt Brecht, of the astonishingly successful *Threepenny Opera*. When first produced, it ran in Berlin for over a year and in fifty other theatres throughout Germany. Wherever it played it caused a sensation – with the sole exception of London, of course, where one critic complained of its 'bald jazz tunes' and of a score 'that contains the most degenerated music one can think of'. But its mockery of the greed and cynicism of German society made Brecht and Weill obvious targets for the Nazis in 1933. Such 'cultural Bolshevism' could not be tolerated, and to escape the inevitable persecution Brecht left for Denmark and Weill for Paris. Arriving with his wife, Lotte Lenya – a singer loathed by the Nazis – Weill was given a commission by the eccentric English patron of contemporary artists Edward James to write the music for a ballet based on the Seven Deadly Sins. It opened in Paris and transferred to London in July 1933, where *The Times* described it as 'fresh if rather crudely obvious'. The contemporary British composer Constant Lambert, however, thought it the most important ballet since Stravinsky's *Les Noces*, and his enthusiasm encouraged Weill to adapt his musical comedy *Der Kuhhandel* for the London stage. It opened as *A Kingdom for a Cow* at the Savoy Theatre in June 1935, but the London critics liked it no better than the *Threepenny Opera*, and the production closed after only two weeks. Weill was bitterly disappointed, as he had taken great trouble to adapt the music to suit a more conservative British audience. But at a time when the most successful contemporary production in London was still *Merrie England*, the public shunned the production and Weill returned to Paris baffled and defeated.

Turning his back on Europe, he now decided to try his luck in the USA and arrived in New York with Lenya in September 1935. But America, as all the cultural refugees found, had still not recovered from the Depression, and new theatrical productions found it hard to get backers. With few commercial offers in sight, Weill was attracted to the Federal Theater Project, which was intended intended to give work to unemployed actors. He suggested that they produce a musical about the history of the Jews called *The Eternal Road*, a project that he had begun in Paris with Franz Werfel. Again, he attempted to score his work for what he thought might be contemporary American taste, but when produced it received the same hostile reviews as *A Kingdom for a Cow* had done in London. Within a few weeks it too was forced to close, and Weill, abandoning his attempt to become a success on Broadway, took the train to California. Since he was a committed socialist, Hollywood represented all that he hated about capitalism with its formulaic productions and reliance on box-office ratings. Nor, unlike Erich Korngold, was he fascinated by the mechanics of film music. In Hollywood he missed the commitment and teamwork that had made his Berlin collaboration with Brecht so creatively satisfying. He did, however, get an immediate offer to work with Fritz Lang on the music for his next film, *You and Me*. While waiting for his contract to be approved, Weill had, like Arnold Schoenberg, made friends with George Gershwin and was equally shocked by Gershwin's premature death at the age of thirty-eight.

As the months passed and his contract for the Lang project failed to materialize, Weill took off in despair for New York. His dream of Broadway success had never left him, and at last his luck changed when he met the man who would become his American Brecht, the lyricist Maxwell Anderson. An old Broadway hand, Anderson was respected as a successful writer for the New York theatre. Intrigued by the opportunity to work with the famous Weill, Anderson proposed that they collaborate on a musical version of Washington Irving's book the *Knickerbocker History of New York*. Weill found an instant rapport with Anderson, and within a few weeks they had completed the adaptation, now entitled *Knickerbocker Holiday*. One of the songs that Weill had written for the star of the show, Walter Huston, was to be remembered long after *Knickerbocker Holiday* was forgotten: 'September Song' is still Weill's best-known Broadway number and still earns royalties for his estate. With Anderson's inspiration, Weill had, at last, found the right formula for success with his score for *Knickerbocker Holiday*. Weill's music blended traditional Broadway melody with American blues and overlaid them both with a hint of the cynicism from his Berlin days. The New York audience loved it and Weill, in turn, now loved them, claiming that New Yorkers were the most responsive and adaptable theatre-goers in the world with a unique capacity to switch from laughter to tears within seconds.

Knickerbocker Holiday ran for over 160 performances in 1938 and was seen by a complete cross-section of New Yorkers, leading the composer to believe that the Broadway musical rather than the Hollywood film might be America's epic theatre after all. But Weill was never destined to rank alongside Rodgers and Hart or Gershwin and Hammerstein as one of the great figures of the American musical. Although his next musicals, *Lady in the Dark* and *One Touch*, were both successful – the latter running for over 500 performances in 1943 and chosen by *Variety* as the musical of the year – his days as a Broadway success were soon to be over. His next production, *Street Scene*, was praised for its witty lyrics but condemned for Weill's 'formulaic' music. It was the end of his Broadway career. Without the control they had been allowed in the Berlin theatre of the 1920s, neither he nor Brecht had been able to recapture in the USA the elusive success they had once enjoyed.

In their diverse talents Weill, Korngold, Bartók, Hindemith, Stravinsky and Schoenberg were among the leading composers of the twentieth century. It is difficult to see any of them fitting into the British music scene in the late 1930s. British musical comedy was too restrained for Weill, as he had proved, nor could the British cinema have supported a Korngold, either creatively or financially; and the serious modern German music of Schoenberg was both unfamiliar and unwelcome to the great majority of British concert-goers. Even Constant Lambert dismissed the work of Hindemith as 'sewing machine counterpoint', and the nation's most eminent music critic, Ernest Newman, condemned Weill's *Threepenny Opera* as having 'the worst faults of more than one bad style and the qualities of not a single good one'.

Britain was at ease with Elgar, Delius and Sibelius but suspicious, as Professor Edward Dent put it, 'of all those dreadful composers ending in -er'. Émigré musicians did, of course, find refuge in Britain, and, in the case of Carl Ebert and Fritz Busch at Glyndebourne, dramatically improved the standards of British opera. Yet some, such as the singers Ilse Wolf and Richard Tauber, were as successful in Britain as they had been in Austria and Germany. Instrumental soloists in particular were welcomed in Britain: the pianists Paul Hamburger, Edith Vogel, Franz Reizenstein and Louis Kentner and the violinists Ida Haendel and Henry Datyner all made successful careers in their adopted country. Among the conductors who joined them were Karl Rankl, Walter Goehr, Leo Wurmser and Walter Susskind. But the only well-known composers of light music who came were Mischa Spoliansky, who became a more low-key version of Erich Korngold, writing the music for numerous British films, and Wilhelm Grosz, who composed the popular tunes 'Isle of Capri' and 'Red Sails in the Sunset'. Perhaps the most influential of them all proved to be the acerbic music critic Hans Keller, who to many assumed the role that Ernest Newman had played in the 1930s as the arbiter of contemporary British musical taste.

But one group of émigré musicians was to have almost as important an influence on British music as the Glyndebourne trio: they were the members of the Amadeus Quartet. Their future leader, the violinist Norbert Brainin, had been ranked second only to the great soloist David Oistrakh as a child prodigy, but as Jews the Brainins were forced to leave Vienna in 1938 soon after the Anschluss. Arriving to join his relatives London, the young Brainin was sent to study under Britain's leading teacher of the violin, Carl Flesch, at the Royal Academy of Music. When Flesch was trapped in Europe in 1939 his place at the Academy was taken by Max Rostal, a gifted teacher who would later be mentor to the whole quartet. Unknown to Brainin, another young musician, Peter Schidlof, arrived in London the same year on one of the transports carrying Jewish children from Germany. With the help of British philanthropists, Schidlof had the good fortune of being awarded a music scholarship at Blundell's School in Devon. The third member of the quartet, Siegmund Nissel, also arrived in Britain on a children's transport. As enemy aliens all three boys were arrested on the outbreak of war and interned on the Isle of Man, where they met many other musicians who had chosen to seek refuge in Britain. The bleak internment camp proved to be a temporary academy for them.

The first members of the future Amadeus Quartet to meet were Brainin and Schidlof. Brainin was said to have been playing a section of the Mozart A major concerto to other internees when he noticed an attentive Peter Schidlof. Brainin offered Schidlof his violin and listened, in turn, while Schidlof responded with his own interpretation of a Bach concerto. Within a week Siegmund Nissel had joined them, and when they were released from detention the following year all three went to London to study under Max Rostal. Their natural technique and thorough approach to music were encouraged by Rostal, and they were soon playing together in concerts arranged by such refugee organizations as the Freie Deutsche Kulturbund. Two years after the war ended, a fourth musician, the young English cellist Martin Lovett, was introduced to them by Rostal.

The four musicians were now encouraged to come together as a quartet by the composer Imogen Holst, who was convinced that they would make an excellent string quartet. At first they called themselves the Brainin Quartet before making their début as the Amadeus in January 1948. From the beginning they attracted both critical praise and enthusiastic audiences. Their biographer Daniel Snowman sees the timing of their arrival on the chamber music scene as being particularly fortunate, given the imminent retirement of the Busch Quartet and the migration of the other leading British-based ensemble, the Griller Quartet, to the USA. A new audience for classical music had also developed in Britain during the war years, encouraged both by BBC broadcasts and by the inspirational series of concerts given by such leading soloists as Myra Hess at the National Gallery in London.

However, there was a more practical reason for the growth of British classical music in the years following the war: Europe had been devastated by the fighting, and the great cultural cities of Berlin, Vienna, Paris and Prague were either still in ruins or more concerned with economic recovery than with the arts. Until the traditional continental venues had been rebuilt, London remained the centre of European music. For this reason many of the world's most eminent musicians, including George Solti, Daniel Barenboim, Alfred Brendel, Yehudi Menuhin and Otto Klemperer now made their homes in Britain. Whereas in the 1930s London had had only two symphony orchestras, there were now five. The BBC alone had twelve orchestras of its own, and Britain's main provincial cities, Manchester, Liverpool and Birmingham, also had their own orchestras of an international standard.

The quartet's immediate success convinced the members of the Amadeus that plans for solo careers should be abandoned in favour of this new partnership. Soon audiences at the Wigmore Hall in London were queuing to hear them, and their British tours were sell-outs. The quartet began making regular appearances at music festivals in Edinburgh, Aldeburgh in Suffolk and Dartington in Devon. Within a year they had made the first of many recordings, and by the mid-1950s the Amadeus was established as the world's leading string quartet. What made them distinctive was their unique sound, which appeared almost uniquely well balanced under the leadership of Norbert Brainin.

For forty years the Amadeus played together until, in the late summer of 1987, Peter Schidlof died at the Wigmore Hall of a heart attack. When they had first formed the Amadeus, all four had agreed that when one of them died the others would not replace him, so, with Schidlof's death, the Amadeus ceased to be. In the mean time it had become not only Britain's but one of the world's most famous ensembles. As Glyndebourne had elevated British opera to the highest rank, so the Amadeus Quartet had earned British chamber music recognition throughout the world and encouraged the growth of a new audience for music in Britain. As David Waterman, cellist of the Endellion Quartet, said in 1988:

> Probably one of the reasons there are so many English quartets at the moment is that a lot of people were inspired to learn to play quartets because of their example . . . they have helped to create an audience which I am sure, when they started, was limited to people who were very much in the know.

8

An Operatic Diversion

Britain in the 1920s had little to offer a dedicated opera enthusiast. Only at Convent Garden was serious opera staged on a permanent basis, but even here productions were invariably repetitive and poorly staged. Everything at Convent Garden reflected the whims and idiosyncrasies of its part-owner, the doyen of British music Sir Thomas Beecham. Manchester, Birmingham, Edinburgh and other major cities were virtually opera-free zones. This situation was in complete contrast to Germany, where every major city from Darmstadt to Dresden had its own opera house as well as at least two theatres for serious drama. To the great majority of British music-lovers opera meant only Gilbert and Sullivan or such undemanding musical comedy as Sir Edward German's *Merrie England*. Anyone interested in more stimulating fare must, of necessity, travel abroad to the great opera houses of Paris, Milan, Bayreuth or Salzburg. But Nazi cultural policy was, unwittingly, about to change all that, and a country manor house in the Sussex Downs was to become the setting for the most important revolution ever seen in British opera.

Nothing better symbolizes the catalytic effect of the cultural émigrés on Britain than what happened at Glyndebourne, where the talent and professionalism of three German refugees, Fritz Busch, Carl Ebert and Rudolf Bing, and the vision of an eccentric Englishman, John Christie, combined to give Britain world-class opera at a permanent and dedicated venue. It began with John Christie, the owner of Glyndebourne and a survivor of the First World War. In 1925 he had travelled to the Bayreuth and Munich festivals and developed a passion for music and, oddly for a Briton, all things German. 'We feel strongly pro-German and anti-English,' he wrote at the time. Inspired by this new-found enthusiasm, Christie decided to start a music festival of his own at Glyndebourne. He began by installing an organ in the music room and presenting a modest programme of opera excerpts to a captive audience of his own farmworkers. Then, in 1931, Christie married an opera singer and promised to build her a proper opera house at Glyndebourne. That he knew nothing about staging opera did not prevent him from starting construction immediately. Only with the building half completed did he realize the need to recruit some professionals who actually knew how to produce an opera. By chance, he was given the name of the German conductor Fritz Busch, younger brother of Adolf Busch, founder of the internationally famous Busch Quartet.

Busch was one of the first leading conductors to leave Germany when the Nazis assumed power. Neither a Jew nor a dissident, his artistic conscience, loyalty to his Jewish colleagues and fierce independent spirit led him to resist the Nazi take-over of German music. When Arturo Toscanini cancelled his engagements at Bayreuth in 1933 as a protest against Jewish persecution, Busch was offered the job. His instant refusal provoked threats from Goering that he might be 'compelled' to perform. 'A compulsory performance of Tannhauser conducted by me would be a most unpleasant experience,' Busch replied. As one of the few leading German musicians to speak out against the Nazis, Busch's protests led to inevitable exile. It was while drifting round Europe in search of work that he heard of Christie's project. Within a few weeks they met in Amsterdam, where Busch's wife recorded her astonishment at Christie's strange Wodehousean appearance: 'This unknown impresario presented an imperturbable figure in his rough, baggy tweeds. His unconventional appearance further accentuated by his pug dog Tuppy which he brought to the interview, under his arm.'

The urbane Fritz Busch found both John Christie and his plans for an opera festival in the English countryside barely credible. Yet something about Christie, perhaps his patent sincerity and enthusiasm for music, seems to have convinced Busch to give it a try. But to Christie's suggestion that music be provided by a string quartet supplemented by an organ instead of a full orchestra Busch was dismissive – he would do it properly or not at all. When the meeting ended Busch had agreed to conduct the first season at Glyndebourne – he doubted there would be a second.

Busch's first request was for a producer. 'And what', asked Christie, 'is a producer?' At that time, the role of the producer in opera was not significant; it was the conductor who dominated not only the musical performance but also much of the stage action. As his producer Busch chose an old colleague and fellow exile, Carl Ebert. A disciple of Max Reinhardt, Ebert was familiar with all the problems of staging such major European music festivals as Salzburg or Bayreuth. A tall man of handsome appearance, Ebert had been a famous actor in Germany before opening his own academy, the Hochschule für Musik, in Berlin. In 1927 Ebert had turned from theatre to opera and was appointed Intendant of the Darmstadt Opera House. Ebert was convinced that opera would, for him, be a heightened expression of drama. Four years later his success at Darmstadt led to his appointment as director general at the Städtische Oper in Berlin. Ebert's acute sensitivity to music was the key to his success as the leading opera producer of his time always apparent in his rigorous approach to rehearsals.

Through his work in Britain Carl Ebert became recognized as the first great opera producer of modern times. Before his arrival, it was the singers and, in a few instances, the conductors who really mattered. Today, the producer dominates in the opera house through-out the world. The careers of such eminent contemporary directors as Peter Hall and Jonathan Miller owe much to Ebert as a role model and to the innovations he introduced at Glyndebourne. George Christie, the son of the founder, described in *The Times*'s obituary for Ebert in 1965 how his method managed to penetrate the inner meaning of each work and then to endow the characters with new significance:

> His *Così fan tutte* at Glyndebourne before the war became a standard
> production in the world of opera shamelessly and in a way blamelessly
> copied in many other opera houses . . . his influence in correcting the
> imbalance which existed as between music and singing on the one hand

and theatre and production on the other was almost certainly more widespread than the influence of any other operatic producer.

By good fortune, Christie had stumbled upon two great professionals in world opera at a time when they were looking for a new cultural focus. In turn, they would make his dream for Glyndebourne into a reality. With them came a third member of the team whose role was to secure for the new opera house many of the world's finest singers, and who would later be the originator of the Edinburgh Festival, Rudolf Bing. Bing was an Austrian Jew who had left Germany in 1933, having worked under Ebert at both Darmstadt and Berlin. Now a jobless exile, Bing gratefully accepted Busch's invitation to join him at Glyndebourne and was signed up as General Manager for a modest £100 fee that included his travel expenses.

When he arrived there Carl Ebert was amazed to discover that the new opera house had no means of flying the scenery in and out of set. Everything had to go through a single door. When originally approached by Christie, Ebert had thought the entire proposition a hoax and did not even bother to reply to Christie's letter. When a second one remained unanswered an anxious Christie resorted to the telephone. Only then did Ebert take this strange Englishman seriously. Now his initial doubts had returned. Did Christie have any conception of the cost of staging an opera or the complicated logistics involved? Ebert was politely told to mind his business and get on with the job – whatever was required would be provided. It seems that neither Busch nor Ebert had met anyone quite as stubborn as Christie before. However, realizing the chaos that could easily occur, they had already obtained Christie's agreement that they alone would have full artistic control of the singers, the repertoire and of rehearsals. Within a week Ebert had produced a realistic budget, which surprised but did not dismay John Christie, who grudgingly approved it.

The programme for the inaugural 1934 season now had to be agreed. Christie, recalling the pleasures of Bayreuth, still hankered for a Wagner season, but Hitler's seizure of power had made all things German even more unpopular in Britain. Nevertheless, the opening season of this new 'English Bayreuth', as the press described it, maintained a heavily Teutonic spirit. Christie had the lavatory doors – the ladies wide enough to permit a crinoline to enter – labelled *Damen* and *Herren*. Later he would often go round knocking on them at the end of each interval. To complete the Germanic atmosphere the wine list was exclusively German. Nor were the Glyndebourne house guests allowed to escape – gentlemen were instructed to wear lederhosen and the ladies dirndl skirts. Christie himself had taken to dining out in such a costume. After much debate Busch and Ebert managed to persuade Christie that his choice of Wagner would be a bad mistake and that Mozart would be far better and the *The Marriage of Figaro* best of all. The press had not taken the pre-opening publicity too seriously, choosing to refer to 'a Captain John Christie, an officer and gentleman who is embarking on an operatic escapade in Sussex'.

From the very beginning, Busch and Ebert were innovators in all that they did. They auditioned the singers together and insisted that the principal artists agreed to both live and work at Glyndebourne for up to two months each season. In doing this they created the feeling of a genuine opera ensemble in which no singer was allowed to dominate. The first opera was to be sung, unusually at that time, in Italian, thus resurrecting the present practice in world opera of performing in the original language. This freedom to innovate was one of the reasons Busch and then Ebert had accepted Christie's invitation. It was also, for them, an opportunity to return to an authenticity of performance. The opening night of *Figaro*, the first opera ever performed at Glyndebourne, was an almost complete triumph – the only disappointment was the poor acoustics of the new opera house. What was obvious to the audience was that Busch and Ebert had set a new standard for opera production in Britain. This professionalism had been made possible by the complete reversal of normal British practice, and involved endless rehearsal and concentration on detail. As Busch and Ebert had decided that *Figaro* should be sung in the original Italian, the cast had to study the work afresh and to put aside all the familiar gestures and movements they had developed in singing in their own language. The effect of this was to give the performers a new insight into the text. There had been over 220 full three-hour orchestral rehearsals alone for *Figaro*, and Busch had endeared himself to the orchestra by dropping his arm at the first rehearsal and saying 'Already it is too loud!'

Through his commitment and understanding of individual needs, Busch was able to inspire not just orchestras but principals and the chorus too. At a time when truth and beauty were becoming beleaguered virtues in Europe, Busch's unique and unshakeable, almost ferocious, determination to make Glyndebourne a success shines out. As the music critic Spike Hughes wrote in 1981:

> He had inspired a spirit and feeling of loyalty among those who first gathered to work at Glyndebourne which was peculiar to the circumstances and conditions of the time, when singers, choristers and stage staff worked until they dropped in what they regarded as almost a Sacred Cause.

It was also a triumph of that peculiarly British quality, team spirit, inspired by two exiled Germans, that had produced near perfection 'from the first notes of the Overture to the last button and bow on the chorus's costumes'. The critics agreed that the whole was immeasurably greater than the sum of its constituent parts. The printed programme for *Figaro*, however, still gave typographical prominence to the name of Fritz Busch above that of the producer, Carl Ebert. Perhaps this was right because Busch, for all his commitment to the team, still believed that the conductor was ultimately responsible to the composer. Good production values alone could not save a bad musical performance, nor could a first-rate performance be totally ruined by poor production. Nevertheless, working together they had achieved a superb sense of unity between sight and sound, with Ebert's contribution always respecting the music. The conductor John Pritchard, a young man at the time, recalls watching from the darkness of the orchestra pit while Ebert and Busch rehearsed that first performance:

> Ebert explaining to the singers exactly what he wanted of them, what he regarded as implicit in the score, what he believed that Mozart expected from the music and da Ponte from the libretto. Busch would continually supplement what Ebert said. They worked together as one man.

The production on the second night was *Così fan tutte*, an opera little known in Britain at that time. The Glyndebourne production was, if anything, an even greater success than *Figaro*, and Mozart's opera was revealed in all its glory. Busch and Ebert had chosen the American-born singer Ina Souez as Fiordiligi, and her success at Glyndebourne won her a Convent Garden engagement the following year. She was to be the first of many discoveries that Glyndebourne was to make. She was also one of the first to discover the doubtful pleasures of the nearby town of Lewes. Busch characteristically always sympathized with the understudies, who never seemed to get the opportunity to sing because 'no stars are ever away at Glyndebourne, even work is more attractive than the night life of Lewes!' John Christie was delighted with the team's success and with the growing numbers who were taking the train down from London, but above all with having bloodied the nose of mighty Convent Garden. Thomas Beecham had said that opera in the country was neither desirable or possible; now he must eat his words. There was, of course, a deficit of £7,000 on the season, a large sum in 1934, but Christie was undismayed – both press and critics were unanimous in that Glyndebourne was here to stay. Above all, the novel experience of the trip down to Sussex had caught the public's imagination, as expressed in Herbert Farjeon's review of the time:

> At five o'clock, in evening dress,
> We catch the afternoon express
> Conspicuous among the press,
> And feeling slightly funny;
> In snowy shirts and showy gowns
> We speed through villages and towns,
> Until at last we reach the Downs
> Where music flows like money.

Presiding over this triumph was John Christie, who, in spite of his many eccentricities, had earned the respect of his colleagues. He undoubtedly had a genuine flair for music which enabled him to appreciate the difference between a good and a bad performance and to spot a promising voice. His immediate interest in opera was closely associated with the technical side of the production: he was fascinated by ingenious lighting and sound-effects and by his pet project, the steam pipes used to make clouds. Basking in the critical triumph of that first season, nothing now seemed impossible to Christie. He even dreamed of opera-lovers uprooting and moving to Sussex *en masse* to be near his beloved Glyndebourne, a suggestion he put into his brochure for the following season: 'Why not come and live within the reach of this Festival Opera. You will have Downs, Sea-air, Woods and "Kultur". If you scatter yourself over England you are too far away to support this enterprise.'

But already the Glyndebourne success was attracting poachers. Even before the 1935 season began Rudolf Bing had received an offer from a Mr Nettlefold, who planned to open a German opera house in London and offered Bing the job of director. For Bing it would have been an opportunity to work again on the level he had enjoyed in Germany, for at Glyndebourne he remained little more than Busch's and Ebert's agent, dealing only with bookings and contracts for the artists. As a refugee he had continued to feel insecure throughout his first season at Glyndebourne as he struggled to master the English language. Christie was happy to recommend him for this new venture, although none of the team wanted to lose his unique skills. When the London project failed to materialize, Busch, Christie and Ebert sought to mollify Bing by appointing him Assistant Producer for the coming 1935 season – Bing would have preferred the title 'Artistic Secretary'.

Although Bing was highly efficient in drawing up and finalizing contracts, he had to contend with John Christie's more leisurely approach. This almost led to disaster before the second season had even begun. Christie, who could not believe that anyone would not jump at the chance of working at Glyndebourne, had failed to send the soprano Ina Souez a contract to sing Fiordiligi again. It was the end of February 1935 before she received it, but she then waited a month before replying with a demand for more money. Fritz Busch, on holiday in Sorrento, was furious when told. He cabled Bing and Christie declaring, in his strange version of English, that if Souez was lost to Glyndebourne he would instantly resign. In the time left he could not guarantee the success of his rehearsal plan with a new singer. 'I know that Ebert will agree with me,' he added, and then went to remind Bing that a singer of Souez's stature should have been signed at the end of the first season with binding contracts for both parties because:

Bad behaviour is the rule among singers, and for that reason Souez is quite right in my opinion to go where she can get more publicity and more money. I demand, if my coming to Glyndebourne means anything, that the five guilty ones do everything with, without or against Beecham, with the help of the King, or Parliament, of friend or foe, no matter HOW: that I have Souez at the necessary rehearsals . . . This IS possible. That is my last word.

(Hughes, 1981)

With just five weeks to the opening, Souez remained under contract to Convent Garden, an institution which Christie had never hesitated to abuse and denigrate. Co-operation from that quarter seemed most unlikely, but a change of programme – even without Busch's ultimatum – would have meant the demise of Glyndebourne almost at birth. In desperation Bing and Christie came up with the name of a replacement soprano, Falconieri. But as doomsday – Busch's arrival on the 10 May – approached, Souez finally relented and Bing raced off to sign her up. The second Glyndebourne season had narrowly survived.

In spite of the initial fiasco it was, if anything, an even greater triumph than the first. *The Magic Flute* had been added to the repertoire and was to many an incomparable experience. As Spike Hughes recalled in 1981:

It had a quality most of us had never encountered before, and few of us . . . since. Between them Fritz Busch, Carl Ebert and Hamish Wilson created what one can only think of as an exceptionally complete performance . . . Busch's conception of the work was so panoramic, versatile and stimulating.

The following seasons confirmed the success of Glyndebourne and the unique talents of John Christie's small team of German exiles. By the end of the 1936 season even the financial deficit was reduced to £4,000. Yet Christie was still managing to irritate his artistic directors by constantly suggesting his own favourite artists. He was described by a friend as being like a small boy who had bought toy trains with his pocket money and was always having them taken away from him when he brought them out of his pocket. Christie's attitude to Germany, however, had fundamentally changed, and he tried in 1937 to persuade Busch, Bing and Ebert to ignore the

Continent and use only British singers. But, true to their artistic principles and in spite of their dislike of Nazi German and fascist Italian artists, all three vetoed the proposition. Yes, they would use British artists whenever possible, but the high standards of perform-ance that Glyndebourne had set must never be compromised. So it was in search of new talent that Rudolf Bing found himself in Vienna at the very moment, 12 March 1938, of the Nazi annexation of Austria. He narrowly escaped with his life. Catching a train back from Vienna he arrived at the Czech border, where all Austrian passport holders were ordered off the train by the Gestapo. By a stroke of luck he had been asked to bring with him a permit issued in Vienna to enable a British Member of Parliament to travel there. Hiding his Austrian passport, Bing produced the permit and passed himself off as the British MP.

When Bing returned to Glyndebourne he found that it had attracted an eminent visitor, Arturo Toscanini. The great conductor had refused to perform in Nazi Europe and had broken his contract to perform at the Salzburg Festival. Watching Busch rehearse Verdi's *Macbeth*, Toscanini praised 'the best little chorus' he had ever heard and reas-sured Christie that there was no better conductor in the whole world – and that included Italy – than Fritz Busch. However, it took clever manoeuvring by Christie to stop the great man running into the other visitor that day, Wilhelm Furtwängler. Toscanini loathed the German conductor, perhaps unfairly, as a Nazi sympathizer and for failing to defy the Nazis as unambiguously as he and Busch had done. With his *Macbeth*, that season Busch opened the ears of the British to the delights of Verdi and overcame the British prejudice against this great composer. With his second production *Don Pasquale*, Busch showed that an audi-ence could not only enjoy but be thoroughly entertained by an opera. Ironically, Donizetti's comic masterpiece had been performed appallingly at Convent Garden the previous year. The Glyndebourne team gave a British audience an unforgettable experience of Italian *opera buffa* at its best. Christie, a little disconcerted that the audience laughed so loud as almost to drown the music, was mollified by the appearance of his pug dog Tuppy, who was rewarded with his own curtain call. The *Daily Herald* the next day headed its review of the opera 'Pug Dog's Hit in Opera'. A disconcerted Fritz Busch demanded to know of his colleagues the next day what this had to do with art?

As war approached, Christie's political naïvety became a constant worry to his colleagues. Of Busch and Ebert, he said in an interview with *The Star* newspaper, 'They are not Jews but left Germany because they refuse to mix politics with art. They feel at present that they cannot go back,' adding that he did not feel that strongly himself, having recently been to Germany to discuss opera. Unfortunately Audrey Christie had agreed to sing in Berlin early in 1939 and later at the Salzburg Festival. Against the advice of Rudolf Bing she insisted on making the trip to Berlin, but, under renewed pressure, agreed to cancel Salzburg. Bing himself was now afraid he would be interned in Britain when war came and considered leaving for the USA, having refused an offer from Thomas Beecham to manage Convent Garden. When war did come all activity at Glyndebourne was suspended for the duration. Of the trio of exiles, only Bing remained resolutely in England, living with Christie at Glyndebourne and commuting to London, where he had a job at the Peter Jones department store that involved fire-watching at night during the Blitz.

Christie had spent £100,000 of his own money on establishing the Glyndebourne Opera, but with the genius of Busch and Ebert he had created an institution that was renowned not just for the novelty of its setting but because it had set a standard of performance and artistic ensemble by which all other festivals would henceforth be judged. Not everyone appreciated this Anglo-European success. The playwright and erstwhile music critic Bernard Shaw, informed Christie in 1940 that, since Glyndebourne was a British institution, it should now employ a British conductor. Others shared his opinion, including an anonymous soldier who early in the war wrote to Christie complaining sarcastically about his involvement with German and Austrian refugees:

> Where are your German Opera directors now? Behind barbed wire we hope. But you must find some more if you can. Don't encourage your country in art – always have German mediocrities or Italians. What you want is a German Bomb under you to knock some sense into you. Not to spend your unearned dividends with the Germans.

Rudolf Bing now determined to build on the triumphs of Glyndebourne when normal musical activity resumed after the war.

Christie had appointed him General Manager in 1944 and had encouraged him to explore his own ideas for an annual music and drama festival at Oxford. When backing was not forthcoming, Christie, as ambitious as ever, came up with a scheme to buy the freehold of Convent Garden Opera House for £100,000 and to transform it into a vast cultural centre to be run by Rudolf Bing. But Bing had other plans. He remembered Audrey Christie's remark on a visit to Edinburgh in 1940, 'What a place for a festival.' So in February 1945, with Christie typically begrudging his rail fare, Bing travelled to Edinburgh on behalf of Glyndebourne with a proposition for the Lord Provost, Sir John Falconer. He suggested forming an Edinburgh Festival Trust that would create the first post-war European international festival of music and drama for the summer of 1947. Bing's timing was perfect, as all the established European festivals – Salzburg, Munich and Bayreuth – would be out of action for some years. With this new festival Edinburgh could seize the opportunity to fill the cultural gap in Europe, and it would be underwritten by the talent and experience of the successful Glyndebourne team. Bing then outlined his plans for a three-week season of opera and drama involving the King's, Lyceum and Empire theatres. Concerts were proposed for the Usher Hall and chamber music and small-scale orchestral performances for the Freemasons' Hall. Open-air events, including Scottish dancing and musical serenades, were also proposed. These would resemble the traditional activities that had taken place at the Munich Residenz in Salzburg before the war. The festival must be financed by Edinburgh itself, as Glyndebourne could not be financially involved. The Edinburgh Trust was impressed by Bing's plan and agreed to form executive committees immediately. As the festival took shape there was much coming and going between Edinburgh and Glyndebourne, with Bing receiving great support from his two new assistants, Moran Caplat at Glyndebourne and Ian Hunter at Edinburgh.

The first Edinburgh Festival opened on 24 August 1947 with eighteen performances of *Macbeth* and *Figaro* produced by Carl Ebert in the cramped King's Theatre. The festival was a great success, a remarkable achievement just two years after the end of the war and a personal triumph for Rudolf Bing. The cost to Edinburgh had been less than £10,000, which the Festival Society found no difficulty in meeting. It was agreed that the Glyndebourne team should act as the artistic management again the following season. Rudolf Bing had at last achieved the prominence and recognition that he desired. He was now General Manager of Glyndebourne Opera and Artistic Director of the Edinburgh Festival. But he was no longer happy at Glyndebourne; for him the atmosphere of the pre-war seasons had gone. He now wanted Glyndebourne to tour but knew that the improvisation that this would have involved would not have suited such a perfectionist as Ebert. So Bing, having overseen the safe launch of the Edinburgh Festival, now accepted the offer of the important post of General Manger of the Metropolitan Opera in New York. Everyone agreed that Bing's departure was Glyndebourne's loss. Ironically, he left at the very time of the return of Fritz Busch, who had stayed away for several years because of a petty dispute with Ebert. Glyndebourne itself continued to build upon success. In 1951 it staged the first ever professional production in Britain of Mozart's *Idomeneo*, in a magnificent Busch–Ebert production designed by Oliver Messel. In the same year *Così fan tutte* was transmitted live in its entirety by the BBC, and their *Don Giovanni* was taken to Edinburgh. That same year Fritz Busch died of a heart attack. John Christie wrote of him in *The Times*:

> Glyndebourne has lost the man who set its original musical pulse. Like Casals he would not return to his native land until the political air had been purged . . . his was an artistic integrity that had no time for the dubious glories of prestige or the luxury of personal vanity.

Busch's hard work and driving enthusiasm was always tempered by a sense of humour shared by John Christie. When there was an argument between Busch and Ebert at rehearsals, Christie would often appear on stage carrying a bowl of ice, which he would place, without a word, between them. The two Germans soon laughed and the incident would be forgotten. At the end of one season the final performance was followed by a dance at which Busch, at the piano, played Viennese waltzes for all to dance to. Beecham once quipped, 'Mozart, like good wine, needs no Busch.' Another Busch characteristic was that he never seemed to be tired; as Peter Gelhorn, chorus master at Glyndebourne after the war, has recalled:

> I watched him rehearsing an orchestra from early in the morning until
> the evening . . . yet after dinner he would say: 'Let's go and play a few
> duets', and he would take me to his green room and we would sit at
> the piano and play until eleven o'clock.

John Pritchard, as Assistant Conductor to Busch at Glyndebourne
in 1950, was deeply impressed by his approach to the operas of
Mozart proceeding from his own vivid and compelling work at the
rehearsal piano. Pritchard observed that as soon as an artist arrived
at Glyndebourne he or she would be summoned to work with Fritz
Busch. 'Glyndebourne', he wrote, 'had a great impact upon singers
because they were far removed from the distractions of a big
city. Busch believed in people living on their job, thinking about the
particular opera they were working on and being free from outside
distraction.'

In 1954, following in his father's footsteps, Carl Ebert's son Peter
produced Busoni's *Arlecchino*. This was the first Glyndebourne opera
not produced by Carl Ebert himself. Much had been written about
Ebert's ability to take the printed page of a score and bring it to life in
such a way that movement and action became, for the singer, a part of
the score. Unlike many of his contemporaries he seems to have made
no division between action and music. Watching him rehearse the
banquet scene in *Macbeth* Peter Gelhorn remembers him saying to the
chorus, 'You must imagine you have come here because you are afraid
to stay away. When you drink the toast your hand goes up mechani-
cally, your face becomes like a mask. Only now and then you watch
your neighbour to see what he is doing.' Sitting in the stalls of the empty
theatre, Gelhorn became quite terrified, as did everyone who later saw
the production.

Today the legacy of Glyndebourne remains. The tradition of excellence that the three exiles began has enabled Britain to become a
world leader in operatic composition, performance and production.
What also remains is the custom of intense preparation for each
production. Some critics have felt it excessive, but most performers
would agree that this discipline enabled them to become fully integrated with their roles. As has often been remarked, at Glyndebourne
performers seemed to act, sing and understand their roles better than
they do anywhere else. The importance of what they achieved at

Glyndebourne can be summed up in John Christie's letter to the West German president when he was awarded the German Bundes-verdienstkreuz prize:

> Our work here was undertaken, not out of personal ambition, but because it was necessary to bring to this country what was normal on the Continent and yet hardly existed here. This, thanks to two Germans, Busch and Ebert . . . has been a success.

Meanwhile the third 'German' was making a new career for himself in New York. Rudolf Bing's arrival at the Metropolitan Opera marked the start of a renaissance for opera in the USA. During the war, with soloists from Germany and Italy no longer available, there had been a need to discover local singers and to recruit American-born musicians to the orchestra. The Met had also benefited enormously from the arrival of the exiled conductors from Europe. By the time that Rudolf Bing took over the management it had become a truly American opera house. He began his tenure by overhauling the complete administration system and introducing a new and more adventurous repertoire. For the first time in his professional life Bing had a large enough budget to enable him to hire the best talent in the world. Yet one of his early innovations was to involve the local direc-torial talent that was readily available on Broadway. His first production was Verdi's *Don Carlos* followed by the popular Strauss operetta *Die Fledermaus.* More importantly Bing had restored *Così fan tutte* and *Don Giovanni* to the New York repertoire. Even Offenbach's *La Perichole* delighted the audience, proving too that, as at Glyndebourne, even relatively unknown, small-scale comic operas could find a place in the repertoire of a major international opera house.

Always an innovator, Bing was influential in introducing the first black American singer, Marian Anderson, as a principal and Thomas Schippers as the first full-time American-born conductor. Yet he kept the repertoire relatively conservative – a quarter of all operas produced continued to be by Puccini – and, perhaps to his detriment, he largely ignored the work of modern American composers. In his first decade in New York Bing made the Met the most fashionable and successful opera house in the world. But his autocratic manner brought him increasingly into conflict with both the singers and the theatrical and musical unions. Even though the disputes led to frequent disruptions, box office returns never fell – no more than 3 per cent of seats remained unsold at any performance. But when the high artistic standard of productions began to decline, Bing was persuaded to retire. He is acknowledged as the greatest opera administrator of the twentieth century with three complete careers in opera – in his native Germany, in Britain and in the USA – to look back on, but it will be his pioneering work at Glyndebourne for which he will be best remembered.

9

Building the Future

Modern architecture first arrived in Britain not as buildings but as images on a cinema screen. Audiences in 1927 were stunned by Fritz's Lang's vision of a futuristic city in his film *Metropolis*. Lang, the son of an architect, had been inspired by what he had seen of the New York skyline on a visit in 1924. With its dense high-rise blocks and bold use of steel and glass structures, the city in his film bore an uncanny resemblance to the contemporary designs of German architects associated with the Bauhaus. Few in Britain had seen anything like it. There were virtually no examples in London of this bold, new architecture that was appearing throughout Germany. A decade after the Great War British architecture was still fifty years behind the times and characterized by conservative 'Banker's Georgian' and suburban mock-Tudor. But soon this architectural backwater would be so transformed that, today, British architects such as Richard Rogers and Norman Foster are considered among the most capable and radical in the world. Their success was largely made possible by the dramatic changes introduced to Britain by the exiled Berthold Lubetkin, Eric Mendelsohn and Erno Goldfinger in the 1930s.

Lubetkin was born a Jew in Georgia and grew up in a revolutionary Soviet Union where architects no longer designed villas for capitalists but built collective housing and crèches for workers' children. Soviet artists and intellectuals believed that their work had a social purpose and that architecture should both inspire the minds and improve the lives of the people. None was more politically committed as a young man than Lubetkin, and it is ironic that he was not only to settle in traditionalist Britain but to live in a Georgian town house in Bristol. Lubetkin's love affair with England had begun fifteen years earlier, when, as a schoolboy, he first visited the country. What fascinated him was not the architecture but London's many parks and open spaces and the game of cricket he saw being played in Regent's Park, 'the green aesthetic of playing fields, a background of bright colours, stripes, score boards, variegated blazers and a whole signalling system of numerals . . . The airy, cool and free confidence which I observed in the parks acted as a powerful visual stimulus' (Lubetkin, 1932).

Back in Georgia Lubetkin trained as an architect then studied in Germany and at the Ecole des Beaux Arts in Paris, where, in 1925, he started his first architectural practice. Although a leading exponent of modernism, he retained a fondness for the idyllic *rus in urbe* that he had discovered in London. Politically, Lubetkin was convinced, as Marx and Engels had been, that Britain was ripe for revolution and that the next phase of the modernist revolution would happen there. Architecturally, British xenophobia had shown signs of abating and such foreign influences as the American beaux-arts movement and modern Swedish classicism were beginning to appear; modernism itself, however, was still being hotly debated in the London architectural journals. This need for a cause explains why Lubetkin chose exile in Britain even before Hitler came to power rather than emigrating to the USA. There his international reputation would have guaranteed him instant commercial success; but in America he could never have become the big fish in the small architectural pond that he was in Britain.

On his first day in London as an exile in 1930 Lubetkin renewed his love affair with British architecture by jumping on a bus and touring the city. From the upper deck he surveyed the architectural panorama – Park Lane, the Dorchester Hotel, the fine early nineteenth-century terraces facing Hyde Park, the streets of Bloomsbury, the Nash terraces of Regent's Park and the grandeur of the Strand. When he wrote of this experience in 1932 his words could have been those of John Betjeman himself:

> Long terraces of cream stucco enclose the endless lawns of Regent's Park. The harmony of the landscape is powerful, impressive and persistent. This is town planning! . . . And yet how superb this grass is! How

agreeable, clean and fresh . . . Urbanity, order . . . Yes indeed, architecture is man's will. And Paris is at least as far from London as Le Corbusier from Ruskin.

Within a year of his arrival Lubetkin had founded the architectural partnership Tecton. With its slogan 'building for a better future', Tecton immediately became the most radical practice in Britain. Lubetkin's wide European experience made him the natural leader of his six young colleagues. 'We were desperately impressed with Lubetkin,' recalled Lindsay Drake. 'I was only twenty-two and at that time he was like a god.' Lubetkin's role became that of unofficial spokesman for modernism in Britain and he immediately attracted the wrath of the architectural establishment. The *Architectural Review* welcomed him with a forthright attack on modernism: 'This banal ideology disguised as freedom of thought.' Compromised by its left-wing politics, Tecton found it hard to survive and needed to be subsidized by its members as they struggled to find commissions. On the verge of collapse, the partnership was saved by contracts to design a banker's house in Hampstead and a clinic in east London.

Tecton struggled on, plagued by lack of finance and disrupted by constant debate on principles. But the architecture its members were producing was beginning to be recognized as the most significant in Britain in the 1930s. Using reinforced concrete and working in partnership with the engineer Ove Arup, they were now producing buildings that demonstrated an unusual unity of purpose and were compared by critics to the finest achievements of Baroque architecture. Tecton's pioneering project in London in 1933 was the first modern high-rise apartment block ever built in Britain, Highpoint Flats at Highgate. The inspiration, Lubetkin claimed, came from the paintings of Braque and Gris that he had seen in Paris in the 1920s. The success of Highpoint led to the commission for which he is best remembered in Britain, the Penguin Pool at London Zoo. Using intertwining ramps and platforms of flowing concrete, Lubetkin married art and architecture in the design. This modest project made Tecton world famous and confirmed the arrival of modernist architecture in Britain. Within a year Dudley Zoo, near Birmingham, commissioned a series of animal houses including kiosks and lion, tiger and polar bear ravines. Again, Lubetkin's solution was innovative and dramatic. 'Even designing a reptiliary, we were doing something of social importance,' he wrote; 'our work was intended not only to inform but to inspire.'

By 1935, following a major exhibition at the Museum of Modern Art in New York, Tecton had gained international recognition, but success failed to temper Lubetkin's radicalism and he remained as firmly anti-establishment as ever. Admired by the artistic intelligentsia, he preferred the company of scientists and became friends with such leading British experts as Rutherford, Chadwick, Cockcroft, Walton and Fleming. He later wrote, 'I formed the impression that England would develop upon scientific principles, and go forward as a fortress of science.' In retirement at his Georgian house overlooking the Clifton Suspension Bridge in Bristol, designed by his acknowledged master, Isambard Kingdom Brunel, the old radical wrote in 1986 (Allan, 1992), 'Looking back it becomes clear to me that our early inspiration to revolt against the old order was certainly historically justified and inevitable; but it did not imply or justify a revolt against order, as such. The old order had to be replaced by a new order, not disorder.'

Even in old age Lubetkin continued to champion change, but Britain's decline as a scientific and industrial force depressed him. 'There is, in this country, an immensely proud tradition of progress', he wrote, 'that has changed the course of world history, but there is also another tradition that brings back the birch, the noose, and the Olde Tea Shoppe.' Induced out of retirement in 1984 to give evidence in support of Lord Palumbo's scheme for a Mies van der Rohe building in the City of London, Lubetkin had lost none of his old fire. In a typically British compromise the scheme championed by Lubetkin was refused but the existing buildings were allowed to be demolished. A week after the Mansion House Inquiry the Prince of Wales launched his famous attack on modernist architecture, and Lubetkin was again moved to defend radicalism with a ferocious condemnation in the press of both the prince's prejudice and his ignorance. Today all Lubetkin's major surviving projects of the 1930s are listed buildings, making him the best-protected modern architect in Britain. Both the Highpoint Flats and the Penguin Pool at London Zoo have been carefully restored as quintessential 1930s icons, securing Lubetkin's pre-eminent place in twentieth-century British architecture. For such a radical it was ironic that his admiration of the English classical tradition never wavered throughout his long life. In the buildings of Inigo Jones, Christopher Wren, William Kent and Robert Adam he saw an authentic, unbroken and still relevant tradition. In 1932 he wrote that the element of classical British architecture that he admired most was the use of brick, a most unmodernist material:

> But what brick! From the softest creams, through scarlets, strong and blood red, to violet purples . . . there, matured by centuries of experience, is the palette from which the English mason composes his masterpieces . . . brick, this material of Pharaohs and a foundation of the English architectural tradition.

The other great influence on British architecture in the 1930s was the German-born Eric Mendelsohn. Although he left far fewer examples of his work in Britain than Lubetkin, his influence was almost as significant. Mendelsohn arrived in London with a formidable reputation as the leading exponent of German modernist architecture. His best-known work was the most visually stimulating and radical building ever attempted in Germany, the Einstein Tower in Potsdam in 1919. Naturally it was anathema to German traditionalists and to the growing numbers of Nazi supporters who loathed both the Jewish-born Einstein and his theories. Mendelsohn's design was seen as a provocation because it sought to demonstrate the Theory of Relativity in the structure of the building. In spite of critical and political hostility the project went ahead, and the Einstein Tower made Mendelsohn the best-known and most controversial architect in Germany in the 1920s. For the first five years of the Weimar Republic the economy boomed and Mendelsohn was in constant demand, turning out designs for office blocks and department stores that transformed the appearance of many German cities. His masterpiece was, according to Nikolaus Pevsner, the Schocken Store in Chemnitz, which Pevsner thought demonstrated Mendelsohn's 'characteristic rejection of ornate detail in favour of simplicity, large windows, modern lighting and bold signs'.

But Mendelsohn, for all his commercial success, remained a key target for the Nazis. Not only was he a modernist intellectual but a Jew and a self-declared Zionist as well. On the eve of Hitler's ascent to power Mendelsohn expressed the feelings of all Germany's modernist architects when he wrote, 'Now prison bars await the free spirit . . . and barbed wire surrounds creative energy.' Torn between Soviet Russia, where he had worked in the 1920s, and Britain, where his work had aroused great interest among the followers of modernism, Mendelsohn finally chose the latter. Arriving in London the day after Hitler became Chancellor, he was welcomed by the same small group of young radicals who were attracted to Berthold Lubetkin. Sensibly he teamed up with a young British-born architect of Russian descent, Serge Chermayeff. Together they entered a competition for the design of the de la Warr Pavilion at Bexhill-on-Sea in Sussex. Quite unexpectedly, given the natural conservatism of the time, the judges chose their bold and innovative plan. Today the Bexhill Pavilion is considered by many to be the most influential modernist British building of the inter-war years. It has been described by the architectural critic Jonathan Glancey as 'white balletic architecture . . . in which Mendelsohn brings many of the elements of his mature German style together and sets them down at the English seaside to great effect'.

The Bexhill project established Mendelsohn's British reputation, and it was soon followed by a commission for a house in Old Church Street, London, whose radical design almost perfectly complemented its Georgian neighbours. Now Mendelsohn was given the opportunity to work on a grander scale with a commission for six tower blocks at the White City, London, and a large hotel incorporating Britain's first multi-storey car park at Blackpool. When his partnership with Chermayeff ended – Chermayeff went on to become a distinguished teacher in the USA, eventually succeeding Walter Gropius at Harvard – Mendelsohn continued working alone but with growing discontent. As early as 1934 he had written 'England is an interregnum', and in spite of being made a Fellow of the Royal Institute of British Architects and granted British citizenship his active Zionism now led him to Palestine. That he was grateful to Britain and tormented by guilt at the prospect of abandoning the land that had given him refuge just as war was imminent is confirmed by his wife, who later wrote that their last winter in London together was the saddest of his life.

Mendelsohn's identification with Zionism and the emergent Jewish homeland had led him to visit Palestine in the mid-1930s, when Chaim Weizmann had invited him to design several housing projects. 'I am planning, I am alive. I am building the country and rebuilding myself. Here I am a citizen and an artist,' he wrote in a letter to his wife from Jerusalem. Yet when he arrived there again in 1939 his conscience prompted him to attempt to enlist in the British Army stationed there.

When his application was refused, he continued with his architecture. But with little new building being commissioned during the war, Mendelsohn felt increasingly frustrated. A few months before the Japanese attack on Pearl Harbor he moved on again, to the USA, which he had visited in 1926 and had met Frank Lloyd Wright. Of all the European modernists, Mendelsohn was the best-known in America. He was given a prestigious one-man show at the Museum of Modern Art in New York and elected to the American Institute of Architects. But for the next five years, with the building industry at a near standstill, he struggled to survive financially. With little to do, he travelled the USA instead, lecturing on modernism and renewing his friendship with Wright. With the defeat of the Axis powers, building recommenced in America, and Mendelsohn was able to resume his career with commissions for a synagogue and a hospital. Granted American citizenship in 1948, Mendelsohn moved to San Francisco and lectured at Berkeley. In his last years in California his most important work was a series of four synagogues that demonstrate not only his ability to involve natural light in a building but his increasing commitment to Judaism.

The third émigré architect to influence the growth of modernism in Britain was the Hungarian-born Erno Goldfinger. Whereas Lubetkin and Mendelsohn built relatively little in Britain, Goldfinger's legacy is still much in evidence in the remaining high-rise blocks of flats and offices that characterized British urban architecture in the 1950s and 1960s. Admired by some but loathed by many, Goldfinger's work occupies a unique, if not altogether popular place in British architecture. Unlike the basically German modernist style of Mendelsohn and Lubetkin, Goldfinger's designs originated in the teachings of the Austrian modernist architect Adolf Loos. Goldfinger had been Loos's pupil in Paris in the 1920s and had joined him in rejecting the beauxarts teaching method as a moribund system that ridiculed modern architecture and ignored the potential of steel and reinforced concrete structures. Of even greater influence on Goldfinger was the avant-garde architect Auguste Perret, who set up his own studio in Paris at Goldfinger's instigation. Perret was also a pioneer in the use of reinforced concrete, and Goldfinger learned from him not only the use of this new material but also the fundamental principle that was to characterize his work for the next fifty years – in Perret's words of 1924, 'He who hides any part of the framework deprives himself of the only legitimate and most beautiful ornament of architecture. He who hides a pillar makes a mistake. He who erects a false pillar commits a crime' (Perret, 1959).

In 1934, wary of the course of events in Europe, Goldfinger moved to London where, like Lubetkin, he refused to compromise his principles by designing 'neo-Tudor or Georgian abominations'. Nor did he subscribe to the 'white box' concept of modernism. 'I want to be remembered as a Classical architect, not a kasbah architect,' Goldfinger wrote at the time. Fortunately his wife was a member of the wealthy Blackwell family (of Crosse and Blackwell, the manufacturers of foodstuffs), and they were able to live in comfort while Goldfinger established his architectural practice in London. His first British commissions were modest: shop interiors, furniture designs and the occasional small house. Much as Berthold Lubetkin is best remembered for a small-scale work, so Erno Goldfinger is now famous for a simple three-house brick-faced terrace in Willow Road, Hampstead, built in the late 1930s. Willow Road was significant in that it was Goldfinger's modernist interpretation of the traditional English Georgian terrace. As with Mendelsohn's Bexhill Pavilion, it provoked initial controversy tinged with thinly disguised anti-Semitism. A seminal work, it was to influence many future developments, including Frederick Gibberd's major terrace developments at Harlow New Town. So important had the Willow Road terrace become that it was made a listed building in 1955 and twenty years later became the first and only modern domestic house to be owned by the National Trust.

Goldfinger's other important contribution to British architecture was in promoting the box-frame method of construction that he had developed in collaboration with Ove Arup. This system allowed fast and efficient construction in the large-scale building projects that became necessary after the return to peace in 1945. Goldfinger had also cautiously explored the potential of the new prefabrication systems becoming available, but he remained wary that they might lower the standards of design. It is significant that in his first high-rise housing project in 1960 he rejected this prefabrication system for the known virtues of poured concrete on site. In the right place at the right time, Goldfinger was now well placed to exploit the post-war building boom. Yet in the first years of peace, his only commissions were, appropriately for a socialist, the new Communist Party Headquarters and the

Daily Worker newspaper buildings in London. These were lean years, but, with the opening of the London exhibition 'This Is Tomorrow' and the removal in 1954 of many of the controls on the size of buildings and the materials used in their construction, his fortunes changed. Goldfinger now became more involved than any other contemporary architect in the large reconstruction projects of the period. Unfortunately he was seen by the press as the leading exponent of the 'New Brutalism' in British architecture.

By the late 1950s Goldfinger was designing flats, offices, schools and hospitals. His ability to work at speed came from the 'big deck' system that he had devised based on his idiosyncratic planning grid of two foot nine inches. It was a simple but highly functional measurement that corresponded to the width of a standard door and its jamb or of a standing man with hands on hips. 'Multiply this by four and I have a grid into which . . . I can fit my whole building,' claimed Goldfinger. His two best-known London projects that used this system, the Albermarle Street office block and Alexander Fleming House at the Elephant and Castle, have been likened, unflatteringly, to the huge Constructivist projects of Stalinist Russia. But Goldfinger's designs were far more commercial, recognizing the need for flexibility of use and realizing that the developer must maximize his profit from an investment. This was the golden age of the property developer, and Goldfinger was the master of providing maximum lettable space, for, as he claimed, 'the client does not care about architecture, he cares whether it works. The architecture is my own private pleasure.'

Where Lubetkin and Mendelsohn had failed in their socialist ideal of building homes for the workers, Goldfinger was to succeed spectacularly. His Watford tower blocks were followed by a commission for another twenty-three high-rise buildings for the Greater London Council. Soon the Goldfinger tower block, preferably set in open parkland, became a feature of the British urban skyline. Building high, he believed, would arrest suburban sprawl and restore London to its past beauty, but it proved an alien concept to the vast majority of the British, and by 1967 Goldfinger's tower blocks were already outdated as low-rise schemes came into favour. Critics felt that Goldfinger's high-rise world, designed with the best intentions for human welfare, had been pushed to the limit and was now an alien and menacing phenomenon. Some even saw aggression in his massive concrete circulation towers, with their ventilation slits a resembling arrow slits in a castle's walls and in his cantilevered rooftop boiler houses a hint of a warship's bridge. As the critic Ian Nairn has said of these strangely un-British buildings, 'they produce respect rather than admiration'. But in recent years Goldfinger's high-rise blocks have been more sympathetically assessed and, where possible, those that remain are being transformed into luxury apartment blocks, for it was not the poorest in society to whom Goldfinger's original concept of a high-rise garden suburb was finally found to appeal but the wealthiest.

Only in the past two decades have the British become grudgingly reconciled to the high-rise buildings in their cities. No such problem, of course, affected the USA, the home of the skyscraper. Because America was used to high-rise buildings, the arrival of the European émigrés had less initial impact than in Britain. Their effect on architectural education, however, was to be profound, and the Bauhaus architects Walter Gropius, Mies van der Rohe and Marcel Breuer were all to play an important role as teachers. All three were also to make a fundamental contribution as practising architects in demonstrating a dynamic reinterpretation of the high-rise building. Unlike their British colleagues, American architects had, since the late nineteenth century, built their cities in a modern, high-rise style, and their skills were acknowledged throughout the world. As the architectural critic Randolph Sexton put it in 1928, 'The skyscraper, an American institution, planned to meet modern American requirements and serve modern American purposes, built of materials of modern manufacture in methods peculiarly American, has finally been made to express Americanism in its design.'

But to some critics this architecture had lost its vigour and had become bogged down in a plethora of of neoclassical shells and pretentious façades that made contemporary skyscrapers look more like high-rise medieval cathedrals or Roman temples. The blame for this was attributed to the beaux-arts tradition that still dominated the nation's architectural training. This search for a false, historic beauty was roundly condemned by the critic Henry Russell Hitchcock, who wrote in the early 1920s, 'For what passes today for architecture is but a blonde wig and gold teeth; no ghost rather, but a soulless imitation of its former body.' But in Europe, encouraged by the Weimar Republic's removal of restrictions on high-rise building, German architects of the time were evolving their own version of the skyscraper. The most radical of German art and design schools, the Bauhaus, was fascinated by the challenge, and by 1921 one of its leading teachers, Ludwig Mies van der Rohe, had already produced a skyscraper design of an almost abstract simplicity for the Friedrichstrasse office project in Berlin.

The Bauhaus philosophy was to seek to unify all aspects of art and design and so eradicate divisions between 'high' and decorative art. Bauhaus students at Dessau and later in Berlin were encouraged to explore the possibilities of the new construction materials now available and to use form and colour in a radical manner. Above all, the Bauhaus philosophy subscribed to the principle that art and design should have a social purpose. The Bauhaus encouraged an architecture that was modern and straightforward, rejecting both ornament and irrelevance. Students were taught to reveal 'the inner logic of a building, radiant and naked, unencumbered by lying façades and trickeries'. This was a radical departure from the beaux-arts tradition and so antipathetic to the German traditionalists, who were among Hitler's most ardent supporters, that the Nazis moved immediately against the Bauhaus in 1933. The majority of the staff were instantly dismissed and their academic and architectural careers virtually ended.

As in all the arts, the Nazis were aware of the need to retain those who would join them or would do their bidding without dissent. Hitler's interest in German architecture was well known and his intimacy with the architect Albert Speer shows the importance he placed in evolving a new German style of building. At first, a deal seemed to have been struck between Goebbels, on Hitler's behalf, and Walter Gropius and Ludwig Mies van der Rohe, the two most senior figures at the Bauhaus. They were allowed to remain at their posts and even encouraged to enter state architectural competitions as long as they kept silent on political issues. A year after Hitler's accession Walter Gropius arrived in London, with the permission of the Nazis, to attend an exhibition of his designs at the Royal Institute of British Architects. When questioned by journalists, Gropius insisted that he was not a refugee and refused to discuss politics or to criticize events in Germany. He was, he declared, merely a cultural ambassador for modernism. Again, when Harvard wrote offering him the prestigious chair of architecture two years later, he discussed it with the Nazi government before accepting the post. In 1934 Gropius travelled to London, where he was invited to stay at the recently completed Lawn Road Flats, the first and only block of modern apartments in London at the time, designed by the English architect Wells Coates. Another local architect, Maxwell Fry, invited him to work with his practice, and they collaborated on several private houses. Their largest project, and the only Gropius building of importance in Britain, was Impington College, Cambridgeshire, built in 1936. But when other projects for apartment blocks and a new Christ's College building at Cambridge were shelved, Gropius decided to move on to the USA.

When he arrived in New York Gropius continued to maintain a discreet silence on events in Germany, whether out of concern for those who were left under Nazi rule or because of some private agreement he had made with Goebbels. In the USA Gropius found a society still suffering from the effects of the Depression and with an architectural teaching system that was out of date and virtually moribund. His appointment as Professor of Architecture at Harvard was to be fundamental in changing all this, and the next generation of American architects was to gain immeasurably from his presence. From the start Harvard gave Gropius the freedom to recruit the best architects, critics, historians and scholars from Europe. Some of the most important figures of modern American architecture – Edward Larrabee Barnes, Ulrich Franzen, John Johansen, Philip Johnson, I.M. Pei, Paul Rudolph and Harry Seidler – were taught by Gropius and his colleagues at Harvard. All that had been missing at the Dessau Bauhaus – generous financial support and an absence of political interference – Gropius found there. He was the most influential and charismatic teacher of his generation, always seeking to reconcile the individual with a fast-changing industrial society. A great believer in teamwork, he encouraged young architects to work with town planners and landscape designers wherever possible. Perhaps his success as an inspirational teacher inhibited his career as a practising architect in America.

In his designs Gropius championed the use of interchangeable prefabricated units for domestic housing, while realizing that complete ready-made houses would never appeal to the public. Working with his old Bauhaus colleague Marcel Breuer, he also conceived and developed his most characteristic building – the slablike multi-storey apartment block of eight to twelve storeys high with the long side resting on the ground. One apartment deep, this light and airy solution to high-density housing set in parkland was to become the most popular type of high-rise development in the USA. But Gropius's first project on arrival was his own house at Harvard. It was followed in 1941 by his first official commission in America, a housing scheme in New Kensington. Four years later he formed a partnership with a group of young architects under the quasi-socialist name of the Architects' Collective. One of their most important projects was the Graduate Centre at Harvard, which the architectural press praised as an important demonstration of European modernist ideas in the USA. Commissions for housing complexes and schools flooded in. Gropius's most important buildings in America include the Pan-Am building in New York and the Boston Bay Center. The latter was the largest project ever associated with him and was remarkable for the fact that all the major architects involved were university lecturers, with some of the original ideas coming from Gropius's own Harvard students – a relationship that was inconceivable before Gropius and Mies van der Rohe appeared. Now American capital, impressed by the skill and authority of the émigré architects, had the confidence to back the innovative ideas that were coming from the institutions where they presided. At the end of his long career Gropius returned to Germany to design the new Porcelain Factory in Hamburg, a project that complemented his first pioneering industrial building, the Fagus Shoe Factory at Atfeld in 1911. Returning to the USA, Gropius remained active in the Architects' Collective until his death in 1969. His most important legacy to America is not, however, his buildings but the unified and modernized architectural education system that he and his fellow teachers devised.

When Walter Gropius left Germany his colleague Ludwig Mies van der Rohe had taken over as principal of the Bauhaus at Dessau. He, too, continued to apply for commissions from the new Nazi regime, perhaps more in hope than in expectation, as his best-known project was his memorial to the murdered communist leaders Karl Liebknecht and Rosa Luxemburg – soon to be demolished by the Nazis. But his international fame rested on the German Pavilion at the International Exposition at Barcelona in 1929, in which he designed everything from the building itself to that classic of twentieth-century design, the Barcelona chair. In an attempt to placate his enemies Mies now joined several Nazi-sponsored institutions and even signed a petition in support of Hitler, but he was unable to save either his career or the Bauhaus itself. His conciliatory actions were later condemned by some of his fellow exiles in the USA; Sibyl Moholy-Nagy said of him, 'He who lies down with dogs gets up with fleas.' Finally, when his submission, bedecked with the obligatory swastikas, for the German Pavilion at the Brussels World's Fair was refused, Mies accepted the inevitable and left Germany for the USA in 1938. Soon after his arrival he was offered a well-paid teaching post in Chicago as director of the Armor Institute, later the Illinois Institute of Technology. Like Gropius he was to play an important role in the future of American architectural education, exercising an authoritarian control over his faculty at the Armor but transforming it, with the help of his Bauhauser Ludwig Hilberseimer, into one of the most prestigious architectural faculties in the world. Hilberseimer himself was one of the world's leading theorists on town planning and much admired for his stark high-rise solutions for the city of the future, based on the critical relationship between population density and open space.

In practice, Mies quickly became the most important architect of his generation, attracting commissions for high-rise apartments, office blocks and institutional buildings. Combining his German intellectual rigour with American opportunism in the use of glass and steel, he produced buildings of purity and simplicity. In the process he coined much-quoted sayings such as 'less is more' and 'God is in the details'. Inspired by Chicago's early high-rises, he went on to create a series of contemporary curtain-wall blocks that include the Secretariat building of the United Nations in New York. But of all his designs in the USA it is the Lake Shore Drive Apartments in Chicago and the Seagram Building in New York that are his masterpieces. As the architectural critic Jan McCallum wrote perceptively of him in 1967 (Fleming and Bailyn, 1969):

> America could not have nurtured Mies, Europe could not have fulfilled his promises, he has perhaps gained more, and given more, to the US than any other émigré outside the realm of atomic physics. He has produced a lyricism of two constituent US psychological facts – unlimited space and unmitigated technology – in a form that . . . can be held up to the rest of the world as an example of a convincing machine-age architecture.

Josef Albers, another Bauhauser, was also to play an important role in the transformation of American architectural education. After the dissolution of the Bauhaus in 1933 he was the first of his colleagues to accept an academic post in the USA, at the newly established Black Mountain College in North Carolina. With him came his Jewish wife Anni, a textile designer of international fame. Their fares and initial financial support were provided by two philanthropic trustees of the Museum of Modern Art in New York, Philip Johnson and Edward M.M. Warburg. Johnson, a convert to modernism, had been stunned at his first sight of the Bauhaus building in Dessau and said of it in 1933, 'It is a magnificent building. I regard it as the most beautiful building we have ever seen . . . the Bauhaus has beauty of plan, and great strength of design. It has a majesty and simplicity which are unequalled.'

When the Albers first arrived, more attention was paid to the wife than to the husband, the *New York Sun* describing her as 'one of the foremost designers of textiles in Europe and a leader in the movement started by the famous Bauhaus in Dessau, Germany, to revive the art of textile weaving'. Although Black Mountain College was located in a remote area of the Appalachians in North Carolina, Joseph Albers's, teaching courses, based on the original Bauhaus curriculum, soon gained it a reputation as a centre for excellence throughout America.

Other Bauhausers followed Gropius and Mies to the USA, and they, too, contributed to America's growing reputation for architectural training. Gropius's pupil, the Hungarian-born Marcel Breuer, also spent a year in Britain in 1936, where he worked with the radical design company Isokon while living precariously on the royalties from his Bauhaus furniture patents, particularly that of the famous tubular steel chairs he had developed in the 1920s out of bicycle handlebars. Although his European buildings had been in the bland International Style – white stucco boxes floating on pilotis (stilts) – Breuer was deeply impressed by the traditional wooden houses of New England and by the work of Frank Lloyd Wright. Breuer now began using more wood and less glass and steel in his designs than other émigré architects. Offered a post by Gropius, he became his celebrated assistant at Harvard and discovered great personal affinity with such specifically American concepts as the modern family home. Another of their ex-colleagues, the Hungarian born László Moholy-Nagy, even set out to recreate the Bauhaus itself in the New World setting of Chicago. The local Association of Arts and Industries (AAI), on Gropius's recommendation, asked Moholy-Nagy to set up a design school based on the Bauhaus principles. This New

World Bauhaus opened in October 1937 with a class of thirty-five students, but within a year it had collapsed because of its director's inability to deal diplomatically with important local sponsors. However, he succeeded in resurrecting the school in 1939 at a new location in Chicago and without the involvement of the AAI. This time he tailored the curriculum more to the needs and values of Middle America. That the school proved to be a success was due to Moholy-Nagy's unexpected ability to raise funds from corporate America. A complex artist, much of his energy in the USA went into product design and other commercial activities. His projects included window displays and showroom renovations for the Simpsons shop in London and the Lanz store in Chicago. For years he had experimented with such unconventional materials as aluminium and glass; now he began experimenting with the new plastics, by incising and painting abstract designs on Plexiglas sheets. Far from Dessau, the misfortune of exile had presented Moholy-Nagy with unexpected opportunities for self-expression without political restrictions. With generous financial backing and surrounded by a society that was open to new ideas, Moholy-Nagy found in the USA a receptive audience for his bold experimentalism.

All the Bauhaus exiles found America a liberating experience after the oppression they had suffered in Germany. They had escaped both political persecution and the entrenched aesthetic conservatism of large sections of German society to find an unexpected freedom in their new home. As the most advanced industrial society in the world, the USA had need of their radical approach to the problems of urban development and the challenge of the motor vehicle. In the 1930s a far larger audience began to see, without realizing it, what Bauhaus design was like. Hollywood films, especially those made by Paramount, were largely designed by German refugees: under the direction of Hans Dreier, Paramount's art department became almost a workshop for Bauhaus design with frequent visual references in their films to the plain white walls, curved glass surfaces and uncluttered minimalism of the original. Not every European contribution to American architecture in the 1930s came from the Bauhaus, however. The universal concept of the shopping mall is said to have originated with the Viennese-born architect Victor Gruen, who created a modern shopping experience at the Northland Shopping Center in Detroit in 1954 by combining space, light and fountains into a modern equivalent of Renaissance piazza.

10

To See Ourselves

A month before Adolf Hitler came to power in 1933 two river steamers packed with 530 boxes containing six thousand books, tens of thousands of slides and photographs and a collection of historic furniture sailed from Hamburg down the River Elbe and out of the clutches of Joseph Goebbels. The contents of the Warburg Institute, Germany's finest archive of art history, was going into exile. In an unprecedented operation the whole institute was moving to London ahead of the predicted Nazi success in the chancellorship elections the following March. The Nazis had already forced the institute to abandon lectures, and its total disbandment was thought to be imminent. Max Warburg, head of the wealthy banking family, who had controlled it since the death of his brother Aby in 1928, looked to the USA for help. But after a new home for the Warburg could not be found there Sir Denison Ross of the School of Oriental and African Studies persuaded London University to offer it a home at the Imperial Institute buildings in Kensington. When the collection was safe in London, it was the turn of the Warburg's lecturers to follow. Soon such eminent scholars as Nikolaus Pevsner, Ernst Gombrich, Frederick Antal and Rudolf Wittkower were lecturing to a new and slightly bemused British audience.

Art history was one of the academic disciplines most affected by the Nazi take-over. More than a quarter of all German art history specialists were dismissed and forced to emigrate as the Nazis seized control of Germany's cultural life. More than a third of them moved to Britain, where the Courtauld Institute of Art in London provided them with teaching and research posts and the *Burlington Magazine*, the leading British journal of arts and antiquities, offered to publish their writings. Six years later, as London's museums and art galleries closed their doors and evacuated their contents for safe keeping during the war, the Warburg Institute repaid its debt to the city by staying open. Throughout the war, using its incomparable photographic archive, the Warburg continued to mount exhibitions and to share its unique collection with the culture-starved London public.

Nikolaus Pevsner – who was to become a British institution in his own right and one of the country's best-loved writers on art and architecture – of all the émigrés in Britain perhaps came closest to becoming an honorary Englishman as he enthused a generation with his commitment to scholarship and his deep affection for the artistic treasures of his adopted country. Pevsner was already an internationally recognized expert on the history of British art when he arrived in 1933, and, recognizing his importance as a scholar of European significance, Professor Sargent Florence promptly offered him a temporary post at Birmingham University that involved writing a critical review of contemporary British industrial design, later published as *An Enquiry into Industrial Art in Britain*. Pevsner's enthusiasm and scholarship impressed everyone he met, and the industrialist Sir Gordon Russell, after one meeting, appointed him as his personal adviser on modern furniture design. In this influential position Pevsner was able to be play a key role in the improvement of British industrial design in the late 1930s.

When war came and German bombers set about levelling much of Britain's architectural heritage, Pevsner was interned on the Isle of Man. On his release Pevsner, to his great delight, was sent to London, where he spent the next two years clearing air-raid rubble from the streets of Kentish Town and working on his book *An Outline of European Architecture* (1956). Regarded as the best architectural history of the Christian period it contains a passage that encapsulates Pevsner's feelings – which may well have been shared by Adolf Hitler – about the importance of architecture:

Architecture is the most comprehensive of all the visual arts and has a right to claim superiority over all the others . . . Neither sculpture nor painting, although both are rooted in elementary creative and imitative instincts, surrounds us to the same extent as architecture, acts upon us so incessantly and so ubiquitously.

At the height of the war Pevsner was given a permanent teaching post and the financial stability he desperately needed by Birkbeck College, London. His lecture subjects in his first term reflect the broad diversity of European scholarship that he brought to the college: 'William Blake', 'Iconography in French Cathedrals', 'Baudelaire and Dramatic Criticism' and 'The Bauhaus'.

Soon after arriving in England Pevsner had begun contributing to the *Architectural Review* and now, with many of its staff on war service, he was offered the post of temporary editor – a remarkable tribute to a man whose first language was German. He was to run the magazine almost single-handedly until the end of the war, his editorship giving him an important voice in in the future of post-war British architecture. Nor did Pevsner ever hesitate before becoming involved in controversy. His main concern was to be the dubious value of the 'New Brutalism' of the 1950s and 1960s and particularly the work of his fellow exile the architect Erno Goldfinger. Pevsner's warnings of the disparity between London's new skyscrapers and the traditional streetscape were largely ignored at the time. What annoyed him most were the tower-block flats that were appearing in every British city. Pevsner disliked both their aesthetics and what he perceived as their shoddy construction, predicting that within sixty years they would rival in squalor the slums of Victorian England. Even that forecast proved to be optimistic, as within twenty years of their construction widespread demolition of urban tower blocks had already begun.

Pevsner's transformation from youthful radical to mature traditionalist may well be due to his later fascination with British architecture. As a young man, he was a committed modernist and would occasionally still champion what he considered to be valuable in modern design, such as Erich Mendelsohn's de la Warr Pavilion at Bexhill-on-Sea. Pevsner idiosyncratically believed that modern architectural and industrial design, generally considered to have originated on the Continent, really had its roots in late nineteenth- and early twentieth-century English design. He expounded these ideas in his influential book *Pioneers of the Modern Movement from Morris to Gropius*, published in 1936. Pevsner's lifelong preoccupation with the influence of fine art on industrial design drew him inevitably to the work and ideas of William Morris, and he was a founder member of the William Morris Society.

When the war ended Pevsner embarked on a punishing round of activity, lecturing at home and abroad for the British Council and helping to establish both the William Morris Society and the Victorian Society. In 1959 he was appointed Professor of the History of Art at Birkbeck College, becoming Emeritus Professor on his retirement in 1969. His distinguished academic career included the Slade Professorship of Fine Art at Cambridge from 1949 to 1955 and a Fellowship of St John's College, Oxford, followed by the Slade Professorship at Oxford, too. All this was due recognition of a man who had helped open Britain's eyes to its heritage. He was made a member of numerous councils and commissions of the great and the good and was lauded, applauded and knighted, but it is for one work that he is best loved and will be remembered by future generations of his adopted country: *The Buildings of England*.

The Buildings of England is a monumental series, but is written with an intimacy rare in a work of scholarship. It is an extraordinary catalogue of England's architecture, county by county. Pevsner began the series with an account of the buildings of Cornwall and Nottinghamshire in 1951 and ended with those of Staffordshire in 1974. The first volume cost a mere 3s. 6d (17.5p) as a paperback; the final volume, now a classic, cost £2 in hardback – both the times and the currency had changed in those two decades. Town by town, village by village, Pevsner describes in detail the architectural and artistic features of every ecclesiastical, public and domestic building of interest, together with a summary of each county's architectural history from prehistoric times. It was a veritable 'Cobbett's Rural Ride' through the length and breadth of England in the twentieth century. Pevsner's inspiration for the series was Dehio's five-volume work on the buildings of Germany that he had read while a student at Leipzig. At dinner one evening with Allen Lane of Penguin books (he had recently edited the *Pelican History of Art*) Pevsner was asked what project he would like to undertake, given sufficient funds. Without hesitation, he suggested a commentary on every building of merit in England. With remarkable foresight and courage (the first twelve volumes of the series lost Penguin £36,000) Lane immediately gave him the commission. In later years he would introduce Pevsner as 'my best losing author'.

Pevsner set out on his 80,000-mile epic journey accompanied by his wife Lola, who made the sandwiches before they set off each morning from their pub or cheap hotel and drove the car. The deal he had agreed with Allen Lane sounds quaint today. Pevsner would pay his own expenses and would research and write the books as a salaried employee of Penguin without a share of the royalties. Twice a year, every year, for twenty-three years, he and Lola left London on expeditions planned with military efficiency, using Ordnance Survey maps backed by thorough research at each county library. His energy was boundless, his itinerary remorseless, although always at risk from the hospitality his visits generated. Each day began with an early walk around the town or village before its proportions became obscured by traffic. In one hand he carried his clipboard, in the other a pen, scribbling incessantly as he went from building to building recording thoughts, impressions, observations. Perhaps those English churches denuded of their stained glass and carved medieval rood screens by an earlier cultural revolution reminded him of Goebbels's more recent auto-da-fé. What Pevsner recorded are not only churches, castles and manor houses but disused Lancashire cotton mills and Art Deco cinemas. As a record it is a modern architectural Domesday Book that will never need repeating, only updating. Already many of the buildings that Pevsner recorded in the early years are gone, swept away by the redevelopments of the 1950s and 1960s.

What gives *The Buildings of England* such lasting appeal is the combination of wide European scholarship and Pevsner's dry wit. Pre-theme-park Alton Towers for instance, built by an Earl of Shrewsbury, is compared to a castle of King Ludwig II of Bavaria: 'But whereas Ludwig glorified royalty, the sixteenth earl's intention was to give form to the highest dreams of Catholic Romanticism.' Of St Bartholomew's in Brighton he wrote in 1965, 'The view from Ann Street prepares us for the impact to come. An immensely high wall with nothing to relieve it . . . One enters and there is the nave 135 ft high, i.e. a good deal higher than Westminster Abbey and nearly as high as, say, Palma Cathedral.'

He can describe a small house in a back street as 'a sweet little thing' or a building he dislikes as 'a horror'. Whereas guidebooks in the past had concentrated purely on antiquarian matters, Pevsner conveyed the excitement of discovering an unusual detail or an unexpected treasure. Pevsner in this respect has much in common with his contemporary John Betjeman. Both men delighted in the then unfashionable glories of the Victorian age and conveyed their enthusiasm for the quaint and out of favour to the British public through book and television; a friend once said to Pevsner, 'I saw something perfectly hideous today, Mr Pevsner; you'd love it!' Of the London suburb near his home in Hampstead he was quite dismissive: 'West Hampstead need be visited only by those in search of Victorian churches. The houses and streets require no notice.'

When his wife died Pevsner's friends and relations took her place on the expeditions until the day in 1974 when, 30,000 buildings later, he stood in a field in Staffordshire at the end of his odyssey. The last building he visited was Butterfield's Parsonage at Sheen, where he clicked his ballpen shut for the last time, picked up a conker from the drive as a souvenir and drove away. The saga was done. The refugee Pevsner had presented the British with a gift that could never be equalled – he had revealed to them their own country. As the journalist Simon Jenkins said of him in his obituary, 'No one today who loves English buildings can love them alone. Enter any cathedral or great house, village street or Victorian factory and Pevsner is at your side . . . To him the story of England was in her buildings.'

Perhaps only a foreigner can truly identify the delights and architectural treasures of a town or country, as Ruskin did for Venice or Sir Harold Acton for Naples. The increased awareness of Britain's architectural heritage and the widespread public support for the National Trust and English Heritage can be directly attributable to Pevsner. Today there is hardly a town or village of any size in Britain where a local trust has not been formed to protect some building of interest.

The second great contribution that Pevsner made to British art history was a detailed definition in his Reith Lectures of 1955 of what constitutes the innate 'Englishness' of English art. Significantly his first public lecture in England had been on that very theme, 'English Art: How It Strikes a Foreigner'. Ideas that he had begun to formulate at Dresden and Göttingen were now developed into a sustained theory of the Englishness that can be instinctively recognized in the music of Purcell, Elgar and Vaughan Williams and more elusively in the paintings of Constable, Gainsborough, Stubbs and Samuel Palmer. Pevsner had found that the only existing book on the subject had been written by the Viennese art historian Professor Dagobert Frey and, bizarrely, published in Germany at the heart of the war in 1942. Given the publication date, Pevsner was amused that *Englishes Wesen in der bildenden Kunst* (*The English Character as Reflected in English Art*) is completely free of any hostile remarks, let alone any Nazi bias. He found that it confirmed to an amazing degree his own views, the criteria he had used to work them out and even the examples he had chosen to illustrate his ideas. Pevsner in *The Englishness of English Art* concentrated on Hogarth, Reynolds, Blake and Constable and on Perpendicular architecture and the Picturesque style of landscape gardening. He started by examining the difference that climate, language and landscape have made to the English character, the mists and rain of the British Isles in contrast to the blue skies of southern Europe; what in fact makes the English 'English'. Not surprisingly the characteristics he identified in 1956 are the ones that would appeal to any refugee from an oppressive totalitarian regime in the 1930s:

> personal liberty, freedom of expression, wise compromises, that is, the two-party system not shaken by communism or fascism . . . the distrust of the sweeping statement and the demagogue. Then the eminently civilized faith in honesty and fair play, the patient queuing . . . a strictly upheld inefficiency in the little business-things of everyday life.

Pevsner believed that there is little Baroque art in Britain because it is a largely Protestant country with a natural distaste for religious art and an inclination to understatement and reticence. Furthermore, an Englishman, as Dr Johnson had remarked, would rather see the portrait of a dog than all the allegories in the world. For Pevsner, the subject of the greatest paintings of the British school are man or nature observed, portrait or landscape, as in the work of Constable, Gainsborough, Turner, Romney, Reynolds, Cotman, Frith and the

Pre-Raphaelites. What they had in common was a keen eye for observation that Pevsner can identify in the grotesque little portraits of man and beast that decorate the margins of English manuscripts of the mid-thirteenth century or in the wood carvings of church choir stalls and in the stone boss carvings of the cathedrals and churches. What made their execution specifically English was the vivid representation, the occasional criticism and the humour. This skill with little things was typically English and would lead to the exquisite small watercolours and the miniatures of Nicholas Hilliard and Isaac Oliver, unequalled anywhere in Europe.

As a German, Pevsner was particularly impressed by the Perpendicular-style parish churches of the late Middle Ages and early Tudor period. Uniquely in the Europe of this period, many of their roofs are of wood rather than stone. Characteristically English, too, are the flat-topped church towers, rarely seen on the Continent. When Pevsner considered in 1956 the work of the English portrait painters of the eighteenth century he found his definitive English characteristic: detachment. Reticence and taciturnity have been recognized as characteristics of the English for centuries and, like the people themselves, 'The English portrait also keeps long silences and when it speaks, speaks in a low voice . . . Or to put it differently, the English portrait conceals more than it reveals.'

Landscape and observation are often combined in the outdoor portrait. The temperance and moderation that distinguish the work of Reynolds and Gainsborough and the pure landscapes of Constable, Pevsner attributes to the moderation of both the climate and the landscape of England. He sees the years between 1800 and 1840 as a prodigious flowering of landscape painting unparalleled anywhere else in Europe. A common treatment of landscape by English artists, what he calls 'the atmospheric landscape', is at that time reaching its apotheosis in Turner's phantasmagoric canvases and in the visionary landscapes of William Blake and Samuel Palmer. Uniquely English, too, is the sporting picture genre in which animal painting, even the racing pictures of Stubbs, has a curious stillness at its heart, the stillness of the landscape, the tranquillity of the English garden at its most picturesque. Long winding paths and serpentine lakes echo the long, gentle, double curve that dominates English art from the Decorated style to the work of William Blake and beyond. Even great buildings are subordinate to the landscape. The typical English cathedral is set in its own precinct, turfed, tree-planted and land-scaped. So, too, are the most important houses, such as Buckingham Palace or Windsor Castle, so unlike the metropolitan palaces of Paris, Rome, Berlin, Madrid or Stockholm.

Pevsner ends his definitive survey of English art with a single reservation:

> A decent home, a temperate climate and a moderate nation has its disad-vantages in art. There is no Bach, no Beethoven, no Brahms. There is no Michelangelo, no Titian, no Rembrandt, no Dürer, no Grünewald. There are no vast compositions . . . What English character gained of tolerance and fair play, she lost of that fanaticism or at least that inten-sity which alone can bring forth the very greatest in art.

But it is to the architecture of England that Pevsner returns. For him, more than painting or sculpture, it is the finest expression of English art. The medieval Decorated style is more brilliant than any contemporary European style, Perpendicular is inferior to nothing of its time, and no Gothic building in Europe of the sixteenth century surpasses King's College Chapel and Henry VII's Chapel at Westminster. It is significant that Pevsner, who brought European scholarship to the undiscovered beauties of English vernacular architecture, chose to live in a small cottage on the edge of Hampstead Heath close to the park-land of Kenwood House, where some of the finest English portraits of the seventeenth and eighteenth centuries hang alongside one of Europe's greatest paintings, the Rembrandt self-portrait of 1661.

Pevsner was not the only art historian of international importance that Britain gained from the Nazi persecution. There was Ludwig Münz, an expert on educating blind children, and Ernst Kitzinger, who worked for the British Museum and helped evacuate its treasures to the country. But the most famous was Professor Ernst Gombrich, OM, who became the world's greatest expert on the psychology of percep-tion and the interpretation of images. His three seminal works – *The Story of Art*, *Art and Illusion* and *The Sense of Order* – have never been out of print and have led to a re-evaluation of the mechanics of our understanding of art.

Gombrich was Viennese. Born in 1909, he grew up in a cultured family: his mother, a pupil of Anton Bruckner, knew Mahler and Schoenberg well; his father was a classmate of Hugo von Hofmannsthal, while Adolf Busch of the Busch Quartet was a family friend. But, instead of becoming a musician, Gombrich developed an interest in art fuelled by his early visits to the nearby Kunsthistorisches Museum and graduated in art history from the University of Vienna in 1933. The proximity of Vienna to Italy had made possible regular trips to the great Renaissance cities in the holidays, and to Mantua in particular. His first post was as assistant to Ernst Kris at the Kunsthistorisches Museum, working on 'the application of wit to the visual arts', a project that was aborted when the Nazis came to power. Realizing the danger to Jews, Kris urged him to look for a job abroad.

In 1936 the director of the Warburg Institute, Fritz Saxl, invited Gombrich to join the them in London to research the papers of its founder, Aby Warburg. With the small grant he received from the institute, Gombrich got married and settled in London. At the Warburg with Gombrich were a number of refugee scholars including Ettlinger, Antal, Wind, Munz and Hodin. The Warburg's main concern was research into the *Nachleben* or 'afterlife' of classical antiquity; it was concerned with cultural history in general rather than the more specialized history of art as studied at the Courtauld. Gombrich began lecturing at both institutions until war broke out. As the threat of German bombing increased, the staff of the Warburg Institute were evacuated to the country, but Gombrich decided to stay on in London as a radio monitor, translating enemy broadcasts from German into English. Not only did his work at the BBC prove an invaluable way to learn his new language; it also provoked in him a lifelong interest in the problems of perception.

During the war Gombrich began researching what was to be his *magnum opus*, *The Story of Art*, the most successful history of art written during the twentieth century. Never out of print since its initial publication in 1950, it has been translated into at least eighteen languages. While still in Vienna, Gombrich had agreed to produce a child's history of art for a Viennese publisher, but the Anschluss put an end to the project. Now in the doldrums following the end of the war and before returning to his academic career, Gombrich accepted an invitation from Dr Horovitz, the founder of the Phaidon Press and a fellow refugee from Vienna, to write a general history of art.

Gombrich went at it with a will, engaging a typist and dictating to her three times a week at considerable speed. Within a few months the book was completed and appeared to both critical and public acclaim. For that publication alone Gombrich can be ranked as the most widely read art historian of the century.

The Warburg, however, was dismayed at Gombrich's popular success. Saxl, the Director, told him to return to research and concentrate on 'proper work'. Gombrich had been able to write the book at high speed almost entirely from memory without consulting reference works. This almost casual approach gave the book its appealing, narrative form. He confessed later to using only illustrations he had to hand, many taken from an old copy of the *Propyläen Kunstgeschichte* encyclopaedia. Gombrich himself attributed the book's freshness to this off-the-cuff method and to his intention that it would not be seen as a textbook.

The rewards were immediate. Tom Boase, the Director of the Courtauld Institute, reviewed it enthusiastically for the *Times Literary Supplement* and then proposed Gombrich as Slade Professor of Fine Arts at Oxford. Duly elected and to great acclaim, Gombrich began lecturing on a variety of topics. At the podium where Ruskin had stood now stood the refugee Gombrich, a world figure in art history with three separate careers to be pursued, as the best-selling author of *The Story of Art,* as a leading scholar of the Italian Renaissance and as one of the leaders in the developing study of the psychology of pictorial representation. Like Pevsner, Gombrich was later elected Slade Professor at Cambridge. He became Director of the Warburg Institute in 1959 and Professor of the History of the Classical Tradition at London University until his retirement in 1976.

Through the mediation of Sir Kenneth Clarke, Gombrich was now invited to give the Mellon Lectures in Washington, and he chose as his subject 'Art and Illusion'. Never having seen himself purely as an art historian, he now explored the basic mechanics of how we actually see art. Gombrich had begun seeking a scientific explanation for what he calls the phenomenon of style not only in art galleries but also in the psychology libraries. As he told an audience at Rutgers University, New Jersey, in 1987:

> The idea that style is simply the expression of an age seemed to me not only to say very little but to be rather vacuous in every respect. I wanted

to know what actually is going on when somebody draws a tree in a particular way, in a particular tradition and in a particular style.

These lectures became the basis for his second book, *Art and Illusion*, in which he applied the recent discoveries in the psychology of perception, linguistics and information theory to the study of imagery. It was a seminal work, its importance recognized by the eminent American psychologist J.J. Gibson: 'The student of perception is tempted to limit his research to what he can experimentally control by methods he has been taught. This book will widen his horizon and stimulate his ambition' (Gibson, 1966).

Gombrich, having tackled representation and perception, now examined form and decoration in his third book, *The Sense of Order*. He saw himself as a commentator on the development of the history of art, having at its centre representation, with symbolism on one side and decoration on the other. What was new about Gombrich's approach was that he saw himself not as the traditional art connoisseur but as a seeker after a scientific explanation of the changing function of the visual image.

The largest contingent of refugee art historians from Nazi Europe were to find themselves in the USA, where the policy of granting visas to academics offered a security that would have been impossible in Britain. Over 130 lecturers and experts settled in America, the best-known being Paul Frankl from Halle and Erwin Panofsky from Hamburg. They were joined later by Max Dvorak, August Schmarsow, Karl Lehmann and Josef Strzygowski of the Vienna School, bringing an unrivalled knowledge of specific European schools of painting with them. Two of the scholars, Hugo Buchthal and Edgar Wind, had first established themselves in London before moving on to America, where Buchthal taught Byzantine studies at the Institute of Fine Arts in New York and Wind went to Smith College before before returning to Britain in 1955 to become Oxford University's first ever Professor of the History of Art.

The most famous of them all, Erwin Panofsky, had lectured in the USA in the early 1930s and was in New York in spring 1933 when news came, in a Western Union cable bearing Easter greetings, of his dismissal from Hamburg University. But within two years Panofsky was back at the top of his profession as a professor at the highly influ-

ential Institute for Advanced Study in Princeton. All of them benefited from the relative wealth of the American academic system and
from the many organizations that were prepared to subsidize their
salaries in the early years. The great majority of the émigré art historians settled in the eastern states, but the prestigious Ivy League
institutions offered them surprisingly little help other than occasional
invitations to lecture. It was not until 1950 that Princeton University
belatedly awarded a full professorship to Kurt Weitzmann and
Harvard appointed Jakob Rosenberg to the Fogg Art Museum. No
refugee art historians were appointed by Yale, Pennsylvania or Brown,
adding to the widely held suspicion that these institutions employed
a discreet policy of anti-Semitism. But the more youthful Institute of
Fine Arts in New York continued its policy of employing visiting
professors from Europe, including Erwin Panofsky, who was instrumental in attracting Walter Friedlaender. In all, the Institute of Fine
Arts employed more than ten exiled art historians, who were largely
responsible for its becoming the most outstanding centre for the study
of European art in America in the 1940s. Predictably there were
attacks on the institute by the more chauvinistic elements of the
American press, who thought it in danger of being swamped by
'Teutonic' influences. Only one other organization, the Institute for
Advanced Study at Princeton, offered so much support to the émigré
scholars.

One of the most important contributions the refugees made was
the broadening of the American academic curriculum. To the traditional subjects of 'antiquity', the Middle Ages and the Renaissance
they now added Mannerism, Early Christian, Late Gothic and
Baroque art. Lecture programmes became more specific to individual artists rather than to schools of painting. But the newcomers found
themselves in an academic tradition different from that they had
known in Europe. The American system placed the responsibility for
success on the teacher rather than on student, and the examination
system was more important than the research-based German tradition.
Where American universities passed on authenticated knowledge, the
German institutions had been more concerned with instilling method-
ological skills. As Richard Krautheimer noted, 'We were used to
graduates of a German Gymnasium [who had] a knowledge of the
monuments gained *in situ*, of the geographical situation, of European

history, and of languages.' Their American students had little of this, but in time the émigrés themselves realized the benefits of this less rigorous system, and both Panofsky's and Krautheimer's later works are more relaxed and more accessible – and by and large dispense with that characteristic of German art histories: reams of turgid footnotes.

11

Pure and Perverted Science

Perhaps the most inexplicable of all Hitler's arbitrary decisions was his determination to rid German science of the Jews in 1933. It is even possible that it cost him the war, for if he had retained his Jewish-born physicists Germany might have developed an atomic weapon before the Allies. But at a time when the German economy desperately needed new scientific research and Hitler's plans for national expansion depended upon a revitalized arms industry, scientists with Jewish blood were summarily dismissed from their posts. The provisions of the Restoration of the Professional Civil Service Act were applied as ruthlessly to the humblest botanist as they were to Germany's most distinguished Jewish physicists.

The writing had been, literally, on the wall for the scientists of Freibourg University soon after Hitler's election to power, when the Nazi students' union put up a poster stating, 'Our most dangerous adversary is the Jew and he who serves him. The Jew can think only as a Jew. If he writes German he lies.' When the rector ordered the posters removed, he was dismissed by the Nazi Minister for Education and his place given to his colleague, the existentialist philosopher Martin Heidegger, a convert to the new regime who told the students to forget the past and put their trust in Adolf Hitler.

So great was the exodus of Jewish scientists from key academic posts under the Restoration of the Professional Civil Service Act that

Germany's most eminent physicist, Max Planck, President of the Kaiser Wilhelm Institute, alarmed at the loss to German science, pleaded with Hitler to reconsider the dismissals. Hitler bluntly replied, 'Our national policy must not be altered . . . even if the loss of Jewish scientists means the end of German science for a few years we must just do without it.' Most dismissed scientists left quietly; others, such as the Nobel laureate James Franck, protested vociferously but found little support from his faculty members. When Franck published an open letter complaining that he and the other Jews were being treated like criminals, forty-two of his Aryan colleagues at Göttingen University responded with a petition branding his letter an act of sabotage and demanding that the dismissals be speeded up. Even outstanding researchers like Hans Krebs, whose paper on the synthesis of urea in the animal body was regarded as one of the classics of medical research, were dismissed. Out, too, to his chagrin, went the chemist Fritz Haber, the most famous scientist in Germany and the first man to synthesize ammonia from the nitrogen in the air.

Before the arrival of Hitler, Haber had never found difficulty in reconciling loyalty to Germany with his Jewishness. His record was exemplary. He had won the Nobel Prize for Chemistry in 1918, with his discovery of the process that enabled artificial nitrogen to be produced, which led in turn to the production of low-cost nitrogen fertilizer. A breakthrough in the battle against world hunger, Haber's discovery had other implications. Germany, cut off from natural salt-petre supplies, was now able to make the explosives without which it would have had to sue for peace early in the First World War. But Haber had more to offer Germany in the field of what Churchill later called 'perverted science'. As the war became bogged down in the trenches, Haber perfected a simple delivery system for poison gas by blowing it from cylinders towards the enemy. His colleagues in the project included James Franck and another future Nobel laureate Gustav Hertz, but Max Born (another laureate who later emigrated to Britain), to his credit, refused to take part. The first battlefield use of chlorine caused 15,000 Allied casualties, 5,000 of them fatal. A few days later Haber's wife Clara, appalled at what he had done, shot herself with his service pistol. When war ended, Haber continued experimenting with poison gas for pesticides, eventually producing, ironically, Zyklon B, the gas that would later be used to exterminate his fellow Jews in the concentration camps. A Prussian in appearance, a Nazi in attitude, Haber's past services to the state counted for nothing in 1933. As he lamented in a letter to Chaim Weizmann that year:

> I have been German to a degree which I feel fully only now. I was more than a great leader of armies, more than a captain of industry. I was the founder of great industries. My work opened the way to the great industrial and military expansion of Germany. All doors stood open to me

As with other scientists, Max Planck pleaded with Hitler on behalf of Haber, but the Führer was obdurate while assuring Planck that he had nothing personal against the Jews. Although Planck had opposed the dismissals, he considered himself a loyal German and was appalled by Einstein's decision to remain in exile and to condemn the Fatherland from abroad. Einstein, he declared, must be thrown out of the Academy immediately. When Planck put the motion for dismissal to his fellow members, all, including Haber, voted with him, with the single honourable exception of the physicist and future Nobel laureate Max von Laue. But fate had not finished with Fritz Haber – within a few months of the vote he suffered the humiliation of having to flee Germany and take refuge in Switzerland. The eminent scientist Max Perutz, who settled in Britain, has speculated that without Haber's synthesis of ammonia Germany would soon have run out of explosives in 1915 – the war would have ended, millions would not have been slaughtered, Lenin might never have got to Russia, Hitler might not have come to power, the Holocaust might not have happened and European civilization might have been spared the horrors of the Second World War.

The internationalism of science meant that the dismissed German academics and researchers were better equipped to find work abroad than their fellow refugees in the arts. Of the twelve hundred Jewish scientists who went into exile, over half decided to emigrate to either Britain or the USA. Those who went to the USA readily found places at the well-funded colleges and universities. The physicists, in particular, found a flourishing environment for their skills, particularly in the wartime Manhattan Project and in the development of microwave radar technology at the Massachusetts Institute of Technology's radiation laboratory. In Britain the scientific establishment, even with its more limited resources, responded immediately by providing over two hundred teaching and research posts. A Society for the Protection of Science and Learning was formed and publicized its activities with a mass meeting at the Albert Hall in London addressed by Lord Rutherford, Albert Einstein and Professor Lindemann, later to become Churchill's chief scientific adviser. Every university in Britain was approached by the society and posts were found at London University for such eminent refugees as Dr Nicholas Kürti and Professor Francis Simon, while Oxford found places for Kurt Mendelssohn and Heinrich Kuhn. Many of these newcomers not only contributed to the advancement of science and learning in Britain but, in the short term, became involved in developing the country's scientific warfare capability.

Among them was Max Perutz, who was involved in an astonishing, and today barely credible, project to make aircraft carriers out of icebergs. An expert on the structure of proteins, Perutz, when released from internment in Canada, was summoned to the Albany in London by the extraordinary Geoffrey Pyke. This amateur inventor and self-appointed scientific adviser to the military told Perutz about his top-secret Habakkuk project. He had been attracted to Perutz by his earlier work on the structure of snowflakes and thought him the right man to perfect the technology that would enable the Allies to establish huge floating airfields made of ice in the mid-Atlantic. To his amazement Perutz was given his own secret laboratory beneath London's Smithfield Meat Market. Here his experiments proved that natural ice combined with wood pulp produced a material that was, weight for weight, as strong as concrete. When demonstrating the strength of this new material to a group of army commanders, one of Perutz's junior colleagues fired a revolver into it the block of ice. So strong was this new 'pykrete', as it became known, that the bullet ricocheted and hit Britain's Chief of the Imperial General Staff in the shoulder, luckily without wounding him.

The Habakkuk project was intended to give air cover to transport planes and shipping in the mid-Atlantic and to handle the bombers that were too large to land on conventional aircraft carriers. With these vast ice airfields in place, planes could be flown across the Atlantic and refuelled half-way rather than having to be shipped across. If Habakkuk worked, Pyke argued, similar floating bases could be used by the Americans in the mid-Pacific to launch the future invasion of Japan.

Nor would large amounts of steel and other costly materials be needed, the basic icebergs already existed and the runway surfaces of pykrete were cheap to make. Floating airfields of ice would be slow to melt and almost impossible to sink by bombing. Churchill, always looking for new ways to fight the war, was enthusiastic when told about the project and gave it his immediate approval. As he told General Ismay in a letter in early 1942, 'I attach the greatest importance to the prompt examination of these ideas . . . The advantages of a floating island or islands, even if only used as refuelling depots for aircraft, are so dazzling that they do not at the moment need to be discussed.'

These floating airfields would have been colossal objects; over fifty feet high, two hundred feet wide, two thousand feet long and able to take the heaviest bombers. Their range was seven thousand miles and their weight over two million tons. These 'bergships', as they were called, would be twenty-six times larger than the world's largest ship, the *Queen Elizabeth*. Geoffrey Pyke saw other uses for them, too. They could be driven into enemy harbours, where the defending troops would be frozen solid by supercooled water sprayed on them from the vast tanks on the bergship. This supercooled water could then be sprayed ashore to form ice walls behind which the advancing Allied troops could safely assemble. Perutz in his memoirs brings Pyke's amazing science fiction down to earth by pointing out that it would have been impossible at the time to have produced even a thimbleful of supercooled water. But such was the desperation of the time that the war leaders were prepared to back even the wildest schemes. So Perutz was hurriedly made a British citizen and sent back to Canada to start the assembly of the bergships. But it all came to nothing when the main supporter of the project, Lord Mountbatten, was made Allied Commander in South-East Asia. Without Mountbatten's support the project was postponed and then abandoned, partly Perutz believes, because of the enormous amount of steel needed to make the refrigeration plant to freeze the pykrete but more likely because of the increasing range of aircraft made such mid-ocean refuelling unnecessary. Perutz returned to Cambridge and continued his distinguished career, disappointed that he had failed in his war effort but consoled by the fact that no one had died as a result of his actions.

Perutz, like most of the 250 leading scientists who took refuge in Britain in the 1930s, stayed on after the war. No fewer than fifty-three of them were awarded fellowships of the Royal Society. Twelve of their number became Nobel laureates, among them Max Perutz, who was awarded the prize for his work on the structure of haemoglobin before going on to help found the Medical Research Council Unit for Molecular Biology at Cambridge. Max Born, a colleague of James Franck's at Göttingen, worked with him to develop the fundamental principles of quantum physics that were to help explain the structure of matter. His Nobel Prize was awarded for his statistical formulation of the behaviour of subatomic particles. Another émigré, Rudolf Peierls, laid the theoretical foundations for the creation of the first atomic bomb along with Otto Frisch.

The contribution of these refugees was particularly impressive in biology and medicine. Not only did Ernst Chain play a fundamental role in the development of penicillin but Bernard Katz's work on the functioning of nerves and muscles won him the 1970 Nobel Prize for Physiology. In British medicine the name of the neurologist Ludwig Guttmann became synonymous with the advanced treatment of spinal injuries that he pioneered at Stoke Mandeville Hospital. Based on Guttmann's experience of treating paraplegics in Germany, the Stoke Mandeville unit rapidly became the country's leading centre for orthopaedic injuries. Hans Krebs, the first refugee from Europe to be appointed to a university chair in Britain, won the Nobel Prize for the discovery of living organisms in the citric acid cycle, which was named the Krebs cycle in his honour. For nearly fifty years he was at the forefront of the intermediary metabolism field of biochemistry. Krebs became thoroughly British in his loyalties and when describing his affection for his adopted land quoted Carl Zuckmayer's saying that home is not where a man is born but where he wants to die. A scientist of almost Prussian rectitude he was, none the less, impressed by the efficient nonchalance of his British colleagues. 'This convinced me again that free coming and going is more conducive to dedicated research than the iron discipline of old Berlin,' he wrote. Unlike Albert Einstein, who refused ever to visit Germany again, Krebs thought being anti-German was almost as bad as being anti-Semitic, and he was instrumental in the re-establishment of contact with German scientists after the war.

But no refugee scientist made a greater contribution to his adopted country than Ernst Chain with his pioneering research in antibiotics.

Alexander Fleming had first discovered its existence in 1929, then Howard Florey demonstrated its therapeutic powers a decade later, but Chain was to develop it as the world's first antibiotic. A short man with a leonine mane of hair and a volatile temperament, Chain arrived in London with just £10 in his pocket. 'I left Germany', he wrote in his memoirs, 'because I felt disgusted with the Nazi gang, not because I thought my life was in danger.' Chain's appearance and manners were those of a mid-European Jew, and he sensed that they provoked an innate anti-Semitism among his new British colleagues. The Academic Assistance Council had secured him a position at Cambridge, but, unlike Krebs, he found the studied informality of British academic life hard to adapt to after the rigours of a German university. But what shocked Chain more was the lack of contact in Britain between industry and the universities. It was his ability to appreciate the needs of the biochemical industry that was to prove so valuable in the commercial development of penicillin. Unlike many of his British colleagues, Chain was able to move easily between the worlds of commerce and academic research. What also shocked him was the poor quality of the equipment that he found in British laboratories. As Lord Rutherford had told him, 'We haven't much money so we've got to use our brains.'

His first encounter with penicillin was at the School of Pathology in Oxford, where he went to work under Howard Florey. For centuries primitive societies had used moulds to treat wounds and cure disease, but not until 1877 did Pasteur and Joubert scientifically assess their antibiotic properties. Fifty years later Alexander Fleming made his famous discovery that micro-organisms from the air could kill off a mass of staphylococcus growing in a Petri dish. Fleming himself was amazed at the result and in the next few weeks regrew the contaminating mould that had supposedly arrived through an open window but had more likely floated up from a laboratory below. Fleming's mould continued to kill off staphylococci even when diluted 800 times, but the difficulty of using penicillin for dressing septic wounds, he wrote, was the amount of trouble involved in its preparation and the difficulty of maintaining its potency for more than a few weeks. This was the problem that Ernst Chain was to solve and for which he won the Nobel Prize for Medicine. But first he had to overcome the British prejudice that chemotherapy should take second place to immunology. As Chain later put it, 'I believe it to be a particularly striking example of how prejudice in scientific thinking can interfere with progress.' After reading Fleming's paper, Chain began his own researches, 'not because I hoped to discover a miraculous drug for the treatment of bacterial infection . . . but because I thought it had great scientific interest'. What also prompted Chain's research was the urgent need to replenish his department's finances. Chain was convinced that by using a freeze-drying process similar to the one recently introduced for drying blood serum, penicillin could be stabilized. By adding a solvent to the resulting brown powder Chain found the process worked perfectly. But a dispute over the next stage of the research led to it being assigned to another scientist. Chain claims that his protests were muted because of his fear that he would provoke more anti-Semitism by which the Jewish community as a whole might suffer.

From the day in May 1940 when it was first used successfully on infected mice, penicillin became a potential life-saver. Chain's paper on the research published that August provoked a visit from Alexander Fleming himself. Both the head of the Medical Research Council and the President of the Royal Society believed it unethical to patent the drug and so restrict its use. Chain disagreed and his case was later proved when Britain had to pay the USA millions of dollars for using its derivatives under licence. This was for Chain yet another example of British academics not wanting to get their hands dirty with industry. Britain, he believed, was giving away a golden opportunity: 'I saw a whole tremendous virgin field and we were the leaders and would remain so if we got enough money.' To Chain it was just as unethical not to take out patents that would protect the British people against exploitation by foreign commercial interests. The broader ethical issue was: should the British government release the basic data about this life-saving drug to the world? With the war at a critical stage, it was decided to keep it from the enemy, but CIBA in Switzerland had already begun developing it themselves, and it was not long before the information was in the hands of the Germans, who, it was reported, had sent details of it by submarine to the Japanese.

Penicillin in bulk was now urgently needed to treat the mounting war casualties, so it was decided to send a British research team to liaise with the Americans. To his chagrin, Chain arrived at the laboratory one morning to be told peremptorily that he was not included. Chain wrote, 'I left the room silently but shattered by the experience of this underhand trick and act of bad faith.' Chain was sent to Moscow instead, with orders to give the Russian allies full details on the development of penicillin. By 1944 it could be produced in bulk and saved thousands of lives when first used in the American landings at Salerno in Italy. Yet it still could not be made by a synthetic process until Chain discovered the molecular structure and it became possible to manufacture cheap, reliable penicillin. When the Nobel Prize for work on penicillin was finally awarded it was given jointly to Ernst Chain, Alexander Fleming and Howard Florey. Personally Chain was satisfied, but he was concerned that Britain would not get the huge financial benefits warranted by its crucial role in the discovery. Chain's proposal was that the government should finance a British antibiotics industry beginning with a national biochemical and pharmaceutical research centre. Starting with penicillin, the state should develop and commercially produce a whole range of the new antibiotics. It was an original proposal at a time when the new Health Act meant that the state had to supply drugs free to the public. Why not, argued Chain, subsidize the cost by producing and selling British drugs abroad and at the same time cut out the huge profits made by the international pharmaceutical companies? With his unique grasp of chemical engineering and his experience of commerce, Chain would have made an ideal head of such an operation. But even for a Labour government with a large majority it was too radical a proposal. Perhaps as a reaction to Britain's lack of interest in his proposals, he accepted an offer to establish the first international centre for research into antibiotics in Rome, where he spent the next fifteen years and in the late 1950s developed the 'tailor-made' penicillins that were further to transform medicine's fight against bacteria.

In 1964 Chain returned to London as head of a new Biochemistry Department at Imperial College. For all his success and recognition in Italy he retained a strong emotional attachment to Britain that had given him refuge in 1933. He was given awards and honours by universities and institutions throughout the world, and in 1969 this most non-English Briton was knighted. Yet he remained a true individualist who enjoyed rocking establishment boats. As he told an American seminar on the purpose of science in 1977:

> No valid conclusion regarding scientific theories can ever be drawn by
> a majority rule. Who tells you that the majority decision is the right one

and the minority decision the wrong one? Usually the opposite is the case. Newtonian physics were overthrown by a very small number of modern physicists including Max Planck and Albert Einstein. Biology is so complex and diverse a subject that we have as yet nothing like an all-embracing theory explaining life in its infinitely large manifestations.

Chain's achievement was to influence the role of government in medical research and to help bring industry and the universities closer together. Perhaps it was only his bluntness and impatience with bureaucracy that prevented him from achieving even more.

Chain was a great loss to German biochemistry, but his departure in 1933 was nowhere near as catastrophic as the loss of the Jewish physicists who had led the world in nuclear research in the 1920s. Many were Jews, among them Lise Meitner and her nephew Otto Robert Frisch. Both had worked with Niels Bohr in Copenhagen, Frisch in quantifying the force produced when uranium is irradiated by neutrons. Meitner and Frisch, in fact, gave the world a new name for this phenomenon: nuclear fission. Both realized the implications of their research: that the enormous amount of energy released could produce an atomic explosion. Fortunately they kept this information to a restricted circle of fellow physicists. When Frisch was expelled from his post in 1933, he travelled to Britain, where he began working with another refugee Rudolf Peierls. In March 1940 Frisch made a vital calculation that just one kilogram of uranium 235 would be needed to make an atomic bomb that could destroy a whole city. Unknown to them, another refugee scientist in their research group named Klaus Fuchs was already passing information, including the Peierls–Frisch memorandum, to the Soviet Embassy in London.

In America another exile was also working on key areas of nuclear reaction. Leo Szilard was a product of the Hungarian Jewish intelligentsia that was to contribute so many brilliant immigrants to America. As a young man he had been so captivated by Albert Einstein's seminars at theKaiser Wilhelm Institute that he switched from mathematics to physics. While still a student he developed the patents for an ingenious electromagnetic pump using fluid metals – later used in the Manhattan Project – and for an early form of linear particle accelerators. When Hitler came to power Szilard was one of the first scientists to leave Germany, even before the Restoration of the

Professional Civil Service Act in March 1933. Szilard went first to Vienna, where he became involved in the work of the British Academic Assistance Council, before moving to a research post at Oxford. A year later, Szilard produced another patent involving uranium fission, which he realized had important military implications. Concerned that it might fall into enemy hands, he assigned it to the Admiralty in London. Szilard's discovery was over four years ahead of that of Otto Hahn and Fritz Strassmann, who had remained in Germany working for the Nazis.

In 1938, while on a research trip to the USA, Szilard heard that Britain had signed the Munich Pact with Hitler and decided not to return, writing to Professor Lindemann at Oxford that October, 'Those who wish to dedicate their work to the advancement of science would be well advised to move to America where they may hope for another ten or fifteen years of undisturbed work.'

Szilard was now haunted by the fear that the remaining German physicists would perfect the technology needed to make an atomic bomb. Then, in 1939, Szilard's fears were justified by the news that Germany had formed the world's first military nuclear fission research unit. What Germany lacked, however, was a supply of uranium, which Szilard suspected it would get by seizing Belgium's uranium mines in the Congo. In a joint letter with Albert Einstein, he wrote immediately to warn the King of the Belgians of their suspicions. A copy was also sent to President Roosevelt. In it Szilard warned about the implications of nuclear fission and that 'this new phenomenon could also lead to the construction of extremely powerful bombs of a new type'. He urged the President to appoint a nuclear supremo to monitor the physicists and to secure as many of the world's uranium sources as possible. Above all, funds should be made immediately available to investigate the catastrophic implications of a chain reaction.

Roosevelt did not hesitate: he appointed one of his scientific advisers, Lyman J. Briggs, as chairman of a study group that included Szilard and the eminent physicist Edward Teller. Szilard's role was to report on the research needed to set off a chain reaction in uranium and to ascertain where in the world suitable supplies of graphite and uranium could be found. Szilard also appealed to the great Italian physicist Enrico Fermi for help. Within six months the research group had established that the carbon atoms in graphite slowed neutrons emitted by uranium fission without absorbing them. These neutrons would then, in turn, induce more fission in other uranium atoms. It was a chain reaction made possible by using pure graphite, and also the key to making a successful atomic bomb. Luckily Szilard dissuaded Fermi from publishing the data and in doing so, as Max Perutz wrote later, could well have saved the world from nuclear destruction. Ironically, the Germans attempted the same experiment but used impure graphite and so failed to produce a chain reaction. Not realizing how close to success they had been, the German physicists decided in 1940 to use heavy water instead (that is, water in which hydrogen is replaced by its heavier isotope, deuterium).

Future generations would owe much to Leo Szilard. Not only did he warn the politicians about the dangers of nuclear fission but he also managed to persuade the scientists involved to keep silent about their discovery. But by this very silence, now enforced by Roosevelt's Defense Research Committee, an astute young Russian physicist on leave from the Red Army and finding no recent American publication on nuclear research in his university library, realized that an American atomic bomb must be imminent. His warning letter to Stalin convinced the Russian leader that he could not afford to let the USA, in the light of the deteriorating political situation, gain an unchallenged superiority in nuclear weapons over the Soviet Union. Stalin ordered work to commence immediately on a Russian atomic bomb, and so the nuclear arms race began. Szilard, given his past services, could have expected to play an important role in what had now become the Manhattan Project, but he found himself marginalized as an ideas man rather than being involved in the heart of the project. The reason was that his eccentricities had irritated General Leslie R. Groves, the Commander-in-Chief of the Manhattan Project. A series of rows between them culminated in Groves persuading the Secretary of State for War to request that Szilard be dismissed and interned as an enemy alien. When the Attorney General refused to take action against a man who had proved both his loyalty and his worth to the USA, Groves personally ordered the FBI to investigate Szilard. None of this stopped Szilard writing a prophetic warning to President Roosevelt in March 1945:

Our 'demonstration' of atomic bombs will precipitate a race in the production of these devices between the United States and Russia . . .

after this war it is conceivable that it will become possible to drop atomic bombs on the cities of the United States from very great distances by means of rockets.

In 1945, however, all that mattered to Britain and the USA was the defeat of Germany and Japan in the shortest possible time and with minimal Allied casualties. In Britain, Robert Otto Frisch and Rudolf Peierls were playing a vital role in the British contribution to the final development of the atomic weapon. Together they had investigated the possibilities of using uranium 238 to create an explosive chain reaction. Initially it was assumed that tons of uranium would be needed, but they were astonished to find that it required only a few pounds. With Frisch's separation system, a pound of reasonably pure uranium 238 could be produced in two weeks. It was at that point, recalls Frisch, that they stared at each other realizing that they had the raw materials for an atomic bomb. When Frisch and Peierls reported their findings to Henry Tizard, the government adviser on scientific warfare, the British government decided to back the production of an atomic bomb without further delay. Most of the scientists now assigned to developing a British nuclear capability were the very physicists dispossessed by the Nazis in 1933; British-born physicists were already fully involved in other vital projects, such as the development of radar. To oversee the work, a committee under Sir George Thomson was formed, known from the start by its members as the 'Maud Committee'. It got its nickname from an enigmatic telegram sent to it from Niels Bohr in Denmark that ended 'AND TELL MAUD RAY KENT'. Convinced that these words were a warning in code or at least an anagram, the committee spent hours trying to rearrange the letters in different ways and coming up with such solutions as 'Radium taken' or 'U and D may react', suggesting that a chain reaction could be caused by combining uranium with heavy water. Not until after the war did they discover that Maud Ray was a real person who used to be a governess in Bohr's house and who now lived in Kent.

Even though Peierls and Frisch were vital to the work of the committee they were, as enemy aliens, technically disbarred from taking part in discussions. It was a ludicrous situation finally resolved by a bureaucratic manoeuvre that established a subcommittee in which the two physicists could participate to discuss the actual technology but not the political implications. Frisch was even more amazed by the almost total lack of security that surrounded the project. There were no guards on any of the offices or laboratories assigned to the physicists or even locked safes in which to store their research data. Students ambled about the laboratories, and Joseph Rotblat, a member of the committee, even talked openly about nuclear fission and chain reactions in his lectures to students. With hindsight, Frisch felt that this very openness was probably their best security and that no outsider had the slightest suspicion about the true nature of their work. Frisch and Peierls were joined in their project by yet another émigré scientist, Franz – later Sir Francis – Simon who, together with Peierls, devised a method of separating uranium isotopes, later used at Los Alamos.

It was now time to combine the Allied resources. The place chosen was Los Alamos in the remote New Mexican desert. From the start, the US government had realized the historic significance of the project, and, along with the many chemists, physicists and engineers, they had provided an artist and a philosopher. At Los Alamos were gathered some of the finest scientific minds of the age, pioneering a new technology and working with dangerous and volatile materials. The first victim of atomic energy was a scientist who broke the rule of not working alone and knocked over some uranium. Within two weeks he was dead. Frisch, who had now joined the team at Los Alamos, narrowly escaped death himself when an assistant switched off a warning device that monitored radiation. The main problem that the team had to solve was how to control a chain reaction from uranium 238 by using a 'moderator'. Heavy water had been shown to work, the route taken by the Nazi physicists, but Fermi chose carbon graphite as a moderator instead. After many tons of pure graphite had been tested, on 2 December 1942 in a squash court beneath the Stagg Field football ground in Chicago, the world's first nuclear chain reaction was achieved. The order was given to make the bomb and large amounts of uranium and graphite were used to produce the kilograms of fission material needed.

The urgency with which the British and American physicists had worked was borne out of the firm belief that Hitler's physicists were close to producing their own bomb. Throughout the war the British intelligence service attempted to monitor the German situation but found no evidence of any large-scale work on any aspect of atomic weapons. Just to make sure, the US Air Force successfully bombed the Kaiser Wilhelm Institute in Berlin and Otto Hahn's Institute for Chemistry but narrowly missed Werner Heisenberg's Institute for Physics. Heisenberg, if anyone, was thought to hold the key to German nuclear research. An American Office of Strategic Services agent had, in November 1942, been sent to Zurich, where Heisenberg was giving a lecture, with orders to kill him if he suspected that Heisenberg was making an atomic bomb. Hearing nothing of any consequence in the lecture, the agent engaged him in conversation and walked back to Heisenberg's hotel with him. The loaded gun remained in his pocket. Only when the war ended did the Allies discover that the German scientists had been unable to create a nuclear chain reaction in a uranium pile and were ignorant of the critical mass needed to make an atomic bomb. All this was revealed in the Farm Hall Transcripts, a series of recorded conversations with the key German physicists captured by US intelligence agents just as the European war ended. Flown in secret to Britain, they were interrogated for a month at an isolated farmhouse in Cambridgeshire. What they revealed proved that, even in 1945, the Germans lacked the understanding of nuclear fission that the British had had four years earlier. When told that the USA had dropped the bomb on Hiroshima they were incredulous. Heisenberg, their leader, then revealed the truth about the German atomic capability. He said to the interrogators that year, 'I was absolutely convinced of the possibility of our making a uranium engine [reactor] but I never thought that we could make a bomb and at the bottom of my heart I was really glad that it was an engine and not a bomb' (Frank, 1993).

Their reliance on heavy water as a moderator meant that they had taken the wrong route from the start. But the underlying reason for the German failure to develop atomic weapons was, they claimed, the nature of the Nazi regime itself. In spite of Hitler's declaration of a thousand-year Reich, Nazi policy in defence procurement relied exclusively on short-term solutions. Developing an atomic weapon would have taken time and money, and the German physicists, particularly Hahn and Heisenberg, claimed that if they had failed to produce results quickly enough their lives and those of their families would be forfeit. They also claimed that there was a second reason for their reluctance to promote an atomic bomb: as scientists they had an ethical responsibility to mankind. They knew that if Hitler had an atomic weapon in his arsenal he would use it ruthlessly and without any considerations for humanity. In the end, Heisenberg insisted, it was the German physicists themselves rather than the Nazi regime who decided that Germany should not have the bomb. But Heisenberg has proved to be as morally ambiguous as Albert Speer. His colleague Carl-Freidrich von Weizsacker later revealed that Heisenberg had told him in 1939 that they must make the bomb or Hitler would lose the war and much of Germany would be destroyed. Scientific opinion now agrees that the main reason the German physicists did not develop the bomb was neither their moral scruples nor the lack of heavy water, nor even the priority of short-term solutions, but Heisenberg's vital miscalculation in believing that huge amounts of uranium would be needed to make it. Ominously, the last experiment undertaken by the the Nazi physicists in late 1944 involved the use of graphite rather than heavy water, and showed a spectacular improvement in their neutron yield.

A strange footnote to the story is Klaus Fuchs, yet another refugee who had joined the German Communist Party shortly before Hitler came to power. As a refugee in Britain he was first interned, then sent to confinement in Canada, then recruited to work on the atomic bomb project at Birmingham University and later at Los Alamos. When the war ended he was given a senior post at the newly established British Atomic Energy Research Establishment at Harwell. Fuchs was a hard and enthusiastic worker and known for his particular concern for security. Then, in the summer of 1949, just before the explosion of the first Russian atomic bomb, the FBI discovered that a British scientist was passing atomic secrets to the Russians. After a long interrogation, Fuchs broke down and confessed that he had told the Russians everything he knew, including the design of the first plutonium bomb. Fuchs had acted according to his conscience, as had Leo Szilard when he became one of the first leading physicists to call for international controls on atomic weapons. Even as the USA had prepared to drop the first bomb on Hiroshima, Szilard had pleaded with President Truman to delay its use. Now it became his obsession; his mission was, he said in a television interview in 1961, to help remove the nuclear threat that he had helped to create. The first step he believed – again he was one of the first to suggest it – was to halt the spread of nuclear weapons. He vigorously condemned the US government's decision to publish the Smyth Report in 1945, which contained, Szilard believed, enough scientific information to allow other nations to build an atomic bomb. A year later he formed the Emergency Committee of Atomic Scientists, with the full support of Albert Einstein, to encourage scientists to make the public aware of the potential dangers of uncontrolled nuclear proliferation. When the anti-communist witch hunt began in the late 1940s, Szilard, recalling what had happened under the Nazis, urged American academics to donate a 1 per cent cut in their salaries to a fund to support their dismissed colleagues.

Although the crisis passed, Szilard persisted with his work for nuclear disengagement and in 1955, together with Albert Einstein and Bertrand Russell, formed the influential Pugwash Group that united scientists on both sides of the Iron Curtain in demanding that their governments enact stricter nuclear controls. He then devised a scheme for twinning American and Soviet cities to exclude them in the event of a nuclear conflict and even managed to lobby Khrushchev personally when the Soviet President visited New York in September 1960. Szilard suggested that the Soviet Union and the West should sign a nuclear ban treaty and that a telephone hotline should be established between Washington and Moscow. The Cuban Missile Crisis would certainly not have escalated as it did had such a link been in place. As it was, Szilard sincerely believed that a nuclear holocaust was imminent, and when the Cuban Missile Crisis broke out he flew immediately to Geneva and informed the director of CERN, the European Laboratory for Nuclear Research, that he was the first refugee of the Third World War. Curiously Szilard, unlike Otto Frisch, believed that scientists were better equipped than politicians to deal with such important matters as international peace. His persistence in pursuing nuclear détente was formidable. He founded a movement called Scientists for Peace and then formed a pressure group, Council for a Liveable World, which continues today. In this work he found common ground with another émigré scientist, James Franck. Based in Chicago, Franck had, like Szilard, urged the US government not to use the atomic bomb on a Japanese city until its full power had been demonstrated on an uninhabited island. This became known as the 'Franck Report' and was one of the first manifestations of scientific concern about nuclear weapons. In his last years as a scientist Leo Szilard abandoned physics and turned to a new interest, molecular biology. Even here his suggestions were prophetic, as his concept for an institution devoted to new advances in applying biochemistry to medical treatment became a reality in the opening of the Salk Institute at La Jolla, California.

Szilard was no ordinary scientist. A true maverick, he combined great intuitive ability with an unusual sense of personal and professional responsibility. His originality of thought and ability to act decisively when confronted with a problem echo those of the great inventor Isambard Kingdom Brunel. Like Brunel, who, having accidentally swallowed a gold sovereign which passed into his lung, designed within minutes an ingenious tool to remove it, Szilard devised his own treatment when diagnosed as having cancer of the bladder. Refusing surgery, he quickly studied the effects of radiation on tumours then prescribed his own successful radiation treatment at a New York hospital. Szilard was never given the true recognition he deserved for his major achievements of the verification of the neutron chain reaction, the behaviour of graphite under neutron bombardment and the design of the first atomic pile. His role as a modern Cassandra of nuclear physics embarrassed many of his colleagues and antagonized politicians. More than any other refugee scientist he had learned a lesson from his own past and saw his mission to warn the world so that history would not repeat itself.

12

Learning from the Past

Four years after the war ended Albert Einstein was invited to rejoin the same Kaiser Wilhelm Institute, now the Max Planck Gesellschaft, that had ejected him in 1933 (Brien, 1996). Einstein replied:

> The crime of the Germans is truly the most abominable ever to be recorded in the history of the so-called civilized nations. The conduct of the German intellectuals – seen as a group – was no better than that of the mob . . . In view of these circumstances, I feel an irrepressible aversion to participating in anything that represents any aspect of public life in Germany.

The great majority of Germany's intellectual refugees agreed with Einstein. Nothing that Hitler had done in restoring the morale of the German people or in reinvigorating the national economy could justify the sheer evil of his regime. As the years passed it became evident that the responsibility for what had happened in Germany could not be attributed to Hitler and the Nazi party alone. Their sophisticated barbarism had only been possible because it was condoned and, in the early years, encouraged by the majority of the German people. In such books as Daniel Goldhagen's *Hitler's Willing Executioners*, historians have revealed how widespread and pervasive this barbarism was. To those driven into exile in the early 1930s even the revelation of the

Final Solution towards the end of the war was but the terrible, predictable and logical outcome of the events they had experienced personally. To someone like the philosopher Hannah Arendt, growing up totally integrated into the cultural life of Germany, it was particularly shocking. Throughout her exile in the USA she sought to explain both the nature of totalitarianism and the moral bankruptcy of the Nazi regime and – to much condemnation from the Jewish community – the passive role that the Jews had played in their own destruction. Where Arendt sought to explain the past, philosopher and fellow exile Karl Popper in his great work *The Open Society and Its Enemies* examined the broader threats to the individual, in both totalitarian and seemingly democratic societies

Arendt and Popper had both been drawn to political activity in their youth. Popper, like many young Jewish intellectuals in Germany, considered himself a communist at the time of the First World War but was horrified by the communist violence he witnessed on the streets of Berlin in 1919. He immediately rejected any form of political extremism, seeing democratic socialism as the only sensible way ahead for the German people. A decade latter, Hannah Arendt, too, was drawn to political involvement, in her case Zionism. With Hitler about to assume the chancellorship, she was asked by the German Zionist Organization to collect information at the Prussian State Library to show how the Nazis had infiltrated that organization and how they were encouraging anti-Semitism in every department. This was illegal under German law, and a few weeks later she and her mother were arrested and held at Alexanderplatz police station in Berlin. An unusually sympathetic police officer procured their release and Arendt, now a target for the Nazis, joined the growing number of Jewish refugees heading illicitly across the Erzgebirge Mountains into Czechoslovakia. In Prague she again involved herself in Zionist activities before moving on, like so many other refugees, to Paris. Here she was again active in Jewish welfare organizations and anti-fascist groups. Then, in May 1940, it was announced by the French government that all refugees from Germany were to be interned. Arendt was sent initially to the Paris sports stadium, the Vélodrôme d'Hiver, along with thousands of other men and women. She had become, as she described it, one of a new kind of human being, the kind that 'are put into concentration camps by their foes and into internment camps by their friends'. When Arendt and her husband were released from internment they made their way, as did so many others, to the south and managed to take Varian Fry's escape route across the Pyrenees to Spain and then on to Lisbon, where, with American emergency visas, they sailed for New York. When she arrived in the USA Arendt was carrying a suitcase packed with the writings of her old colleague Walter Benjamin. These she took to his friend Theodor Adorno, who had re-established his Frankfurt Institute for Social Research in New York. It was to be an important contribution to American scholarship.

By then Karl Popper had become convinced that the freedom of the individual was threatened by state socialism. To Popper this freedom mattered more than any concept of equality because, as he wrote, 'if freedom is lost, there will not even be equality among the unfree'. Popper's concern for individual freedom was matched by his fascination with scientific method. As a student he had attended a lecture given by Albert Einstein in Vienna that revealed to him the difference between the dogmatic approaches of Marx, Freud and Adler and Einstein's own method of testing scientific theories. Popper's interest in scientific theory took him to Britain in 1935, where he lectured at the London School of Economics and discussed his ideas with Bertrand Russell and other British intellectuals, who were to prove useful contacts when he came to seek permanent exile in Britain. A year later, 1936, he met the Danish nuclear physicist Niels Bohr, who explained to him that quantum mechanics could not be understood in the same way as traditional physics. But Popper's speculations were interrupted by the assassination of his colleague Moritz Schlick by a Nazi student. Schlick was the leader of the Viennese circle of philosophers that had championed the principles of the Enlightenment. As a Jew and a colleague of Schlick's, Popper realized the danger he was now in and, rejecting an offer to lecture in philosophy at Cambridge, chose instead to join his Viennese colleague Fritz Waismann at the University of Canterbury in New Zealand. Far from Europe, Popper used the war years to develop his understanding of the probability theory and of quantum physics. He had also come to see that historicism was at the root of both Marxism and fascism, and *The Open Society and Its Enemies* warns of its dangers. Just before the war ended Popper returned to Britain, where he lectured at Cambridge and pursued a stormy relationship with his fellow Austrian émigré, the eminent philosopher Wittgenstein.

As a student at Heidelberg Hannah Arendt had studied with the philosophers Karl Jaspers and Martin Heidegger. It was their colleague Kurt Blumenfeld who first inspired her to discover her Jewish identity. Her relationship with Heidegger was to be the most influential of her life. Heidegger shared with Arendt a love of German culture and literature that would lead him to identify with much of the new Nazi regime. In the late 1920s Arendt was emotionally obsessed by Heidegger, both as a man and as a powerful intellectual influence. Not until she moved to Berlin in 1929 did she allow herself to realize the full import of Heidegger's fascination with National Socialism. For a man who was Germany's most important contemporary philosopher to embrace the crudities of Hitler's nationalism seemed, even to his contemporaries, ludicrous. But Heidegger's contempt for the modern world and his obsession with the lost pastoralism of a historic and rural Germany led him to believe, initially, in national rebirth under Adolf Hitler. He shared with Arendt a passion for German, which he described as 'the most powerful and most spiritual of languages'. To Arendt he was 'the last German Romantic'. Yet, in spite of the extreme polarity of their beliefs, Arendt maintained an affection for Heidegger, seeing him as more comic than evil, that even survived the war and her realization of the full horror of the Nazi crimes. Seventeen years after they had parted they met again in post-war Freibourg, and she found that the bond had endured, kept alive by their mutual love of the German language.

This enigmatic relationship with Heidegger was emblematic of Arendt's attitude to Germany. in 1946, in an attempt to understand the rise of Nazism, she began to write her book *The Origins of Totalitarianism*, in which she concludes that the rise of Hitler was the logical outcome of the combination of German imperialism and endemic anti-Semitism. Totalitarian regimes, she suggests, are characterized by their use of concentration camps. These are not the protective-custody camps and the internment camps that Britain had resorted to in the Boer War, nor the internment camps that the Allied powers established in wartime, because these did not exist to cause terror. What the Nazi regime and Stalinist Russia had produced was something quite different: 'Both Nazi and Soviet history provide the evidence to demonstrate that no totalitarian government can exist without terror and no terror can be effective without concentration camps.' These conclusions led her to propose a more detailed inquiry into the subject, which became the Research Project on Concentration Camps. The change in Russian attitudes towards their democratic allies at the end of the war she found attributable to the very nature of totalitarian regimes (Arendt, 1951):

> It is only now beginning to be realized that what makes Russian policy so hostile to the Western world is not a conflict between national inter-ests and not even a mere antagonism in general ideology, but the fact that a totalitarian state ruled by terror cannot possibly feel secure in a non-totalitarian world.

It was this reliance on terror institutionalized as the concentration camp that Arendt believed distinguished the totalitarian state from the democracy. What mattered was not the conflict between East and West, socialism and capitalism, or even one social class against another, but the conflict between governments that respected civil liberties and those that relied on terror and imprisonment. It was these same ideas that were preoccupying Karl Popper in Britain. Throughout her time in the USA Hannah Arendt never courted popularity, as her later writings show. She was highly critical of the militant Jewish nationalism that had led to the ejection of the Arabs in Palestine, which, having

> started a half a century ago with ideals so lofty that it overlooked the particular realities of the Near East and the general wickedness of the world, has ended — as do most such movements — with the unequivo-cal support not only of national but of chauvinistic claims — claims not against the foes of the Jewish people but against its possible friends and neighbours.
>
> (Arendt, 1951)

Nor was she any less critical of what she saw as Jewish co-operation in their own destruction by the Nazis. In particular she condemned the Jewish leadership of the time that had betrayed its people by appeasing the Nazis and failing to rally the people into some form of armed resistance to the tyranny. Later she wrote that it would have been better for the Nazis to have selected their own victims rather than the Jewish leaders doing the dirty work for them. Nor did she agree with the concept of sacrificing a hundred people to save a thousand. The Jewish socialists, too, she believed, had been more concerned with experimenting with kibbutzim than with forcing the British to make Palestine a sanctuary for their fellow Jews. The only way ahead for the new Israel, she believed, was for the Jews to co-operate with the Arabs. In a shrinking world, 'we are bound to share with peoples whose histories and traditions are outside the Western world'. Her words echo, in some ways, those of the anti-Nazi Weimar satirist Kurt Tucholsky who had committed suicide in exile in Sweden. Tucholsky, in his last days, had railed against what he saw as the historic Jewish cowardice in allowing themselves to be driven into the ghetto and lamented that his own generation would not live see freedom restored to the Jews.

Arendt's opinions scandalized the Jewish community, but her courage in questioning events that were still painful for the great majority of Jews brought her many admirers. Nor did she confine her comments to the events of the past. In March 1953 she attacked the US Attorney General for announcing that over ten thousand American citizens, many of them European exiles, were being considered as political undesirables and that even the American Committee for the Protection of the Foreign Born itself was under investigation by the FBI. When the civil rights movement erupted in the 1960s she wrote of her sympathy for the black children who had, like the Jews, to endure race hatred while their parents, like the Jewish leaders in Nazi Europe, hesitated to act.

Her dispassionate approach to emotional dilemmas was to characterize her coverage of the Eichmann trial in Tel Aviv in her book *Eichmann in Jerusalem*. Her phrase 'the banality of evil' was to many the appropriate epitaph for Eichmann and his kind. Again she questioned the role of the Jewish leaders and even speculated on the political motives of the Israeli government in bringing Adolf Eichmann to trial. Her objectivity brought charges of being anti-Israel and anti-Zionist, and her questioning of the legal process itself was thought by some to be no more than arrogant self-publicism. Above all, she was fair to Eichmann, accepting that he was indeed the archetypical bureaucrat driven by duty and incapable of discriminating between right and wrong. Eichmann had simply obeyed the diktats of the state. She did not dispute the final guilty verdict but thought that existing laws could not adequately deal with men like Eichmann who had participated in such 'administrative massacres'. She also speculated on how the moral corruption of this totalitarian regime had tainted other countries and individuals, including the Jews themselves. She did not, however, believe in German collective guilt and disagreed vehemently with her old Berlin colleague Leo Strauss when he urged all Jews to shun Germany. This she thought both arrogant and irrelevant. The German nation must not be excluded from the future of Europe and should become part of the world democratic community.

Arendt's writings were at the heart of all subsequent studies of the Holocaust, as historians sought to explain the calamity that had overwhelmed the Jews. This applied, in particular, to her conclusion that extreme evil is unpunishable because no punishment can be adequate or commensurate. Such evil, she maintained, is unforgivable because it arises from motives that are beyond normal human comprehension. Evil had become 'banal' because in the Nazi state anything and everything had been permitted against the Jews, and human life had become superfluous. With *Eichmann in Jerusalem* Hannah Arendt had become one of the most controversial figures in the USA, attracting praise and condemnation in equal measure. Her life continued that of the scholar teaching at the University of Chicago's Committee on Social Thought and at the Graduate Faculty of the New School for Social Research. She wrote for the *New York Review of Books*, joined anti-Vietnam War organizations and founded the Committee for Public Justice. Her love for the USA never wavered, nor did her respect for Britain, the only nation, she said, to have survived the Second World War morally intact. She expressed the profound insight of the émigré when she said of her adopted country in 1973:

> This republic . . . is a living thing which cannot be contemplated or categorized, like the image of a thing which I can make; it cannot be fabricated. It is not and never will be perfect because the standard of perfection does not apply here. Dissent belongs to this living matter as much as consent does. The limitations of dissent are the Constitution and the Bill of Rights . . . if you try to 'make America more American' or a model of a democracy according to any preconceived idea, you can only destroy it.

No such dramatic events troubled the life of Karl Popper as he concerned himself the same fundamental examination of the nature of totalitarianism as Hannah Arendt. An academic for the rest of his life, he was appointed Professor of Logic and Scientific Method at the University of London in 1949 and the following year made his first visit to the USA, where he discovered the same sense of personal freedom that Arendt had found. His concern with scientific method was stimulated by meeting both Einstein and Bohr again at Princeton and discussing with them his new thinking on indeterminism, which he expounded in *The Logic of Scientific Discovery* in 1959. But it was *The Open Society and Its Enemies* that transformed the experience of the European tragedy into a warning for the future, not just against totalitarianism but also against the less dramatic, if more insidious, encroachment on individual freedom by the modern democratic state.

Popper contrasted the open society with the closed society. The open society was not a modern Utopia but an imperfect democratic system that nevertheless allowed the individual the greatest possible freedom. There was nothing new in this, but Popper warns against even the encroachments of a modern liberal democracy where free speech can be threatened by a new political correctness which dictates that an individual may say anything he or she likes provided it does not offend anyone. Popper had seen the power of the bureaucracy in both Nazi Germany and Soviet Russia; it was one of the reasons that he rejected communism and was central to his suspicion of socialist regimes. His own experience of bureaucracy in the First World War coloured his attitude to what he called the 'power problem' of society. In post-First World War Vienna Popper, working in a home for destitute children, had needed some iodine for a disinfectant. To obtain a new bottle it had been necessary to apply to a magistrate in person by travelling to the other side of Vienna. He had then been required to travel on again to a doctor who, after much questioning, reluctantly wrote a prescription. Finally Popper had to take the prescription to a nearby hospital and to pick up the bottle of iodine. It was the start of Popper's lifelong hatred of bureaucracy and taught him, he claimed, that society's administrators are principally concerned with their own advancement rather than in helping the people. Once again ahead of his time, Popper pointed out that, while claiming to help the individual, many government organizations and charities often waste the bulk of the their finances on bureaucratic administration.

Having witnessed the tragedies of the twentieth century, Popper suggested that the people should not only be vigilant of the state but should treat it with a degree of healthy distrust. Its power must be confined within recognized limits and must not be allowed to grow out of control. For Popper, power does indeed corrupt. In the end it is only the vigilance of the citizens that can keep any society open and free. Our duty as citizens is 'to watch and see that the state does not overstep the limits of its legitimate functions'. For this reason, he suggests, we must expect the officers of the state to become corrupted and we must always have replacements ready, as he puts it (Popper, 1966):

> Even a well-designed and well-functioning democracy is not so much justified as the best of a bad lot. Its primary virtue is not that it provides us with the best leaders. It usually does not. Its primary virtue is that it provides us with a regular and peaceful mechanism for replacement.'

Karl Popper believed that society should not only tolerate dissenting opinions but also respect and protect them. He was also convinced that science should not be the exclusive possession of scientists. Albert Einstein would have agreed with both these propositions, as his life in the USA became a very public demonstration of his support for an open society and of his unique understanding of the moral limitations of scientists.

Einstein had arrived in New York on 17 October 1933 to take up his position at Princeton on a generous salary secured for him by Abraham Flexner. From the start, Einstein's presence in the USA attracted both adulation and hostility, beginning with a petition to Washington – even before he left Europe – from a right-wing group attempting to have him banned from entry as a communist. Einstein countered by issuing an ultimatum stating that he would cancel his travel plans unless his visa was ready by noon the next day. If he failed to appear, the USA would then be the laughing stock of the world. Even in 1933 Einstein was aware that his fame extended far beyond his importance as a scientist and that attempts by the Nazis to portray him as a pariah had served only to enhance his moral status. What Einstein thought mattered to the world, and his willingness to associate himself openly with peace manifestos and anti-Nazi movements had earned him international respect. 'But now', as he told Max Planck in Germany, 'the war of annihilation against my defenceless Jewish brothers has forced me to place whatever influence I have in the world on their side of the balance.'

Einstein had always claimed that his principal concerns were international peace and the welfare of the Jews, but, as the Nazis began to threaten, his natural pacifism began to wane. 'If I were Belgian I'd not refuse military service under the present circumstances,' he told an audience in Brussels before leaving Europe. He went even further by adding that, now Germany was preparing for war, it was the duty of every citizen to undertake military service and to contribute towards saving European civilization. In response to the constant accusations that he was a communist or, at best, a fellow traveller, he admitted that in the past he had been taken in by pacifist or humanitarian organizations that were little more than mouthpieces for Russian despotism but denied that he had ever supported communism because, like fascism, it was intent on enslaving the individual. This did not stop him offering his support for the loyalists in Spain in their heroic struggle or condemning the Western democracies for largely ignoring fascist aggression. Einstein was now totally disillusioned by traditional pacifism, and he warned the American League against War and Fascism that British pacifists were endangering democracy by opposing British rearmament. In this his views were no different from those of Winston Churchill.

Now an American citizen, Einstein, whose theoretical work had first revealed the possibilities of nuclear power, was not involved in the race to produce an atomic bomb. Instead, he was invited to work for the US Navy's Bureau of Ordnance as a $25-a-day consultant. 'I am in the Navy,' he told friends, 'but I was not required to get a Navy haircut.' Einstein was happy to play a positive role, even forgoing his annual leave from Princeton to concentrate on his task of developing electromagnetic devices to explode naval torpedoes. Einstein was now a committed activist against the Nazis, made all the more determined by the news from Max Born in Edinburgh of the systematic slaughter of European Jews, the starvation and murder of thousands of Americans by the Japanese and, later in the war, by the news that the son of his old colleague Max Planck had been tortured and executed for his involvement in the failed attempt on Hitler's life.

When the war ended, Einstein's participation in the Emergency Committee of Atomic Scientists at the behest of Leo Szilard marked a return to his natural pacifism. His involvement in an organization that sought to outlaw atomic warfare brought him renewed attention from the FBI. As chairman of the committee, Einstein, with Washington's permission, wrote to Stalin in May 1945. He deplored the deterioration of relations between East and West and suggested that Stalin broadcast his ideas for reconstruction to the American people and back a proposal for regular meetings between Russian and American scientists. Einstein also asked Stalin to help rescue the Swedish diplomat Raoul Wallenberg, who had saved 20,000 Jews from the Nazis and who had disappeared when Soviet troops entered Hungary. 'As an old Jew,' Einstein wrote, 'I appeal to you to find and send back to his country Raoul Wallenberg [who], risking his own life, worked to rescue thousands of my unhappy Jewish people.'

Einstein's other concern, the establishment of a Jewish homeland, moved towards a resolution when, on 29 November 1945, the United Nations voted to divide Palestine between the Arabs and the Jews. Yet the 600,000 Jews in Palestine were heavily outnumbered and faced powerful Arab armies. Once again, Einstein confused his friends and delighted his enemies by giving open support to the Haganah terrorist group. When the state of Israel was declared on 14 May 1948 and was immediately recognized by the USA, Einstein shared the joy of Jews throughout the world. It did not, however, stop him advising the new state of Israel to give recognition to its own conscientious objectors.

Since his arrival in the USA Einstein had courted controversy, never missing a chance (unless his loyal aides managed to shut him up) to give his opinion on any matter of national or international concern. The arrival on the US political scene of Senator Joseph McCarthy made Einstein an obvious target for investigation, but his reputation as the scientific conscience of the world gave him a degree of immunity that other refugees lacked. When the Soviet Union tested its first plutonium bomb in 1950, it further escalated the arms race as the USA produced the hydrogen bomb in response. It was a bad time for Einstein to have chosen to join Linus Pauling and Thomas Mann in protesting against the harsh treatment given to the attorneys who had defended those leaders of the American Communist Party accused of sedition. It was Einstein who bore the brunt of a fresh barrage of accusations that their action provoked. 'Einstein Red Faker, Should Be Deported, Rankin Screams,' declared the *New York Post*, quoting an enraged Mississippi congressman. A hesitant J. Edgar Hoover now felt confident enough to order a discreet investigation of the great scientist in 1950. It revealed that:

> Einstein is affiliated with at least thirty-three organizations that have been cited by the Attorney General, the House Committee on Un-American Activities, or the California House Committee on Un-American Activities. He is also affiliated in one way or another with approximately fifty miscellaneous organizations which have not been cited by any of the three above-mentioned. He is principally a pacifist and could be considered a liberal thinker as indicated by his connections with the various organizations indicated above.
>
> (Schwartz, 1983)

There was nothing here that could justify further FBI action, although the Immigration and Naturalization Service did consider revoking Einstein's citizenship when the *Tablet*, a Catholic journal, revealed to American readers that Einstein had opposed their fellow Catholic, General Franco, in the Spanish Civil War and had sponsored the Spanish Refugee Relief Campaign, which the House Committee on Un-American Activities had denounced as a communist front organization. Far greater damage could have been done to Einstein's reputation by a report that linked him to the British atomic spy Klaus Fuchs, until it was shown that the two had never met. But Einstein continued to associate himself with unpopular causes by pleading for clemency for the American atomic spies, Julius and Ethel Rosenberg, while not speaking out for the nine Soviet doctors – six of them Jews – who were on trial in Moscow accused of plotting to kill Stalin. The Jewish doctors were also charged with being part of an international Zionist spy ring as Stalin sought to capitalize on the innate anti-Semitism of the Russian people. One right-wing magazine put the accusation of bias to him succinctly in a telegram: 'Note you support the Rosenbergs clemency. In name of human rights we ask you make equally forthright condemnation anti-Semitic Prague trial and imminent execution Soviet Jewish doctors.' Einstein's reply unreservedly condemned Soviet injustice but pointed out the impotence of Western opinion in influencing

Russia. Far better, Einstein advised, for such condemnation to come from scientific or academic bodies in the West that were obviously independent of politics. Luckily the accused doctors were freed a month later after Stalin's sudden and unexpected death. All of this led J. Edgar Hoover, still too wary to question him face to face, to order the FBI to summarize their huge file on Albert Einstein, which ran in the abridged version to over a thousand pages of fact and bizarre fantasies.

But even Albert Einstein could not save the Rosenbergs. As he told Bertrand Russell, public opinion in the USA was so convinced of a 'red threat' that the President dare not commute their death sentence, even though General Leslie Groves of the Atomic Energy Commission had testified that the secrets betrayed were of little value. Nor did this experience deter Einstein from espousing other unpopular causes. When Albert Shadowitz, a physicist, was accused by Senator McCarthy of starting a trade union as a cover for potential Russian espionage he sought Einstein's advice and support. Einstein advised him to declare to the investigators that he was not a spy but, under the First Amendment, he had the right to keep his political views to himself. At the hearing Shadowitz did as he was bid, citing the First Amendment, 'following the advice of Professor Einstein'. Public opinion was divided on Einstein's involvement, some seeing it as ingratitude in return for the refuge that the USA had given him. Others praised his upholding of one of the tenets of the American Constitution. Shadowitz's family, however, saw it as an act of great humanity and arrived at Princeton to hug and kiss the highly embarrassed Einstein who was, declared Shadowitz's wife, 'like a superman to our Jewish community because he exemplified all those things which we would like to see in Judaism'.

Einstein saw in 1950s America the same threat to democracy that he had witnessed in the Germany of the early 1930s. Unless public figures spoke out for an open and tolerant society all would again be lost. For this reason he seldom hesitated to defend those he considered were being unjustly treated. Again, when Robert Oppenheimer was accused by McCarthy of being a communist sympathizer, Einstein openly defended him. So wary had his staff become of his tendency to speak out without considering the consequences that his secretary Helen Dukas ran out in the street one day as he returned to face a picket of television cameramen and reporters shouting, 'Professor Einstein, they are newsmen, don't talk, don't talk!' Dukas herself now came

under investigation as the FBI continued their nine-year quest to impli-
cate Einstein in seditious activity. It was alleged that back in Berlin
Einstein had two secretaries, one of whom had been a communist
agent. Finding no corroborating evidence, the Newark Office of the
FBI finally concluded that neither Dukas nor Einstein had been, or
were now, implicated in any illegal activity. Hoover accepted their
report and closed the file on Einstein for good. As Richard Alan
Schwartz wrote in the *Nation* in 1983:

> The amount of money spent to pay people who devoted countless hours
> to clipping newspaper items, typing summaries of public statements
> and following up absurd leads must have been enormous . . . Perhaps
> most perplexing is the way in which history is ignored. The Depression,
> the rise of Nazism and World War II might never have happened as far
> as the FBI was concerned. That someone might have supported com-
> munist causes during the 1930s in response to an economic crisis that
> represented at least a temporary failure of capitalism or to the spread
> of fascism is not even considered.

With the collapse of McCarthy's power after Edward R. Murrow
had denounced him on television in February 1954, Einstein was at
last left in peace. A reconciliation with Germany now seemed possible
in spite of his almost unshakeable conviction that it was 'a land of mass-
murderers'. He approved of the rebuilding of the German economy
and the measures taken to restore the country to membership of the
world community. But he never returned to Europe and lived out his
days in the USA as one of the tiny handful of people whose fame and
appearance made them instantly recognizable anywhere in the world.
Of his unequalled contribution to science he was characteristically self-
effacing. Once, when asked to comment on the importance of science,
he said that if Newton and Leibniz had not lived we would still have
differential calculus but without Beethoven we would not have had
the *Eroica Symphony*.

13

The Legacy of Exile

The description 'exile' contains the possibility, at least, of an eventual return, but for the cultural refugees from Nazi Europe, particularly the Germans, there was little to return to in 1945. The society and culture that they had known was gone for ever, swept away by the Nazi broom as thoroughly as the Allied bombers had levelled Germany's architecture. The occupied nation was now divided in two. In the East, Nazi totalitarianism had been exchanged for communist, and in the West democracy had returned. Austria was free, but Czechoslovakia and Hungary were enduring a new cultural winter. Yet the logical destination for those German-born émigrés disillusioned by American capitalism and dismayed by its growing political intolerance was still East Germany. Many who had retained their communist allegiance in exile now returned, among them Leonhard Frank, Alfred Döblin, Hans Eisler and Bertolt Brecht. All had been promised influential posts in the new German Democratic Republic, and Heinrich Mann had been offered the important post of President of the German Academy of Arts in East Berlin. Those who had not demonstrated their commitment to communism in exile were unwelcome in East Germany, and such political turncoats as Arthur Koestler and his old boss the political activist Willi Munzenberg were vilified by the state-controlled media. Some who hesitated to leave the USA in 1945 had their minds made up by virulent McCarthyism.

By the early 1950s the West German economic miracle had begun, and the increasingly prosperous Federal Republic was able to offer lucrative posts to returning exiles, particularly the much-needed teachers. Among those who came to terms with the past and accepted the offers were the sociologists Theodor Adorno and Max Horkheimer, who both returned to the University of Frankfurt; the writer Alfred Döblin, who was to play an important role in West German education; and Erwin Piscator, who assumed a theatrical role in the West similar to that of his old colleague Bertolt Brecht in the East. All found that the German people had acquired a collective loss of memory and that the Adenauer government was more concerned with fostering a virulent anti-communism than in raking over the past. In contrast to the thousands of American émigrés who left for Europe, only a small percentage of those exiled in Britain decided to return. Among the first to go were the politicians who had been part of the governments-in-exile such as the Czech leader Edvard Beneš.

By 1947 Maurice Maeterlinck, André Maurois, Jules Romains, Emil Ludwig, Wieland Herzfelde, Leonhard Frank, Erich Maria Remarque, Alfred Neumann and Carl Zuckmayer had all returned from the USA. Those who could not face living in either of the two Germanies settled, like Thomas Mann and Remarque, in Switzerland where they could again speak their native language. Many now lived in modest security on the reparation payments provided by the West German government. But all had suffered in exile. As Chaim Bermant has written, 'The number of the dead is not the sole measure of the Jewish tragedy; there is the vast unhappiness which engulfed so many of the living.' Many had faced xenophobia and anti-Semitism in their countries of refuge, which added to their lack of self-esteem and the diminution of their creative powers. Only a minority would have agreed with Egon Schwarz that exile had led him away from the insularity, provincialism and narrow-mindedness of his middle European existence. This neurosis of despair in exile had been recognized as early as 1937 in Ernst Stern's book *Emigration as a Psychological Problem*. Later, a British report on exile revealed that the suicide rate for refugee males, even after the war, was almost ten times that of other citizens. Nor were time, drugs or therapy effective healers for those who had suffered persecution and the loss of their homes or family members. Another report in 1950 came to an even more dramatic conclusion: the victims of 'forced emigration' had been almost as badly affected psychologically as had survivors of concentration camps. It was not surprising, then, that some had succumbed to despair and had taken their own lives – Kurt Tucholsky, Walter Hasenclever, Ernst Weiss, Carl Einstein and Walter Benjamin, for example. As Hasenclever had lamented, 'We are banished, we are homeless, we are cursed. What right do we have to live?' Stefan Zweig, staring at the Brazilian jungle with a bottle of veronal in his hand, gave poignant testimony to this despair.

When the exiles left Europe in the early 1930s the whole of Western European culture was under threat. If Britain had, like France, fallen in 1940, then only the USA would have remained to carry the torch of political and intellectual freedom in the West. As it was, the exiles were to help America assume this role by having an important and catalytic effect on American culture. Fortunately the nation already possessed the most dynamic economy in the world and was easily able to provide for the material needs of the refugees. But the USA still lacked self-confidence in the arts and continued to look to Europe for inspiration and guidance. As the writer Laura Fermi has put it, 'Although in some areas she had overtaken Europe, on the whole she looked deferentially upon European culture with its rich heritage.' Who in Europe, after all, knew the name of an American painter or a composer other than Sousa before 1945? The international credibility that the exiles helped to give an emergent American culture led to national self-confidence in the arts and the flowering of native-born American talent in the 1950s and 1960s. The impact on architecture, for example, of Gropius and the other Bauhausers was dramatic, as they helped reinvigorate American architecture's increasingly moribund concept of high-rise building. Their success resulted from a belief, shared with their hosts, in the possibilities of modern technology and the value of experiment. The USA's affluence turned ideas into realities unhindered by the political and ideological pressures that had frustrated their work in Europe.

Whereas the scientist Ernst Chain found it impossible to persuade the British authorities to endorse his far-sighted plan for a state pharmaceutical industry to produce the new post-penicillin antibiotics, László Moholy-Nagy had little difficulty in persuading the local Chicago businessmen to underwrite the establishment of his New

World Bauhaus. Consequently the USA benefited from the presence of the refugees in every branch of the arts and sciences. Without the presence of the Surrealists and the other exiled European artists New York would probably not have become the centre of world art in the 1950s. Nor would American music have enjoyed such international success but for the presence of so many composers and musicians. Their arrival coincided with a sudden demand for music that many feel amounted almost to a minor cultural revolution. Much of it was the result of new technology that enabled symphonic music to be broadcast across the USA in the late 1920s. This advance in mass communication was followed by significant improvements in recording techniques that allowed a new and enthusiastic audience access to high-quality recorded music. The musicians played an important part in all this, with the exiled conductors, in particular, not only bringing the established classics to the rapidly expanding American audience but also introducing them to radical new works. Throughout this period American symphony orchestras were strengthened by the presence of refugee musicians, veterans of some of Europe's finest ensembles, who were only too eager to find regular or permanent positions. Consequently, even industrial cities such as Pittsburgh and Cleveland found that their symphony orchestras were gaining a world-wide reputation for excellence. Add to this the influence of such eminent teachers as Schoenberg, Hindemith and Milhaud, who introduced their American pupils to their own pioneering modernism, and it is apparent that American music had been revitalized.

But the greatest contribution the exiles made was to higher education. Culture was no longer the preserve of the wealthy, nor, by the 1930s, was a college education. New establishments were springing up that needed skilled teachers at a time when Nazi policy in Europe was forcing so many academics into exile. What greater catch could the newly established Black Mountain College in rural North Carolina have made than the celebrated Bauhauser exiles Josef and Anni Albers? Britain, at the time, was unable to provide anything so comprehensive as Alvin Johnson's University in Exile. Almost uniquely it kept together, when the natural tendency was for dispersal, a body of exiled scholars who were later able to examine the cultural roots of fascism. Its scholars also developed the economic concepts that were to be invaluable to Roosevelt's New Deal policy. Throughout the country there was scarcely a faculty in any college, university or academy that did not benefit from the presence of at least one refugee teacher. With them they brought a different attitude to learning and scholarship. Based upon the more disciplined and comprehensive German system, this approach reached its apotheosis in Leo Strauss's Neoplatonic school of political thought at Chicago. So distinctive and rigorous was his methodology that his disciples were known ever after as 'Straussites'. By the time the war ended the enhanced reputation of American universities – much of it due to the émigré teachers – made them a Mecca for European students whose own establishments still suffered from the devastation of the war. Science students, in particular, were attracted to the USA by such institutions as the Massachusetts Institute of Technology and the California Institute of Technology, where the presence of so many European scientists had swung the emphasis from practical to theoretical research. Nor would the USA's own students ever again feel the need to seek advanced education in Europe as their parents had done in the 1930s.

Britain in the 1930s lacked the new centres for advanced learning that proliferated in the USA. Whereas the latter was able to provide its refugee intellectuals with the financial security of teaching posts at all levels in all disciplines, Britain could offer her exiles little more than the prospect of finding a position on the open market. Only in science and, particularly, in medical research – mainly at the traditional universities of Oxford and Cambridge – were the exiles offered immediate opportunities to continue their careers. Culturally, the nation seemed to have little need of the Continental-based ideas that the refugees brought with them. Modernism and a radical approach to ideas held little appeal to a Britain that had reached its apogee as a colonial power and was already becoming obsessed by a nostalgia for a lost past. Yet, for the six years of war against Germany Britain became the moral leader of the Western world, a role that was as rare as it was unexpected. The nation's strength in adversity came not from any identification with new and radical ideas but from a fundamental belief in its own past. What Nikolaus Pevsner later revealed to the British about their own vernacular architecture in the 1950s encapsulated much of what the nation had been fighting for. Yet British cultural life was subtly changed by contact with the intellectual refugees. They brought with them not only unfamiliar ideas of modernism but a disciplined and

comprehensive attitude to learning that immediately produced a grudging respect in the more lackadaisical British.

As the distinguished art historian Sir Denis Mahon recalls, 'You've
no idea the benefit we derived from the dreadful Nazi persecution of
the Jews. Brilliant men, human beings who were thoroughly awake,
came over here . . . I was lucky in Pevsner.' When they met at the
Courtauld Institute of Art in London in the late 1930s, Mahon was
both astonished and impressed by Pevsner's rigorous and professional
approach to scholarship. It clearly rubbed off, as Mahon went on to
become the greatest expert on seventeenth-century Italian painting in
the late twentieth century. Such encounters were typical. Carl Ebert's
insistence on repeated rehearsals at Glyndebourne, the thoroughness
of Ernst Chain's research on penicillin and Otto Frisch's experiments
in nuclear fusion both surprised and impressed their British colleagues.
It was an approach born out of the German academic system, in which
application and methodology were prized and amateurism treated with
suspicion.

But these new thinkers also opened British eyes to modernism in
all its forms and particularly in architecture. No one in Britain, for
instance, had ever seen a building quite like Mendelsohn's de la Warr
Pavilion in Bexhill, and it remains a national icon of modernism. The
clash between tradition and the new styles introduced by Mendelsohn,
Lubetkin and Goldfinger was perhaps the greatest, and certainly the
most visible, impact of modernism. Although admiration of traditional
style continues in the work of such architects as Quinlan Terry,
modernism prevails to such an extent that projected public buildings
in London are more likely to be criticized for their lack of radicalism
rather than for it. Ironically it is a British modernist architect, Sir
Norman Foster, continuing the tradition of Mendelsohn and Lubetkin,
who was chosen by the German government to restore the ruined
Reichstag building in Berlin. But few in Britain in 1933 had even met
a European intellectual, and the great majority of the people retained
an endemic suspicion all things continental. As a Somerset Maugham
character put it, 'It is good to be on your guard against an Englishman
who speaks French perfectly.' This ignorance and disregard for continental Europe was common at the highest levels of British society. Even
the Prime Minister Neville Chamberlain could say of the Czech crisis
in 1938 that it was 'a quarrel in a far-away country between people of

whom we know nothing'. When the intellectual refugees arrived it was not only their professionalism that startled the British but also their outspokenness and natural lack of reserve. Their concern with ideas rather than with manners and convention surprised and impressed their hosts. A grudging admiration was born, followed by a curiosity and respect for them as the bearers of an alien but no less valid cultural tradition. No better example exists than that of John Christie and his émigrés at Glyndebourne.

An American historian of the period, Laura Fermi, feels that the exiles accomplished more in the USA than they would have done if they had remained at home in Europe, which is arguable, but her contention that no other country but the USA was large enough or rich enough to have accommodated or supported such a vast migration ignores the contribution that Britain made. Despite having fewer resources and a fraction of the land mass, as well as lying three thousand miles closer to the danger of Nazi Europe, Britain took in more than half the number of refugees that settled in America; this at a time when Britain was increasingly threatened by German expansionism and was desperately seeking to rebuild its military defences. Britain was also, unlike the USA, faced with the imminent prospect of war, bound as it was by treaty to intervene when Hitler finally invaded Poland. There was little to be gained by the hard-pressed nation in taking in such a large proportion of the refugees; it was, rather, a humane response to their plight. But in spite of the petty bureaucracy and an innate suspicion of foreigners Britain did provide that first and all-important refuge in the early and mid-1930s. Many celebrated creative intellectuals such as Albert Einstein, Walter Gropius and László Moholy-Nagy, who later went on to embellish American culture, found initial safety in Britain. Many of the refugees, of course, remained in Britain and continued to influence its culture in the following decades. What endeared them to the ordinary British was their willingness to share the dangers and privations of war. As Britain became an armed camp in 1940, it was the British-born celebrities who remained safely in Hollywood – such as Gracie Fields and Charlie Chaplin – who were condemned by the people, and refugees like Private Arthur Koestler of the Pioneer Corps and Rudolph Bing fire-watching on the roof of a shop in Chelsea who gained their respect.

Such an event as the mass emigration of Europe's persecuted

intellectuals is unlikely ever to happen again; the circumstances that produced it were peculiar to the time. Not only has Western society, it is to be hoped, rejected totalitarianism but modern communications make such an event unnecessary. Again, as Laura Fermi noted in 1968:

> The cross-fertilization of ideas between the continents is achieved less by settlers from distant lands than by airplane travellers with return tickets in their pockets. They go to meetings by the thousands and hop from Paris to Chicago or Tokyo with greater ease and less mental preparation than were required to go from Paris to London thirty years ago . . . The learned men moving from Byzantium to Italy, or from Göttingen to America, will no longer be the principal instruments of cultural diffusion abroad.

It is possible that in their exile the European-born émigrés achieved more than they would have done at home. Some historians feel that they gained over the British and Americans by acquiring a second culture and a second identity. Perhaps the story of one individual best encapsulates this experience of exile. Stephen Lacner, the writer and art historian, was, as a teenager, taken into exile in the USA. When it entered the war he enlisted in the army and fought his way through Europe as a GI in a tank crew. When he returned to the USA he no longer thought of himself as an exile. He and his family were now Americans but, as he says, with German accents. Santa Barbara became their home, and Stephen Lacner began writing in English as well as in his native German. Lacner went on to become a successful novelist and scholar, often visiting Europe, able to make friends with young Germans but never growing roots there again. He completes his autobiography with these words:

> Now, at eighty-six, I can't leave California anymore. Occasionally I remember the most deeply touching verses in the *Odyssey*. The hero is stranded far from home, pining 'to see just once again the smoke rising from Ithaka's hills and then to die.' Even this last, modest pleasure was spoiled for me by Hitler's cohorts. The sight of smoke rising from a German chimney cannot evoke nostalgia, but only horror.

Select Bibliography

Abbey, William, *Between Two Languages: German Speaking Exiles in Great Britain 1933–45* (Stuttgart: Verlag Hans-Dieter Heinz, 1995)

Allan, John, *Berthold Lubetkin: Architecture and the Tradition of Progress* (London: Royal Institute of British Architects Publications, 1992)

Allen, John, *Erno Goldfinger* (London: Royal Institute of British Architects Publications, 1997)

Allday, Elizabeth, *Stefan Zweig: A Critical Biography* (London: W.H. Allen, 1972)

Arendt, Hannah, *The Burden of Our Time* (London: Secker and Warburg, 1951a)

Arendt, Hannah, *Crises of the Republic* (Harmondsworth: Penguin, 1973)

Arendt, Hannah, *Eichmann in Jerusalem* (New York: Viking, 1963)

Arendt, Hannah, *The Origins of Totalitarianism* (New York: Harcourt Brace, 1951b)

Aris, Stephen, *The Jews in Business* (London: Cape, 1970)

Ashton, Rosemary, *Little Germany* (Oxford: Oxford University Press, 1986)

Barron, Stephanie, *Degenerate Art* (Los Angeles, Calif.: Los Angeles County Museum of Art, 1991)

Bentwich, Norman, *The Refugees from Germany: April 1933 to December 1935* (London: George Allen and Unwin, 1936)

Berghahn, Marion, *German-Jewish Refugees in England: The Ambiguities of Assimilation* (New York: St Martin's Press, 1984)

Berghaus, Gunter (ed.), *Theatre and Film in Exile: German Artists in Britain, 1933–1945* (New York: St Martin's Press, 1989)

Bogdanovich, Peter, *Fritz Lang in America* (London: Studio Vista, 1976)

Bogdanovich, Peter, *Who the Devil Made It* (New York: Ballantine Books, 1997)

Boyers, Robert, *After the Avant Garde* (Philadelphia, Pa.: Pennsylvania State University Press, 1988)

Brandon, Ruth, *Surreal Lives: The Surrealists 1917–1945* (London: Macmillan, 1999)

Brecht, Bertolt, *Poems 1913–56* (London: Methuen, 1979)

Brien, Denis, *Einstein: A Life* (Chichester and New York: John Wiley, 1996)

Ccsarani, David, *Arthur Koestler: The Homeless Mind* (London: Vintage, 1999)

Chambers, Iain, *Migrancy, Culture, Identity* (London: Routledge, 1994)

Chappell, Connery, *Island of Barbed Wire* (London: Corgi, 1986)

Christie, Ian, *Arrows of Desire: The Films of Michael Powell* (London: Faber and Faber, 1994)

Clark, Ronald, *The Life of Ernst Chain* (London: Weidenfeld and Nicholson, 1985)

Coe, Peter, *Lubetkin Tecton* (London: Arts Council of Great Britain and University of Bristol, 1981)

Collaer, Paul, *Darius Milhaud* (London: Macmillan, 1998)

Corvi, Roberta, *An Introduction to the Thoughts of Karl Popper* (London: Routledge, 1997)

Dizikes, John, *Opera in America* (New Haven, Conn.: Yale University Press, 1993)

Drazin, Charles, *The Finest Years: British Cinema of the 1940s* (London: André Deutsch, 1998)

Duchen, Jessica, *Erich Wolfgang Korngold* (London: Phaidon Press, 1996)

Duggan, Stephen and Betty Drury, *The Rescue of Science and Learning: The Story of the Emergency Committee in Aid of Displaced Foreign Scholars* (London: Macmillan, 1948)

Dunett, James and Gavin Stamp, *Erno Goldfinger* (London: Architectural Association, 1983)

Elderfield, John, *Kurt Schwitters* (London: Thames and Hudson, 1985)

Elwall, Robert, *Erno Goldfinger* (London: Academy Editions, 1996)

Farrer, David, *The Warburgs* (London: Michael Joseph, 1975)

Fermi, Laura, *Illustrious Immigrants: The Intellectual Migration from Europe* (Chicago: University of Chicago Press, 1968)

Fiedler, Leslie, *An End to Innocence* (Boston, Mass.: Beacon Press, 1955)

Fleming, Donald and Bernard Bailyn, *The Intellectual Migration: Europe and America 1930–1960* (Harvard, Conn.: Harvard University Press, 1969)

Foot, Michael, *Loyalists and Loners* (London: Collins, 1986)

Frank, Charles, *Operation Epsilon: The Farm Hall Transcripts* (Bristol: Institute of Physics Publishing, 1993)

Friedlander, Saul, *Nazi Germany and the Jews* (London: Weidenfeld and Nicholson, 1997)

Fry, Varian, *Surrender on Demand* (New York: Random House, 1945)

Gibson, J.J., *Leonardo* (New York, 1966)

Giedion, Sigfried, *Walter Gropius: Work and Teamwork* (Oxford: Architectural Press, 1954)

Gillman, Peter and Leni, *Collar the Lot* (London: Quartet Books, 1980)

Golomstock, Igor, *Totalitarian Art in the Soviet Union: The Third Reich, Fascist Italy, and the People's Republic of China* (London: Collins Harvill, 1990)

Gombrich, Ernst, *Kokoschka in His Time* (London: Tate Gallery, 1986)

Guggenheim, Peggy, *Out of This Century: The Informal Memories of Peggy Guggenheim* (New York: Dial Press, 1946)

Guilbaut, Serge, *How New York Stole the Idea of Modern Art: Abstract Expressionism, Freedom, and the Cold War* (Chicago, Ill.: University of Chicago Press, 1983)

Heilbut, Anthony, *Exiled in Paradise: German Refugee Artists and Intellectuals in America from the 1930s to the Present* (New York: Viking, 1983)

Hirschfeld, Gerhard (ed.), *Exile in Great Britain: Refugees from Hitler's Germany* (Atlantic Highlands, NJ: German Historical Institute, 1984)

Hochman, Elaine, *Bauhaus: Crucible of Modernism* (New York: Fromm International, 1997)

Holms, Frederic, *Hans Krebs* (Oxford: Oxford University Press, 1993)

Houseman, John, *Unfinished Business* (New York: Columbus Press, 1988)

Hughes, Spike, *Glyndebourne: A History of the Festival Opera* (Newton Abbot: David and Charles, 1981)

Jackmann, Jarrell C. and Carla M. Borden, *The Muses Flee Hitler: Cultural Transfer and Adaptation* (Washington, DC: Smithsonian Institution Press, 1983)

James, Kathleen, *Erich Mendelsohn and the Architecture of German Modernism* (Cambridge: Cambridge University Press, 1997)

Jay, Martin, *Permanent Exiles* (New York: Columbia University Press, 1985)

Johnson, Paul, *A History of the Jews* (London: Weidenfeld and Nicholson, 1987)

Johnson, Philip, *Architecture in the Third Reich* (New York: Hound and Horn, 1933)

Kahn, Lothar, *Insight and Action: The Life and Work of Lion Feuchtwanger* (London: Rutherford Fairleigh Dickinson Press, 1975)

Kent, Donald, *The Refugee Intellectual: The Americanization of the Immigrants of 1933–94* (New York: Columbia University Press, 1953)

Kentgens-Craig, Margret, *The Bauhaus and America* (Cambridge, Mass.: Massachusetts Institute of Technology Press, 1999)

Kokoschka, Oskar, *Letters* (London: Thames and Hudson, 1992)

Lakner, Stephan, *Max Beckman* (New York: Harry N. Abrams, 1977)

Lubetkin, Berthold, 'L'Architecture en Angleterre', *L'Architecture d'Aujourd'hui*, Vol. 10, pp. 3–23 (Paris, 1932)

Lyon, James, *Bertholdt Brecht in America* (Princeton, NJ: Princeton University Press, 1980)

MacDonald, Kevin, *Emeric Pressburger: The Life and Death of a Screenwriter* (London: Faber and Faber, 1982)

McGilligan, Patrick, *Fritz Lang: The Nature of the Beast* (London: Faber and Faber, 1998)

May, Derwent, *Hannah Arendt* (Harmondsworth: Penguin, 1986)

Milne, Hamish, *Bartók: His Life and Times* (Tunbridge Wells: Midas, 1982)

Nicholas, Lynn H., *The Rape of Europa: The Fate of Europe's Treasures in the Third Reich and the Second World War* (London: Macmillan, 1994)

Notturno, Mark, *Science and the Open Society* (Budapest: Central European University Press, 2000)

Oliver, Michael, *Igor Stravinsky* (London: Phaidon Press, 1995)

Perret, Auguste, *Concrete* (London: Faber and Faber, 1959)

Pevsner, Nikolaus, *The Buildings of England* series (Harmondsworth: Penguin, 1951–74)

Pevsner, Nikolaus, *The Englishness of English Art* (Oxford: Architectural Press, 1956)

Popper, Karl, *The Open Society and Its Enemies* (London: Routledge, 1966)

Prater, Donald, *European of Yesterday: A Biography of Stefan Zweig* (Oxford: Clarendon Press, 1972)

Prater, Donald, *Thomas Mann: A Life* (Oxford: Oxford University Press, 1995)

Read, Herbert, *The Politics of the Unpolitical* (London: Routledge, 1943)

Richmond, Sheldon, *Aesthetic Criteria: Gombrich and the Philosophies of Science of Popper and Polanyi* (Amsterdam: Rodopi, 1994)

Rose, Paul, *Heisenberg and the Nazi Atomic Bomb Project* (Berkeley, Calif.: University of California Press, 1998)

Rosen, Charles, *Schoenberg* (London: Marion Boyars, 1976)

Said, Edward W., *Identity, Authority, and Freedom: The Potentate and the Traveller* (Cape Town: University of Cape Town, 1991)

Sawin, Martica, *Surrealism in Exile and the Beginnings of the New York School* (Cambridge, Mass.: Massachusetts Institute of Technology Press, 1995)

Schwartz, Richard, 'The FBI and Dr Einstein', *The Nation*, vol. 237, no. 6 (September), 1983

Scorsese, Martin, *Interviews* (Jackson, Miss.: University Press of Mississippi, 1999)

Sexton, Randolph, *American Commercial Buildings of Today* (New York: Brentano's, 1928)

Skelton, Geoffrey, *Paul Hindemith: The Man Behind the Music* (London: Gollancz, 1975)

Snowman, Daniel, *The Amadeus Quartet: The Men and the Music* (London: Robson Books, 1981)

Steinweis, Alan E., *Art, Ideology, and Economics in Nazi Germany: The Reich Chambers of Music, Theater, and the Visual Arts* (Chapel Hill, NC: University of North Carolina Press, 1993)

Stevens, Austin, *The Dispossessed* (London: Barrie and Jenkins, 1975)

Strauss, Herbert, *Jewish Immigrants of the Nazi Period in the USA* (New York: Saur, 1978)

Szilard, Leo, *My Version of the Facts: Selections, Recollections and Correspondence* (Cambridge, Mass.: Massachusetts Institute of Technology Press, 1978)

Tashjian, Dickran, *A Boatload of Madmen: Surrealism and the American Avant-garde* (London: Thames and Hudson, 1995)

Taylor, John Russell, *Strangers in Paradise: The Hollywood Emigrés* (London: Faber and Faber, 1983)

Taylor, Ronald, *Kurt Weill* (London: Simon and Schuster, 1993)

Timms, Edward, *Austrian Exodus* (Edinburgh: Edinburgh University Press, 1995)

Toller, Ernst, *Letters from Prison* (London: John Lane, 1936)

Wechsberg, Joseph, *Opera* (London: Weidenfeld and Nicholson, 1972)

Weidenfeld, George, *Remembering My Good Friends* (London: HarperCollins, 1995)

Weld, Jacqueline, *Peggy: The Wayward Guggenheim* (New York: Dutton, 1986)

Whitfor, Frank, *Oskar Kokoschka: A Life* (London: Weidenfeld and Nicholson, 1986)

Willett, John, *Brecht in Context* (London: Methuen, 1984)

Woodfield, Richard (ed.), *The Essential Gombrich* (London: Phaidon Press, 1996)

Young-Bruehl, Elizabeth, *Hannah Arendt: For Love of the World* (New Haven, Conn.: Yale University Press, 1982)

Zevi, Bruno, *Erich Mendelsohn* (Oxford: Architectural Press, 1985)

Zolotow, Maurice, *Billy Wilder in Hollywood* (London: W.H. Allen, 1971)

Index of Names